12⁰⁰
EC

D0282496

Communication and Society
Series Editor: Jeremy Tunstall

Journalists at work

*This book is the first volume in a series
edited by Jeremy Tunstall and devoted to
explorations of the interrelationships between
society and all forms of communications media.*

JEREMY TUNSTALL

Journalists at work

specialist correspondents: their
news organizations, news sources,
and competitor-colleagues

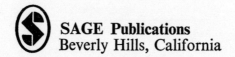

SAGE Publications
Beverly Hills, California

Copyright © 1971 by Jeremy Tunstall

All rights reserved. No part of this book may be reproduced
or utilized in any form or by any means, electronic or
mechanical, including photocopying, recording, or by any
information storage and retrieval system, without permission
in writing from the publisher.

For Information Address:
SAGE PUBLICATIONS, INC.
275 South Beverly Drive
Beverly Hills, California 90212

Printed in Great Britain

International Standard Book Number 0–8039–0322–7

Library of Congress Catalog Card No. 73–87745

First Printing

PN
4797
.T85
1973

A64   10.00

10-25-74

Acknowledgements

This book could not have been written without the financial support of the Leverhulme Trust Fund. I would also like to thank Peter Townsend, who supported my grant application, and Oliver Boyd-Barrett, whose work as research assistant on the project is further described in the Appendix on Methods. Others who read and provided helpful criticisms on earlier drafts of this book include: James Curran, Harry Christian, Jack Goody, Colin Seymour-Ure, David Shapiro and Gavin Weightman.

J.T.

139194

EMORY & HENRY LIBRARY

Contents

1

Introduction

'Not every reader of every newspaper cares to know about or could understand all the activities of mankind. But there are some readers, specialized in some subject, who have to be alerted to important developments of even the most specialized activities.

'For this, the profession of journalism is becoming specialized. . . .

'The journalist is becoming subject to the compulsion to respect and observe the intellectual disciplines and the organized body of knowledge which the specialist in any field possesses.

'This growing professionalism is, I believe, the most radical innovation since the Press became free of government control and censorship. For it introduces into the conscience of the working journalist a commitment to seek the truth which is independent of and superior to all his other commitments.'

Walter Lippmann (1965)

Two hundred specialist newsgathering journalists – employed by national British news media in 1968 – are the subject of this book. One need not necessarily agree with Walter Lippmann that the appearance of subject specialists has been the single, most important development in journalism in recent times. Nevertheless in any attempt to assess the 'Pictures in Our Heads'[1]* about a number of public issues, it would be difficult to deny specialist journalists an important part in drawing the pictures.

This research project set out to collect data from *all* the full-time specialist journalists who worked in certain selected fields for *all* 23 general news organizations at the national level in Britain. These selected fields were Politics (Lobby), Aviation, Education, Labour, Crime, Football, Fashion and Motoring; also included were Foreign correspondents working for London news organizations and stationed in four foreign cities: Bonn, Rome, New York and Washington.

Few of us know intimately Westminster politics 'behind the scenes', or watch at close quarters the making of national aviation policy, or spend our days following the twists and turns of national negotiations between trade unions and employers; few of us have any close acquaintance with daily politics in Washington or Bonn. Even those

* References are on p. 283.

of us who do have such close acquaintance with one area are not intimately involved in the other areas of news. All of us who want to know about such subjects must rely heavily upon the journalists who cover them.

Although we may rely upon journalists for information, this does not mean that they alone draw the pictures in our heads. There is plenty of evidence that people selectively perceive new information and tend to file it away in such a manner as to leave their existing beliefs undisturbed. Nevertheless the many studies which have reported the media to have little or no 'effect', for instance in changing audiences' political attitudes, have mostly looked only at short periods. Such studies largely ignore what are probably two of the most important influences of media messages (and hence of specialist journalists): Firstly, long-term audience effects, which are difficult to study rigorously; secondly, the effects of the media on the political system – changes in the overall relationship between political leaders and followers, and changes in political leaders' perceptions of, and responses to, 'public opinion'.

In a separate short study of one of the categories of specialist journalist included in this more general study it has been suggested that national journalists (and news organizations) play a prominent part in defining political 'crises'.

(1) From various possible crises available, the media play a large part in selecting which will become publicly defined as crises.

(2) A political crisis involves a government in problems of explaining its behaviour to the electorate, and the media – which play the major part in communicating such explanations – are sucked into the area of dispute.

If all or most of the media define a new political 'crisis', the government cannot easily ignore it. Major political crises are often first signalled by journalists who, collectively, move more quickly than politicians or legislatures:

'Thus in 1962 the early phase of the *Spiegel* Affair was dominated by the reactions of the West German press; it was only after a huge wave of press criticism of the Government's arbitrary actions in arresting the Editor and seizing the magazine that the political phase of the crisis developed.

'By catching a government unprepared and off-balance, damaging press coverage of this kind can destroy a government's plans of presentation and gain the initiative in defining the scope and nature of the crisis; moreover, by dictating a new timetable such coverage may lead to further hasty and ill-considered government decisions.'[2]

But the part which the news media play in defining major political 'crises' occurs also in other fields of news. Indeed, compared with crises in national politics the relevant specialist journalists in other fields of news probably play a larger part in crisis-definition – since both the national legislature and media organization managers are likely to be less prominently involved or interested.

When we first hear of some 'crisis' involving a national strike, or some major planning development, or some business conflict, or some educational dispute, or the impending cancellation of an air-craft project – in each case the news comes to most of us from one or more members of a small group of national specialist journalists. But such 'crisis-defining' is only one aspect of specialist journalists' activities. 'Our Aviation Correspondent' talks to us not only when 'Cancellation Crisis Looms' but also at other times and on more humdrum aviation topics.

Before we can fully evaluate what the specialist correspondent is saying we need to know something about his newsgathering activities. This book reports an attempt systematically to investigate specialist newsgatherers at work and to compare specialists from different fields of news.

1. SOCIOLOGY FOR WHOM?

This study is aimed first at sociologists and other social scientists. Secondly it is intended for journalists themselves and other communicators. Journalism is a segmented, outward-looking occupation; most journalists only have personal experience of a few limited areas of the whole occupation. Studies such as the present one may help journalists to place their own experience in a wider comparative framework. To an outsider one of the most striking characteristics of British journalism is its ignorance of itself.

Thirdly this book is aimed at a wider audience – especially those people in many areas of life who have, or who have had, some contact with journalists. Journalism touches society in many sensitive areas. Most people come into contact with journalists only when they themselves are involved in unusual circumstances of personal excitement or distress. It is perhaps partly for this reason that so many people who adopt moderate attitudes on many topics nevertheless are willing to make strident and sweeping assertions about journalism and journalists.

2. How many media voices?

'... the only way to neutralize the effect of newspapers is to multiply their numbers. ... There is hardly a hamlet in America without its newspaper. Of course, with so many combatants, neither discipline nor unity of action is possible, and so each fights under his own flag. ... There are other equally noteworthy effects of this division of the forces of the press; starting a paper being easy, anybody may take to it; but competition prevents any newspaper from hoping for large profits, and that discourages anybody with great business ability from bothering with such undertakings.'

Alexis de Tocqueville, *Democracy in America*

Much has changed since de Tocqueville wrote of the American press; in particular a *national* journalism has arisen in America – the syndicated news services and columns, the news agencies, news magazines, and the radio/TV networks. In Britain the news industry is more centralized than in any major nation, except possibly Japan. The *national* newspapers in Britain collectively have much bigger sales than the local dailies, most of which are both local monopolies and London owned. Broadcast news, news agencies, magazines and books are also London dominated.

The decreasing number of voices has been a subject for public concern for many years. During the 1960's new monopoly legislation came into effect; nevertheless *The Times* was taken over by Thomson. Moreover IPC, which at the time owned three national newspapers, some 200 magazines, plus book, TV and other media interests, was taken over by the Reed Group. During the 1960's a new type of *multi-media* organization emerged, of which IPC was the leading example, and these multi-media organizations have vigorously expanded into the new electronic media fields. There are several possible ways of regarding such developments; one can point to the many monopoly or duopoly situations in limited fields; or there is the much larger number of voices in other, more broadly defined, fields. One can point to the increasing dominance of some organizations in press retailing or in electronic research and development, but there is also the relative ease of entry to some fields such as magazines.

The present study can offer new evidence relevant to one segment of the large question of monopoly and competition in the media. The occupational behaviour of communicators is basic to some common assertions. For instance, it is sometimes argued that communicators are independent and competitive and thus the apparent 'number of voices' is the real number. But it is also suggested that the competing communicators in fact co-operate with each other in a restrictive manner which makes the effective number of voices less than the apparent number. The first argument suggests that communicators constitute a 'countervailing' power against monopolistic tendencies. The second argument suggests that communicators themselves constitute a monopoly.

3. A SOCIOLOGICAL ANALYSIS OF SPECIALIST NEWSGATHERERS

Much of the best empirical work on the mass media was fired by concern as to the use of the media by Hitler's regime in Germany. A decline in such concern may be partly related to a decline in the quality of American research on the mass media since about 1950.

In Britain the quantity of work on the mass media has been much less than in the United States – but the quality of some British work on the television audience has been excellent. Britain – with its centralized media pattern – is also an especially suitable research site for studies of *national* media organizations and communicators.[3]

The situation in 1965, at the beginning of this study, was that not a single social science study of any aspect of British journalism existed. There was no study of any type of specialist journalist, no study of a communications organization,[4] and no study of recruitment to the occupation.[5] Nor was there any general history of Fleet Street that could satisfy a sociologist or a social or economic historian. The several scholarly studies of specific historical topics were mainly written by American historians.[6]

The situation in America was, of course, quite different. There, a large number of studies of many aspects of journalism existed; but most dealt with journalism at the state or local level. At the national level the American literature was much weaker; despite numerous books on Washington journalism, there was no comparative social science study of the various kinds of political and semi-political journalism in Washington. The literature was still weaker on New York. Nor was there any adequate organizational study of typical newspapers or broadcast stations; there was also no satisfactory broad social science study of the occupation of journalism in the United States.

The present study sets out, in the case of British journalism, to investigate certain aspects of a relatively small sub-group – specialist newsgatherers on national newspapers constitute about 15 per cent of the personnel in those organizations, but only perhaps 2 per cent of all British journalists. This small sub-group had to be approached over terrain completely uncharted by social science. Most of Chapter 2, which sketches a broad picture of journalism as occupation and organization, is, then, hypothesis rather than finding.

At this stage it is worth summarizing what the present study does and does not attempt to do. It is not a study of the whole occupation of journalism in Britain; nor is it a study of news organizations. The study is primarily an exploratory one, which includes the following objectives:

(1) The study is firmly sociological – which is in itself unusual, since most studies in this area have either a social psychology or political science orientation; it aims to use sociological theories and concepts, and to indicate ways in which sociology can contribute to mass media research – as well as *vice versa*.

(2) It aims to establish an intimate familiarity with the subject matter. To this end it deliberately uses more than one research method.

(3) It aims to develop hypotheses for future studies of communicators.

(4) It develops a conceptual framework which would be suitable for such studies.

4. THEMES, CONCEPTS AND RESEARCH DESIGN

A central theme in this, as in studies of members of other occupations, is that much occupational behaviour can be seen in terms of responding to *uncertainty*. One of the most important forms of uncertainty surrounds 'news values'. Related to the theme of uncertainty is the *speed* at which journalists have to work; much of what happens in journalism (and, even more important, much which fails to happen) has to do with chronic time scarcity. A third theme is that specialist journalists seek to maintain and increase their *autonomy*; they do this by balancing pressures exerted on them in one work role against pressures in another work role. However, the amount of autonomy they enjoy is itself uncertain.

Some of the main concepts used in this study are as follows:

(1) The *news organizations* in this study were 7 general national Sunday and 10 daily newspapers, plus 2 London evening newspapers, 2 broadcast news organizations (BBC and ITN) and 2 national news agencies (Press Association and Reuters) – a total of 23 national news organizations. The concept of 'news organization' refers only to editorial departments – it does not, for instance, include such technicians as printers or TV cameramen. News organizations are distinguished from larger and more encompassing 'media organizations'.

(2) *Goals* of news organizations are seen as related to the unusual financing of news organizations – especially the advertising/sales dichotomy in revenue and the important non-revenue aspects. Thus news organizations are seen as having three types of goal:

(a) Advertising revenue goal
(b) Audience (or sales) revenue goal
(c) Non-revenue (or prestige) goal

These three goals are seen as the subject of internal bargaining and coalitions. Certain types of specialist newsgathering are seen as having a primarily advertising revenue goal (such as motoring and fashion), others as having a primarily audience revenue goal (such as crime and football), others as having a primarily non-revenue goal (such as foreign correspondence) and some as having a mixture of goals (such as aviation, labour and education).

(3) The work carried on within the occupation of journalism is seen as being *non-routine*.[7] It emphasizes personal qualities, and inter-personal skills – rather than being capable of systematization. Nevertheless, although the news organization is involved mainly in non-routine work, its encompassing media organization is primarily involved in *routine* work (such as printing newspapers). There is a basic tension between the routine and the non-routine.

(4) *Newsgathering* journalism (of which specialists and general reporters are the main components) is contrasted with *news-processing*; whereas newsgatherers are oriented towards news source organizations and news source individuals and 'performers' outside the news organizations, the news processors are involved in processing material within the news organization.

(5) *Competitor-Colleague* as a concept is more specific than any of the many varieties of 'reference group'. Newsgatherers acquire not merely some of their values from the group; the competitor-colleague group is operationally defined as a group of journalists each employed full-time by one of the 23 national news organizations covering a single specific news source area. From this group the specialist receives regular, usually daily, acts of competitive (and co-operative) behaviour.

(6) The concept of *frequency* refers to the periodicity (weekly, daily, hourly, etc.) of output under which a news organization operates. From this follows the urgency of 'deadlines', and the unusual daily *timetables* on which journalists operate.

(7) Finally the concept of *exchange* is introduced at various points – the notion that specialists, for instance, exchange information for

publicity with news sources and exchange information for information with competitor-colleagues.

The research methods are described in an appendix, so a very brief account will suffice here. This was designed as a comparative study of *all* the correspondents in each of the specialist newsgathering fields. No sampling was involved.

The main form of data collection was a mailed questionnaire, sent out in May 1968. Usable completed questionnaires (22 foolscap pages) were received back from 207 correspondents. The successful response rate for London-based specialists was 76 per cent; for Foreign correspondents 58 per cent. The overall response rate was 70·2 per cent.

The mailed questionnaire was preceded in the great majority of cases by an unstructured interview. Additional preliminary unstructured interviews were completed with non-specialist journalists; there were other unstructured interviews – for instance with business executives and national Editors. Direct observation sessions took place inside 11 news organizations.

2

Journalism: occupation and organization

---

1. JOURNALISTS AND SOCIETY

'. . . the ingenious fraternity of which I have the honour to be an unworthy member. I mean the news writers of Great Britain. The case of these gentlemen is, I think, more hard than that of the soldiers. . . . They have been upon parties or skirmishes where our armies have lain still. . . . They have made us masters of several strong towns, many weeks before our generals could do it. . . .'

Joseph Addison, in *The Tatler* 21st May 1709

'The journalist belongs to a sort of pariah caste, which is always estimated by "society" in terms of its ethically lowest representative. Hence, the strangest notions about journalists and their work are abroad. Not everybody realizes that a really good journalistic accomplishment requires at least as much "genius" as any scholarly accomplishment, especially because of the necessity of producing at once and "on order" and because of the necessity of being effective, to be sure, under quite different conditions of production. It is almost never acknowledged that the responsibility of every honourable journalist is, on the average, not a bit lower than that of the scholar. . . .

'Nobody believes that the discretion of any able journalist ranks above the average of other people, and yet that is the case. The quite incomparably greater temptations, and the other conditions that accompany journalistic work at the present time, produce those results which have conditioned the public to regard the press with a mixture of disdain and pitiful cowardice.'

Max Weber, *Politics as a Vocation* (1919)

Two hundred and fifty years after Joseph Addison mocked the inaccuracy of his fellow 'news writers', prominent journalists were still often the most outspoken critics of their fellow workers. The quotation from Max Weber also illustrates a recurring theme in attitudes expressed about journalists; Weber, in common with many other outsiders who have had some inside view of journalists at work, is willing to note their 'responsibility' and to think their dubious public image undeserved. To point out that Weber was primarily referring to the 'responsibility' with which German journalists had supported the German cause during 1914–18 is not necessarily to destroy the force of his comment. Nevertheless it does point to a fundamental problem: Responsible for what and to whom?

A passive approach to journalistic activity can be interpreted as supporting the existing political and social system. An active, investigative or watchdog interpretation of journalistic activity implies that to some people the 'watchdog' will seem to be a wolf. Other obvious bases of public ambivalence derive from the familiar dichotomy between 'comment' and 'news'; the conflict between the democratic ideal of an informed electorate and the output which many millions of people are willing to consume day after day; another obvious source of public ambivalence lies in the difference between what people think or say they want to read, hear or view and what they nevertheless do read, buy, switch on and view.

a. An indeterminate and segmented occupation

When an occupation deals with a fairly specific line of activity it becomes possible to lay down specific training and other regulations and hence to make the occupation more determinate still. Such determinate occupations include ones like 'medical doctor' or 'plumber'. 'Indeterminate' occupations include jobs like 'sales representative', which cover a very wide range of activities and lack prescribed arrangements for entry or training. In journalism, also, 'the range of expected tasks' is wide and is likely to change 'from one workplace to another'.[1]

In journalism there is no single clear 'core activity' (in Everett Hughes' terminology). News itself is a vague entity and on a national daily about half the journalists are not gathering news at all – but processing it, or acting as executives and deskmen. Although individual journalists may show some interest in the overall occupation of journalism, they are usually oriented mainly towards a more specific segment of journalism, or of the world outside, or both.

Indeterminate occupations also often contain elements which become interested in narrowing down the range of work tasks, specifying training, restricting entry and raising status. The main body attempting this in Britain is the National Union of Journalists; but a trade union is presented by an indeterminate occupation with some acute and perhaps insoluble problems. Efforts to make the occupation more determinate involve efforts to limit the power of employing organizations.[2] But news organizations seem likely to retain much power over journalists – at least in Britain – and for many journalists their work situation drives them into some degree of identification with the organization. Newsgatherers tend to become more, but not entirely, oriented towards the fields where they gather news. And the national newspaper Football specialist may feel he has little in common with the Knitting columnist on a women's magazine, or, for that matter, with the Editor of a rural weekly newspaper.

Journalists tend to rate journalists in other sub-fields in terms of the prevalent level of criticism. *National* journalism aimed at general audiences is generally believed to be the best and the most critical. Journalism which is either local or aimed at specialized audiences is believed in most cases to be less critical and of lower quality. *'House journals'* are believed to be highly uncritical and are scarcely regarded as being journalism at all. Another separate segment of journalism is the world of *consumer magazines*, which are believed by many other journalists to be an extension of the advertising world rather than of journalism. The *trade and technical magazines* are a separate world again, with each one oriented primarily to the interest or industry which provides not only its readers and its advertising but also its news sources. Many journalists on these publications have previously worked in the industry about which they now write. *Provincial daily* newspapers are more highly regarded by national journalists – although primarily as a training ground for London journalism.

Even within a national newspaper there is a high level of segmentation. The editorial is largely cut off from the commercial departments. Among the journalists there is a basic distinction between *gatherers* and *processors*. Newsgathering journalists are also divided by time, place and the kinds of stories they cover. An Aviation correspondent may not know a Football correspondent who has a desk twenty yards away. The Financial specialists spend all their time at a separate office in the City of London; the Political men are always down at Westminster; the Foreign correspondents are at their foreign postings. The open floor office system which is designed to speed face-to-face communication appears to do so only between people in closely related work roles.

In broadcast journalism segmentation is no less marked than in the press. Firstly, broadcast journalism is physically separate from the press in Fleet Street. Secondly, the two broadcast news services are separate from each other. And, thirdly, the BBC in particular is internally segmented.

b. British journalism, 1855–1955: a century of London dominance

Dominance of London in British journalism[3] is maintained by the dominance of London in other fields including the 'creation' of news;

the great majority of newspapers sold each day in Britain are printed in London or one of its major satellite printing centres – Manchester and Glasgow. Most of Britain's population lives within a two-hour train journey of one of these three centres.

How did this system of national journalism – more centralized than that of any other major nation except possibly Japan's – ever become established? It began this way and, with geography assisted by government policy, has so remained. During the period 1855 to 1955 there were only a few minor challenges to London dominance. In the period up to 1855 *The Times* was allowed a virtual monopoly in the daily newspaper field in Britain. After the removal of the 'taxes on knowledge' other daily papers appeared – notably *The Daily Telegraph*, which was for the middle class what *The Times* was for the upper class, and it was also London based.

Around 1890 Manchester became a major newspaper centre. But in 1896 Northcliffe launched his *Daily Mail* for the lower middle class; it succeeded – with luck, falling newsprint costs, editorial techniques previously used only in evening papers, American promotional methods, and Boer War hysteria. In 1900 Northcliffe began printing the *Daily Mail* in Manchester and the pattern of *national* popular papers was set when the *Daily Express* also began a Manchester printing.

For over a decade after 1940 the British government rationed newsprint in a way which retarded any circulation changes. Provincial newspapers were thus artificially protected, but the removal of rationing during the 1950's led to the closure of many provincial dailies and a local daily monopoly in all English cities outside London. In 1955 there appeared the second television channel – which despite a 'regional' structure was (like the BBC) London dominated. Its news service – ITN – was even more London dominated than the remainder of the new network.

c. Journalists in Britain: the labour force employed

Frequent Fleet Street references to journalism as a 'declining industry' tell more about journalists' pessimism than about the changing numbers in the labour force. The census for England and Wales showed that 'Journalists and Authors' made up 1·0 per 10,000 population in 1861; 2·3 in 1881; 3·4 in 1921; 5·5 in 1951 and 7·3 per 10,000 in 1961. The increase from 2,000 in 1861 to 34,000 in 1961 suggests that both authors and journalists had been increasing in total numbers quite fast. The best estimates for the late 1930's are a total of either 9,000[4] or 10,000[5] journalists; and for the late 1960's about 20,000 – that is a doubling in thirty years. From 1964 to 1969 the number of national newspaper journalists increased by 18·6 per cent.[6]

National newspapers accounted for under a fifth of all journalists employed (Table 2.1). However, one must include some of the news agency and broadcasting journalists as national; then daily and Sunday *national news journalism* probably employed about a quarter of all British journalists. The number of journalists employed by specific national daily newspapers varies from 440 working for the *Daily Mirror* to 140 for the *Financial Times* (Table 2.2). Table 2.3 shows a more detailed breakdown for three national daily newspapers which each had an average of 294 employees. The same table also includes similar evidence from three provincial dailies; of these provincial dailies one had a circulation of about 100,000 – and one of more, one less. The national dailies each employ about 300 journalists while the provincial dailies each employ only about 60.

TABLE 2.1

APPROXIMATE NUMBERS OF FULL-TIME JOURNALISTS
IN BRITAIN, JANUARY 1969

National dailies and Sundays (London)		2,800
National dailies and Sundays (Manchester)		750
National newspapers	TOTAL	3,550
Daily, Sunday and Weekly *Provincial newspapers*	TOTAL	9,700
British news agencies		450
Independent Television News (ITN)		50
ITV programme companies (regional)		125
BBC (TV and radio)		500
Agencies and Broadcast	TOTAL	1,125
Periodicals, magazines		4,000*
Full-time freelances		2,000*
Other journalists	TOTAL	6,000
All journalists	TOTAL	20,375

* National Union of Journalists' estimate, dated September 1968.

Main Source: National Board for Prices and Incomes, *Journalists' Pay* (1969).

TABLE 2.2

NATIONAL NEWSPAPERS: CIRCULATION AND NUMBERS
OF JOURNALISTS EMPLOYED IN 1968

Media Organization	Newspaper	Average daily circulation	Number of journalists employed
Associated Newspapers	*Daily Mail* (a.m.)	2,067,000	364
	Daily Sketch (a.m.)	900,000	151
	Evening News (p.m.)	1,138,000	166
Beaverbrook Newspapers	*Daily Express* (a.m.)	3,820,000	415
	Sunday Express	4,222,000	82
	Evening Standard (p.m.)	626,000	173
IPC Newspapers	*Daily Mirror* (a.m.)	4,992,000	440
	Sunday Mirror	5,076,000	86
	The Sun (a.m.)	1,038,000	293
	The People (Sunday)	5,480,000	60
Telegraph	*The Daily Telegraph* (a.m.)	1,393,000	371
	The Sunday Telegraph	730,000	57
News of the World	*News of the World* (Sunday)	6,161,000	60
Manchester Guardian and Evening News	*The Guardian* (a.m.)	275,000	174
S. Pearson Newspapers	*Financial Times* (a.m.)	160,000	140
Observer	*The Observer* (Sunday)	878,000	79
Times Newspapers	*The Times* (a.m.)	408,000	300
	Sunday Times	1,451,000	108

Source: National Board for Prices and Incomes, *Journalists' Pay* (1969).

TABLE 2.3

JOURNALIST STAFF OF A NATIONAL DAILY AND
A PROVINCIAL DAILY NEWSPAPER

	National Daily	Provincial Daily	National Daily	Provincial Daily
	No.	No.	%	%
Executives/Deskmen				
General executive	11	4	4	7
Assistants	8	1	3	2
Gathering executives	4	1	1	2
Assistants	12	1	4	2
Processing executives	3	1	1	2
Assistants	13	2	4	3
TOTAL	51	10	17	17
Gatherers				
Foreign correspondents	8	0	3	0
Financial specialists	8	0	3	0
Other News specialists	21	2	7	3
Sports specialists	8	0	3	0
General Sports reporter	7	3	2	5
Photographers	27	5	9	8
Leader writers	4	0	1	0
Columnists, Cartoonists	4	0	1	0
Feature writers, Critics	18	4	6	7
General reporters	30	10	10	17
Regional Sports, News reporters	18	17*	6	28
TOTAL	153	41	52	68
Processors				
News and specialist subs	60	9	20	15
Sports sub-editors	20	0	7	0
Features sub-editors	10	0	3	0
	90	9	31	15
TOTAL	294	60	100	100

* In the case of a paper sharing branch office staff with a partner daily paper, half the numbers were included.

Source: Staff lists of three national dailies and three provincial dailies.

2. THE FLOW OF NEWS

News flows within countries and between countries in a way which has several similarities with the flow of other sorts of communication – such as telephone communication or transportation. There is an especially heavy volume of traffic across the North Atlantic – between USA and Western Europe.

News organizations act as magnets for news or would-be news. The number of words which flows into a national news organization each day may be ten or twenty times the number of words which goes out to the audience – 90 or 95 per cent of available material is not used. Even in Britain there are over 100 daily newspapers, plus many agency and other news organizations serving them and competing with them; each of these news organizations has several editions. If one wants to investigate the flow of news within Britain (including the news which in the case of each publication did not become 'news') for just 24 hours, then one is considering tens of millions of words. If one then considers a country like the United States, with more than 10 times the number of daily newspapers, the problem becomes much larger again.

Faced with these niagaras of words (and pictures) the numerous social science studies of the flow of news have concentrated on a selection of news media – such as afternoon newspapers in one American state; secondly they have concentrated on one type of news – for instance, news about specific foreign countries or political leaders. Many studies have also concentrated on the output of the news agencies. Nevertheless, the findings of news flow studies are sufficiently extensive to make even a summary impossible here.[7] One simple generalization, however, can be made. The news flow results from the interaction of supply and demand.

a. News: demand and supply

'. . . the things which most of us would like to publish are not the things most of us want to read. We may be eager to get into print what is, or seems to be, edifying, but we want to read what is interesting.'

Robert Ezra Park

'Wherever there is a good machinery of record, the modern news service works with great precision. There is one on the stock exchange, and . . . a machinery for election returns. . . . It will be found, I think, that there is a very direct relation between the certainty of news and the system of record.'

Walter Lippmann, *Public Opinion* (1922)

Information, or gossip, or invention is in most urgent demand when the 'news' in question will have a direct impact on the audience member, or upon people of direct personal interest to him; this demand is strongest in situations of the greatest uncertainty. In these demand circumstances 'rumour' also thrives. Tamotsu Shibutani in his study of *Improvised News* defines rumour as:

> 'A recurrent form of communication through which men caught together in an ambiguous situation attempt to construct a meaningful interpretation of it by pooling their intellectual resources. It might be regarded as a form of collective problem-solving.'[8]

Rumours tend to occur when there is an imbalance between an urgent demand for information and a failure in the supply. Rumours thus arise in stock markets – where early information is in demand for financial reasons[9] – and in situations of crisis, disasters, 'miracles', drama and conflict. Institutionalized news media sometimes dispel rumours, but sometimes also carry rumours in the form of stories attributed to 'substantial bodies of opinion', 'usually reliable spokesmen' and the like. A more extreme form of this phenomenon occurs frequently in Roman Catholic countries in press and TV interviews with children who have seen the Virgin Mary or a miracle.

War is the biggest source of rumour because the multiple individual crises of war produce the greatest demand for information. An extreme disequilibrium between the supply of, and the demand for, news occurs under military occupation when institutionalized news media are controlled and censored. The resulting underground press tends to survive the torture and execution of some journalists and readers. There are, of course, other kinds of 'underground' press; one is the humorous paper of suspect taste, accuracy, legality and financial soundness which may lurch from one legal action to the next, via financial crises, to an early death, or which may prosper and acquire more socially approved taste, accuracy, legality and finance.

Institutionalized news is expected, at least by the immediate audience involved, to be more reliable than rumour; it is believed that such institutionalized news organizations as newspapers have proved more or less reliable in the past, have a 'name' to protect and have superior ways of gathering news.

How can the news organization meet the demand for news, with a supply of news that is new, not prohibitively expensive to collect and both interesting and 'reliable' enough to keep the customers paying for more of the same (but different)? As Walter Lippmann indicated long ago, the tendency is to post journalists at fountains of interesting 'facts'. What Lippmann calls precision is also known by journalists as 'hard news' – scores, dates, number killed, votes counted, sums of money spent or robbed, the numerical results of contests. Another type of fact fountain is the prominent individual – whose words are 'factual' in the sense that at least this was what 'the mayor told our reporter last night'.

News has to seem interesting and new in some way or other. But it must not seem too new, too surprising, or the news organization will fail to notice it. When Orville Wright made the first aeroplane flight in December 1903 it did not go completely unreported, but most American papers failed to use a short Associated Press item on the flight. Robert Park wrote in his essay 'News as a Form of Knowledge':

> 'If it is the unexpected that happens, it is not the wholly unexpected that gets into the news . . . births and deaths, weddings and funerals, the condition of the crops and of business, war, politics and the weather. These are the expected things, but they are at the same time the unpredictable things . . . things that one fears and that one hopes for. . . . News is characteristically, if not always, limited to events that bring about sudden and decisive changes.'

The latter point covers the often noted phenomenon that a man is seldom so newsy as when he dies.

Although a daily newspaper is in marketing terms a 'repeat purchase product' of great perishability, and although newspapers offer what is new and are accused of supplying what is trivial, nevertheless the relationship between news supply and news demand is one of extraordinary stability. Newspapers seldom change their circulation by more than a few per cent per year. Butler and Stokes found in their surveys of British political behaviour that newspaper reading was the most stable variable apart from sex and date of birth.[10] These contrasted aspects of novelty and stability will reappear in a later discussion of routine media organizations and non-routine news organizations.

b. *Word-of-mouth, élite personalities, blood on the streets*

> '. . . and we'll live,
> And pray, and sing, and tell old tales, and laugh
> At gilded butterflies, and hear poor rogues
> Talk of court news; and we'll talk with them too,
> Who loses and who wins; who's in, who's out. . . .'
>
> William Shakespeare, *King Lear*

> 'Human interest is the universal element in the news. It is what gives the news story its symbolic character.'
>
> Robert Park (1940)

The most well-worn definitions of news tend to stress that news is something the audience talks about – 'what makes the reader say "Gee-whiz"'. Charles A. Dana, Editor of the *New York Sun*, defined news as 'something that will make people talk'.

Many studies of mass-media audiences indicate that word-of-mouth communication remains of great importance. The 'two-step flow' school of communication research has produced evidence that much of the impact of the mass media comes about only in combination with the personal advice of a local 'opinion leader'.[11] The very rapid diffusion within the United States of the news of President J. F. Kennedy's assassination resulted from a combination of radio and TV news – plus individuals who had heard the broadcast news quickly telling others (often by telephone) about it.[12] Other evidence shows that in situations – such as the Soviet Union during the Stalin period[13] – where many people doubt the authenticity of mass-media news, there is a particularly strong flow of word-of-mouth communication.

In order to produce news which 'will make people talk' journalists use the device of personalization. Thus events which can be presented through personalities are more likely to become news, especially if the audience can be expected to *identify* with the personalities in question. Again the device is one used not only by journalists, but by communicators in drama, entertainment, sport and educational and cultural output.

The personalities presented tend to occupy élite positions in society, because more events can be related to a few élite individuals and widely spread audiences are expected to identify more with élite individuals, although the opposite case of the 'common man' personality also has appeal within a variety of social systems. Concentration on top people of various kinds also appears among the fictional characters on American television. In his investigation of the occupations of characters portrayed on American television, De Fleur found that men in professional, technical and managerial occupations made up 62·9 per cent of the TV labour force – as against only 18 per cent in the real life labour force.[14]

De Fleur also found that fictional TV concentrated heavily on people occupationally concerned with the use and control of force in society:

'By far the most frequent form of work turned out to be occupations associated with the enforcement or administration of the law, with nearly a third of the televised labour force involved. . . . The characters portrayed on television faced constant crises, in which they were frequently embroiled with the law. Large numbers of legal specialists, enforcement personnel, and "private eyes" toiled night after night to untangle these legal snarls.'

In this respect TV drama has much in common with Greek tragedy, Shakespeare and other fictional writing. Conflict (often between élite individuals) makes the news story, just as conflict makes the plot in fiction.

A British journalist commenting on the lavish media coverage of the 1965 riot in the Watts area of Los Angeles said: 'That was a story which commanded attention. Blood on the streets. You can't do better than that.' Riots in which many people are killed (in a place with whose white inhabitants the intended audience can be expected to identify) fulfil all of the requirements of a big news story. But a war does so even more fully and over a longer period. War has a special place in the news. Modern journalism was largely invented during the American Civil War. New techniques of newsgathering, such as the interview, new electronic forms of story transmission, and other features of modern journalism, were all well developed by the end of the war in 1865. The American Civil War's impact on circulations created the world's first mass-media audience. The Boer War played a similar part in British journalism.

Foreign news reported by staff correspondents has always been dominated by war and threats of war. At any time there is always in the world one leading centre of violence or war, which is covered by the largest collection of Foreign correspondents (during most of the 1960's it was Vietnam); a good deal of the time of Foreign correspondents stationed elsewhere is connected indirectly with this one leading centre of violence. Frequently the war will become the leading story of the day; and other stories which pre-empt it in the headlines will often be other forms of violence – riots, natural disasters, plane crashes, murders – which on the particular day offer a greater, or more sudden, or in some other way more interesting, dose of violence.

c. What, then, is the news? Foreign, domestic, TV

'The Structure of Foreign News'[15] is an analysis by two Norwegian sociologists of the presentation of the Congo, Cuba and Cyprus Crises (1960, 1964) in four Norwegian newspapers. It sets forth a number of hypotheses, such as:

(1) The more similar is an event's *frequency* (time-span needed for event to unfold) to the frequency of the news medium, the more probable it will be recorded as news. Sudden death and dramatic climaxes are thus more newsy than long time span events.

(2) There is a threshold of *amplitude* – so that a certain level of violence, size, or numbers, is required.

(3) The *less ambiguity*, the more the event will be noted.

(4) The more *meaningful*, in the sense of culturally proximate or relevant, the more likely news will result.

(5) The more *expected* – in the sense both of predicted and wanted – the more an event will become news.

(6) The more unexpected or rare, within a certain range of what is meaningful and consonant, the more newsworthy.

(7) Events will continue to be news for some while even after the amplitude is reduced.

(8) There is an element of *composition* – of producing a 'balanced' diet of news for the audience.

Further hypotheses indicate that events concerning élite nations, élite people, events which can be seen in personal terms and negative events will be more likely to become news items. It is suggested that *negative* events satisfy the frequency criterion (e.g. sudden death); negative events are consensual and unambiguous; negative events fulfil some latent or manifest need of many people; negative news is more unexpected.

All content studies have serious limitations. Some specific limitations of the Galtung and Ruge study are: (1) It deals only with news explicitly concerned with three foreign crises; (2) almost all the news originated through the four western international agencies – AP, UPI, AFP, and Reuters; (3) the study is based on news in only four Norwegian newspapers. More general limitations of the study include the following: (4) It concentrates on a few major 'crises' – whereas the day-to-day coverage of lesser events may be more important; (5) it looks at only the content *explicitly* concerned with the selected area; (6) it ignores fundamental aspects of news presentation – such as the *editionizing* phenomenon; (7) it ignores the visual aspect altogether, whereas, quite apart from television, high quality dramatic pictures not only take space but also affect the content of written material.

An unusual strength of the Galtung and Ruge study is its presentation of a coherent set of hypotheses which can be applied to crises other than the selected foreign crises. Indeed these hypotheses could probably be applied not only to the domestic news content of national news organizations but also to local coverage in weekly newspapers. The latter case suggests that the probability of events becoming news may depend upon scoring high on a minimum of one or two of the chosen variables. For instance, any event which scores very high on cultural proximity may not need to be violent or negative (much news in local papers is positive).

Although their study explicitly deals only with newspaper content, the Galtung and Ruge scheme could also be adapted to the case of television. Ways in which television news content differs from press news include:

(1) The visual is given pre-eminence. The possession of new film material will often greatly increase the prominence given to an item.

(2) News items which include film of 'our own reporters' either interviewing a prominent protagonist (or himself 'talking straight to camera') are preferred.

(3) Television uses only a small fraction of the *number* of stories the newspapers have, and even major TV items are also on average very short.

(4) There is a strong preference for 'hard' stories or actuality on television news.*

Television has its own technology and also special arrangements for social and political control and 'neutrality'. But such Galtung and Ruge variables as personalization, cultural proximity, unexpected-ness-within-predictability (cameras must be present), and frequency, are all highly relevant to TV. Television 'news' also involves 'composition' in relation to other than news output on television.

Here again we return to the point that any sharp distinction between mass-media 'news' and other mass-media output is arbitrary. Much that appears in newspapers or even on short TV news bulletins would be regarded by most journalists as not news but 'features', 'colour journalism' or something else. On even a loose definition of 'news' probably less than half of most newspaper content could be called news – when one remembers the advertisements, poetry, syndicated fiction, travel pieces, and so on.

d. The structure of news and the discretion of journalists

'News does not have an independent existence; news is a product of men who are members of a news-gathering (or a news-originating) bureaucracy.

* These points refer to TV news bulletins of at least daily 'frequency'.

> . . . But until we understand better the social forces which bear on the reporting of the news, we will never understand what news is.'
> Walter Gieber, *News is What Newspapermen make it* (1964)

Any social science scheme for classifying categories of news and predicting what categories will most often become news will never do more than show broad probabilities. There will be much room for the exercise of discretion by journalists. Even though news may not be what journalists alone make it, journalists constitute one of the important categories of people who make news.

Kurt Lewin's work on social channel and field theories[16] has been used as the main theoretical backing for a series of studies dealing with news 'gatekeepers'. It has been used especially to analyse sub-editing selections by a journalist who chooses from material supplied by the big American news agencies. White analysed the activities of a copy-editor, 'Mr Gate', who was selecting news from the (then) three major American news agencies on a 30,000–circulation daily newspaper in the American midwest. Mr Gate in one week used 1,297 column inches out of 11,910 inches supplied – about one-tenth. Asked about prejudices which might influence his gatekeeping, Mr Gate said:

'. . . I dislike Truman's economics, daylight saving time and warm beer, but I go ahead using stories on them and other matters if I feel there is nothing more important to give space to. I am also prejudiced against a publicity-seeking minority with headquarters in Rome, and I don't help them a lot. As far as preferences are concerned, I go for human interest stories in a big way.'[17]

Despite such cheerful admission, probably as important as the 'prejudice' of the gatekeeper, or the 'policy' of the paper, was the pressure of time; the nearer to edition time, the progressively 'stronger in news value a story needed to be for Mr Gate not to reject it with the explanation "no space" '.

Other likely candidates as influencers or shapers of the news content include the publisher, proprietor or other owners; the audience – its characteristics and prejudices as perceived by both journalists and business executives; advertisers – and their requirements and prejudices as perceived within the news organization. Lewis Donohew found among Kentucky afternoon newspapers, using Associated Press stories on the Medicare issue in 1962 (when the US Congress was handling a Medicare bill), that 'publisher attitude' accounted for about half of the variance[18] – when other variables such as socio-economic characteristics of the audience in the circulation area were also included. Nevertheless, the Donohew study, despite some excellent qualities, has great weaknesses.* One might think that a publisher who did not have any influence on such an ideologically salient issue as Medicare in USA in 1962 could scarcely be expected to have much influence on other political issues. It may never be possible to solve all of the methodological difficulties in the gatekeeper type of study. A major difficulty is presented by the pressure of deadlines; when the gatekeepers are under greatest pressure, events are too complex and happen too fast either for direct observation or subsequent recall.

The gatekeeper concept implies a *processing* rather than a *gathering* view of journalistic activity. It tends to take the existence of a flow of news as given – whereas the present study of national news-gathering concerns people placed at the initiation of the flow. Nevertheless, the flow approach remains useful.

3. NEWS ORGANIZATION AS NON-ROUTINE BUREAUCRACY

The lack of any substantial studies of news organizations is a serious gap in the organizational literature†, since on several organizational dimensions they seem to represent a sociologically important deviant case. Nevertheless, some small-scale studies provide interesting data. The most frequently quoted of these is Warren Breed's analysis of journalists' conformity – 'Social Control in the Newsroom' (1955) – which is based on a doctoral thesis at Columbia University (1952). Breed interviewed 120 journalists on small daily newspapers (10,000 to 100,000 circulation) in the north-east United States. Another study by Rodney W. Stark (1962) is a participant observation study of a 200,000-circulation daily – which sounds like the California Oakland *Tribune*. This newspaper was owned by a family with extreme Republican views, which produced sharp internal conflict, a situation in strong contrast to that reported by Breed. A third organizational study of newspapers, by Matejko (1967), a Polish sociologist from the Cracow Press Research Centre, is based on interviews with 100 journalists on a Warsaw daily and weekly, and a Cracow daily and weekly.[19] Although these newspapers carry high status in Polish journalism, there is a sense of frustration partly induced by the policies of the Communist party and government authorities which suggests some similarities to the American journalists' sense of frustration induced by Republican policies. While the small daily American Editor may have to spend much time with a Republican publish-

* For instance, the 14 newspapers included one paper accounting for about half the total circulation.
† E.g. James G. March (ed) *Handbook of Organizations* (1965) lists organizational studies by over 2,000 authors. Only one of these, Warren Breed, is the author of a news organization study.

er, and a Polish Editor is similarly involved with Communist authorities, in the American national TV networks all Vice-Presidents in charge of News 'are heavily concerned with relationships with the Federal Government'.[20]

Among the numerous existing studies there is little agreement upon the definition of 'organization'. Is a commercial broadcasting 'network', or a company which publishes over 200 separate newspapers and magazines, one 'organization'? The definition even of a 'newspaper' is unclear; for instance, a regional company with a dozen weekly newspapers all of which have some pages in common, and some pages unique to a local area, could be regarded either as one or a dozen separate publications.

For the case in hand – primarily national newspapers, but including also news agencies and broadcast news – a distinction appears necessary between the *editorial department* (staffed primarily by journalists) and larger encompassing organizations.* These editorial departments will here be called *news organizations*; whereas *media organization* will describe the encompassing unit (made up of perhaps several news organizations and such other communications organizations as magazine companies). Between these two levels or functional categories of organizations there can be expected to be other major differences. We will look briefly at two:

Firstly, there will be different goals. Media organizations will have goals of a more commercial nature, whereas at least some news organizations will have less commercial goals.

Secondly, there will be fundamental differences in the work orientations, in hierarchical arrangements and on other dimensions of bureaucracy. The editorial news organization will have a basically *non-routine* character, whereas the overall media organization will be much more routine.

'Routine' and 'non-routine' are the terms of Charles Perrow, who looks at organizations in terms of the technology or the work done on raw materials. Perrow's routine/non-routine dichotomy is comparable with Max Weber's bureaucratic/charismatic distinction, the mechanistic/organic categorization of Burns and Stalker (1961), the 'small batch and unit'/'large batch and unit' categories of Joan Woodward (1965) and the uniform/non-uniform approach of Eugene Litwak (1961). Crucial to Perrow's analysis, however, is a concern with two major aspects of technology:

(1) The number of *exceptional* cases encountered in the work.

* It is quite possible, of course, for a major national publication to be printed on contract—and thus by an organization of which the relevant editorial department does not form a part.

(2) The nature of the *search* process undertaken when exceptions occur. The search may be logical, systematic, analytical (routine). Or the problem may be so vague that it is virtually unanalysable, in which case no formal search occurs and emphasis is placed on experience and intuition, or 'chance and guesswork' (non-routine).[21]

Perrow's *non-routine* category fits fairly closely the work done by journalists in the news organization. The overall media organization with its quite different work done on quite different materials – for instance the manufacture and sale of several million newspapers a day – conforms more closely to Perrow's *routine* category.

a. Routine media organization

In the complete operation of the writing, printing and the financial and other management of a large newspaper, the total labour force involves only a smallish minority of journalists. One breakdown of total staff on a national newspaper[22] was as follows:

	%
Journalists	11·5
clerical and other non-journalist staff in editorial department	9·5
Business staff (advertising, circulation, accounts)	15·1
Production/Printing staff (compositors, foundry, machine room, publishing)	63·9
Total	100
Total number	1,931

From the point of view of the media organization, a newspaper – both in terms of numbers employed and costs* involved – is *primarily* a manufactured product consisting of paper and ink processed by printing presses and printing workers. In terms of Perrow's two major technological variables, this primarily manufacturing media organization is much more routine than is the editorial department. Firstly, the number of exceptional cases encountered in this very large scale type of printing is fairly low. Secondly, the search processes which are

---

* Newsprint, ink and production costs make up about 60 per cent and editorial costs about 15 per cent of total costs of national newspapers. Economist Intelligence Unit (1966), Part II.

undertaken when exceptions occur can be logical, systematic and analytical – for instance with quality control of ink or paper and the servicing of machines.

Media organizations, however, do not fit the routine category very closely. Perrow quotes tonnage steel mills and screws and bolts as having routine technologies (as against the non-routine aerospace industry). Media organizations have several unusual organizational characteristics; printing workers are unique among traditional crafts,[23] and printing unions are unusually strong[24] – as are the technical trade unions in broadcasting. These characteristics follow partly from the connection between media organization and its constituent news (or other communications) organizations. Seen as a manufacturing enterprise the media organization is presented with the unusual problem of a product which, although produced in large numbers, is redesigned several times a day (in the case of a paper with several editions).

Media organizations are unlikely to fit very neatly into any broadly applicable organizational categories. Partly this depends upon what period of time and sort of units of output are considered – one day or one year, one regional page or the whole newspaper. In Perrow's scheme it depends also upon how 'search' and 'exceptions' are defined. Clearly the advertising, circulation and accountancy functions are also partly shaped by the non-routine news organization. Consequently on some criteria the media organization is not routine.* But it will always be much more routine than the news organization.

One media organization will usually contain more than one news organization (see Table 2.2) plus other sorts of communications organizations (e.g. magazines, books). These different communications organizations will have differing output frequencies (daily, weekly, monthly), and thus the media organization – at its encompassing and overall level – will be less directly tied to one very high frequency of output which is the most characteristic feature especially of a *daily* news organization.

b. Non-routine news organization

Journalism is *non-routine* work. Firstly, 'exceptional cases encountered in the work' are numerous – news values stress the exceptional. Secondly, 'search' is not logical, systematic or analytical; on the contrary 'search procedures' in journalism stress talking to people on a non-systematic 'personal' basis; 'experience' and 'intuition' (or 'news sense') are highly valued.

* It may have some of the characteristics of Perrow's 'few exceptions but unanalysable problems', (or *vice versa*), boxes.

In non-routine work (personal services, symbol processing, inno-
vating, or 'one-off' production) the hierarchy may be unclear – in
sharp contrast to the pyramidal Weberian bureaucratic model. Non-
routine work favours an unclear authority structure, shallow hierarchy, and broad lateral span. The emphasis on innovation and
creativity requires quick communication with the top – and hence
non-routine work follows a shapeless, or apparently 'chaotic',
arrangement.

Journalism has such working arrangements. There is no steep
hierarchy, but a large bulge in the middle. This can be seen in terms
of pay in Table 2.4, which shows that 78·5 per cent of all London
newspaper journalists were earning around (one-third more or less
than) £45 a week. Moving away from this bulge at the middle (or
lower middle) one notices in Table 2.4 smaller numbers higher up
the pay scales, but an interesting category of 7·4 per cent in the top
pay grade. Apart from a few star specialists and others, these highly
paid journalists are primarily editorial 'executives'. It is only over-
simplifying a little to say that there are just two main levels inside a
typical national news organization.

Firstly, about 20 senior men (mainly executives) and averaging
£100 a week or more.

Secondly, about 280 other journalists – all averaging around £45
a week.

There is also a *third*, non-journalist, category (secretaries, messeng-
ers and other clerical workers) – perhaps 200 of them – averaging
£20 a week or so.

Figure 2.1 simplifies somewhat since the London and Manchester
offices are combined. But the most obvious mechanism through
which 20 or so executives 'control' 280 or so other journalists is the
'desk'. This (imaginary) news organization has seven desks – news,
picture, night, foreign, feature, sports, and financial. The 'desk',
equipped with files and other impersonal apparatus, will be recognized by any student of Max Weber as an element of bureaucracy.
How then can we still call news organizations non-routine, if the impersonal desk is such a key managerial mechanism?

As Perrow himself says:

'Organizations uniformly seek to minimize exceptional situations.'[25]

Moreover, just as the non-routine editorial (or design) department,
by redesigning the product so frequently, influences what happens

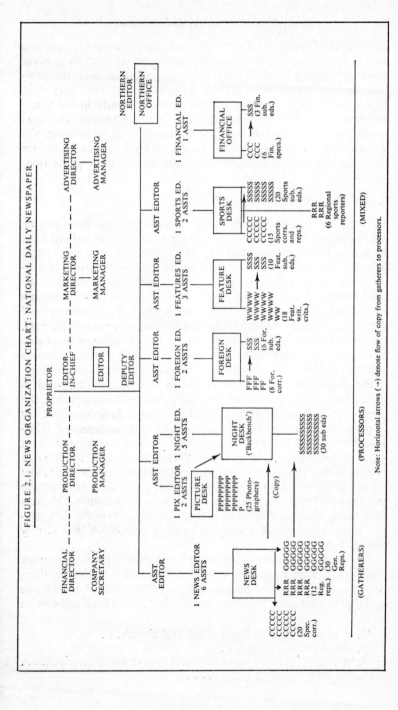

FIGURE 2.1. NEWS ORGANIZATION CHART: NATIONAL DAILY NEWSPAPER

Note: Horizontal arrows (→) denote flow of copy from gatherers to processors.

in the encompassing media organization, this relationship operates in two directions. The routine media organization, with its production, distribution, and finance problems, requires that the non-routine news organization arrange its operation to meet very rigid deadlines. These remorseless edition deadlines timetable and shape all the non-routine work activities of the news journalists. The non-routine bureaucracy involves a continuing struggle between the demands on the one hand of the routine media organization and on the other hand of its constituent non-routine news and organization.

c. *News processing: audience orientation*

The typical national daily newspaper employs nearly five times as many journalists as a provincial daily; both news organizations have 17 per cent of their staffs working as executives or deskmen (Table 2.3). But the national organization has twice the proportion of processors (and 10 times the absolute number) compared with the provincial. Provincial papers have much more of their staff in branch offices, gathering news from local sources which then goes into fixed slots in the paper; provincials also use more agency copy. Nationals, on the other hand, use more freelance material, which is re-written by sub-editors. Most nationals have more complicated edition changes and the popular nationals generally use more aggressive sub-editing.

The divide between sub-editors and all other journalists, which is the major internal functional boundary within the occupation, depends partly on different work functions and partly upon differences in previous career and future expectations. One fundamental difference is the orientation towards different outside groups and different organizational goals. The gatherers are oriented towards their news sources, the processors towards the ultimate audience. The processors regard gatherers as over-involved in their particular subjects; the gatherers see the processors as playing *down* to the audience. This conflict, partly concerned with the overall goal of the organization, cannot easily be resolved since most news organizations lack clearly defined goals.

Sub-editors and other processors on newspapers prepare copy for the printers. They work later hours, inside the office, under the direction of a night editor and his assistants – the 'backbench'. Here is one senior processor describing the characteristics of an ideal sub-editor:

'1. A capacity to check and check and check. . . .
2. An organized mind. . . .
3. A sense of time. A good sub must always watch the clock. . . .
4. An understanding of type. . . .

TABLE 2.4

AVERAGE WEEKLY EARNINGS OF NATIONAL NEWSPAPER JOURNALISTS
(LONDON OFFICES ONLY) JANUARY, 1969

Weekly earnings	Editorial executives & assistants	Feature and specialist writers	Photographers	Reporters	Sub-editors	Other journalists	All journalists
	%	%	%	%	%	%	%
Below £30	—	1·8	1·3	2·6	2·0	2·4	1·8
£30–40	4·5	16·8	64·0	48·9	30·8	32·5	29·1
£40–50	13·5	33·7	28·7	37·5	50·5	33·4	34·0
£50–60	20·6	21·8	4·7	7·8	15·4	14·6	15·4
£60–70	18·7	11·7	1·3	2·1	1·2	7·5	7·7
£70–80	13·5	6·6	—	0·9	0·2	4·7	4·7
£80+	29·2	7·8	—	0·2	—	5·0	7·4
Total	100	100	100	100	100	100	100
Total Number	438	606	150	536	507	425	2,662

Source: National Board for Prices and Incomes, Journalists' Pay (1969)

5. An ability to assess length. . . .
6. An ability to count headlines. . . .
7. An ability to write clearly in a well-ordered way. . . .
8. An ability to write bright headlines. . . .
9. The knack of getting to the heart of the story. . . .
10. A clear understanding of when re-writing is necessary and when it's not. . . .
11. A continuing sense of excitement about change. . . .
12. A capacity to cope with dull stories and get the best out of them. . . .'[26]

The gatherers accuse the processors of cutting stories needlessly, lacking judgement, and being envious of gatherers. The sub-editor's basic pay is slightly higher than the reporter's (Table 2.4) and a daily man can increase it by working on Saturday as a 'casual' for a Sunday paper. But the gatherers' incomes vary more – partly according to their inclination to do extra work.

Over half the national newspaper sub-editors have been in their present job for less than four years – whereas specialist gatherers are much less mobile (see Table 3.9). More than gatherers, sub-editors conform to the 'provincial tradition'. A sub-editor would seldom be hired on to a national without previous daily experience. He is also much less likely to have been educated beyond 17 than a gatherer. Among sub-editors university graduates are rare. Some newsgatherers claim that most sub-editors lead mole lives in the outer suburbs of South-East London, which they leave only during the hours of darkness, and where they share a socially and sexually frustrated existence with a wife whom they met years ago when working on a small provincial newspaper. Sub-editors are accused by gatherers of thinking that the reader always wants to see a few more square inches of female flesh.

In 1965 a *Financial Times* journalist got six times as many column inches into his paper as did a *Daily Express* journalist, five times as much as a *Daily Mirror* or *Sun* man and twice as much as a *Guardian* or *Times* journalist. There were strong inverse correlations of column inches per staff member with both total numbers of journalists and size of circulation. On a paper like the *Daily Express*, where each member of editorial staff produced only 3·2 column inches per working day, the processing of news was much more aggressive than on the *Financial Times* where each man got over six times as much – 19·8 inches – into the paper.*

*This assumes 250 days of work per year. These figures should, in detail, be treated with scepticism, since 'editorial staff' appears to include substantial and differing proportions of non-journalist staff. See Economist Intelligence Unit (1966), Part I, p. 67.

The usual physical arrangement of the night-desk is a 'backbench' – such senior processors as the Night editor, deputy night editor and chief sub-editor – facing two or more long tables of sub-editors. Much of the work must be done in about three hours. During this intensive period no one man can read all the words which will constitute the first edition of a daily newspaper. Large quantities of material will be rejected – or 'spiked' – so total reading is even more impossible. Further, the processors do not merely read but also cut, re-write, update stories with new matter, check spellings and write headlines. There is some division of labour: *Firstly*, by pages – front, sports, features, etc.; *secondly*, processors specialize according to the stage in the flow. Some processors gatekeep for others farther on in the flow. After the copy has left the news-desk it will be 'copytasted'*; if not rejected, it then goes to an executive (e.g. deputy night editor) who will give it a 'catchline' (preliminary title) and a rough indication of the number of words required; a sub-editor then does the detailed processing. The processed story is next returned to the backbench where, if accepted and of suitable size, it will be allotted perhaps half a column on page 3 by an executive – say, the cheif sub-editor – who is 'laying out' this page. Later still, yet another gatekeeper, a 'stone sub-editor', with proof in hand and the story set in the composing room, may make another cut. So, after leaving the news-desk the piece of copy passes perhaps five or six gatekeepers before reaching print.

Such specialization of gatekeepers at different stages in the flow (and at different hierarchical levels) contrasts with newsgathering, where specialization is primarily by subject-matter. A senior gatherer will deal with just one subject, but a senior processor may deal with all the 'inside' news pages – for which he will select 'page leads' from political, crime, human interest, aviation, beauty queen, animal, and other stories. Processors must also consider appearance. Within a very few minutes a chief processor will (in consultation with his picture editor) select a picture of a photogenic kitten, while throwing a pile of glossy dog, panda and pony pictures on the floor; next he selects one girl who provides the best combination of leg quality and photographic quality, while other assorted starlets and débutantes join the ponies and pandas on the floor; then he interrogates the office lawyer about possible libel in a crime story; next on to a late arriving United Nations story.

Pages are made up around advertisements, with pictures and headlines especially affected. Using blue pencil, scissors and paste, processors must rapidly butcher copy upon which other men and women have spent their whole day. There is some specialization by subjects

* There are 'copy-tasters' on news-desk as well as night-desk (or 'backbench').

(e.g. sport), but much less than in gathering; newspapers like the *Daily Express* and *Daily Mirror* which had substantial staffs of Foreign correspondents nevertheless process their foreign and domestic news together. The 'splash' sub-editor processes the front-page lead story regardless of its subject. A story is assigned to a sub-editor primarily according to its importance and to his seniority 'up the table' (that is physically closer to the backbench).

The gatekeeping role of copy-tasters includes regulating the total flow to the processing executive – according to space available at the time and date (which depends on the amount of advertising, the number of pages for that day's paper and whether it is a busy or slack day for news). Further on in the processing flow is the 'revise' sub-editor or 'prodnose', who reads proofs, and checks for matters of house style, policy or inconsistencies between stories.

As each edition time approaches, the processing team works at great speed and pressure. If a reporter hands his copy in at the newsdesk, but does not see it in the paper next morning, all he will know is that it disappeared somewhere in the processing process.

d. Newsgathering: source orientation

Processors have a distinct hierarchy and a basic orientation towards audience and revenue. Gatherers, however, are primarily oriented towards performers in entertainment, politics, or some other field of performance.

Among newsgatherers the *feature writers* claim to deal with background, perspective and the like. A feature writer – who may do a political story this week, and an aviation story next week – tends to see himself as more independent of news sources than is a *specialist* newsgatherer who will need the source again tomorrow. Feature writers see specialists as often uncritical and superficially factual, while the specialists see feature writers as piratical and usually ignorant intruders.

The *columnist* may specialize in politics, finance, sport or show business. Although unlikely to achieve the status of the national American columnist – whose strength is based on syndication in many local publications – the Fleet Street columnist is encouraged to be 'independent', outspoken and personal. His seniority, his 'name', his licence to pontificate and his fixed space leave him free of much processing; his prominence and previous career will have established favourable contacts with sources; being defined as general but 'prestige', his column need not appeal to any narrowly defined audience group. His major orientation is likely to be to the broad world on which he comments.

Diary writers or 'gossip columnists' usually work in an anonymous team. Diaries, like features, tend to be 'locked up' early and to conflict with other gatherers in the same news organization; juicy gossip items may be 'poached' or dull items may be 'dumped' on the diary. Many diary items are based on following up previously reported events for an additional personal angle. Gossip journalists may have family connections in gossip-source areas – such as literature or diplomacy. The orientation of diary journalism to its source area is also noticeable in the stage vocabulary of some gossip writers.

General reporters (10 per cent of national daily newspaper journalists) mostly do not wish to remain permanently as ordinary general reporters. Some are aiming for the job of their current boss – the News editor; and there is a hierarchy leading up through the news-desk assistant posts. Other career ambitions include becoming a specialist newsgatherer, or a feature writer, or perhaps a star reporter – doing some foreign 'fireman' trips plus unusual reporting assignments within Britain.

General reporters come to the news-desk for assignments each day, and return their completed copy to the news-desk; when out of the office, on a story, reporters are expected to telephone in at regular intervals. A general reporter may on the first day of the week be assigned to cover an unofficial strike meeting, the next day a beauty show for dogs or girls, the third day a mystery explosion, the fourth day a story about petty criminals in the East End, the fifth day a 'colour' story about the demolition of an ancient factory. However, even general reporters tend to specialize a little. Some deputize on the Aviation, Crime or Labour correspondent's day off. Especially good shorthand, or being female, or having a particular social background may seem (to the news-desk) relevant to some categories of story. Most general reporter's assignments are those which specialists do not think adequately interesting. But there is always the chance – even for a junior reporter – that his story will turn into the front-page splash. One ambition predominates among young general reporters – to become a Foreign correspondent. There is much competition to get these few jobs which cost the news organization more than can be justified in revenue terms. This reflects the prestige of the Foreign correspondent's job, as well as the marked lack of revenue-orientation among most young general reporters.

The *News editor* is a senior executive in newsgathering, although an 'assistant editor (news)' may come in the hierarchy between him and the Editor. The news-desk may have a normal staff of the News editor, plus his deputy, plus three assistants. But, since the news-desk on a national daily paper is manned day and night six days a week, the total regular news-desk staff will be nearer to ten. An important object on the news-desk is the list of local correspondents (some are freelance agencies, others news editors or branch-office men on local papers). Another prop is the 'Enter Ups' – a filing system of forth-coming events, appropriate invitations, and notes to check back on fresh developments. Across the news-desk there flow even larger quantities of paper than across the night-desk. A major news-desk activity is the 'copy-tasting' of material from agencies, stories phoned in by stringers (and typed out by 'copytakers'), and various kinds of public relations material. During one day at a news-desk an estimated 75 to 90 per cent of this material was rejected without even reaching the News editor. If material does reach the News editor it then has a fair chance of being assigned to a reporter.

There is a tendency for News editors on 'popular' media to have come up through the more junior jobs on the news-desk, and for prestige paper News editors to have been senior specialist news-gatherers. To the source orientation which a newsgathering background normally entails, the News editor must add an ability to match the personality of an available reporter to a news source's anticipated type of personality. His work role thus forces the News editor (and his staff) to remain primarily source-oriented.

e. Rapid internal communication: benefits and costs

Internal communication is especially central if the organization's own product is communication. The output of a communications organi-zation is usually highly *observable*. Mistakes and successes occur in public, and are especially open to the observation of other members of the organization.

Both observability and continuous product change are especially marked in *news* organizations. Broadcast news bulletins occur at set times, are fairly brief, and contain some 'live' material. A newspaper is also extreme in observability; unlike the diverse output of some other communications organizations, the newspaper drops in an in-tegrated package on to the reader's breakfast table. It has only one splash story, one front page, and one major 'editorial' article. Consequently the product of a news organization communicates a great deal to an organizational member. A journalist – even on holiday abroad – can read the newspaper and see who's just flown out to Africa, who's got the splash story, and how the number two Industrial man is outshining his number one. A journalist can also observe how his own organization is faring against its main competi-tors.

The product communicates, to the people who produce it, many different things. One is political policy. But probably more important will be the general vision of the world which the organization communicates to its members. The product also provides continuing minor revisions of the house 'rules'. If a sub-editor wants to know the organizational rule as to how one refers to the current President of a small African nation – the preferred spelling, the degree of familiarity approved, the political policy line if any – all of this can be found in the 'cuttings'. Some inaccurate information in the cuttings may get repeated on several subsequent occasions. This illustrates the strength of the rule book on many matters of detail.

The product also signals changes in the balance of power between various types of gatherers – such as specialists, reporters, and feature writers. It communicates information about the probable demand for particular types of story. If a specialist notices that his news organization is making a big build-up for a royal wedding, a murder trial, or the opening of a sponsored exhibition, on the day in question he will know – without even consulting his desk – that fewer words are required of him.

Information about the current competitive position comes to the journalist through the *final* product of his news organization. Changes from the first edition as a result of what competing news organizations are doing in their first editions make clear to the journalist how his organization is currently responding to its competition. The content also communicates how the news organization is currently defining its goals. Journalists say you can tell when the popular newspapers are worried – they increase still further the space devoted to naked female flesh.

The 'by-line' is the running organizational honours system. Leading gatherers, such as senior specialists, almost invariably get by-lines. The name of a well-known political correspondent attached to the story is believed to give it more 'weight'. But with general reporters a by-line may be a fairly unusual honour. The star treatment occurs when the face or biography of the journalist is projected with the story. In television the equivalent of the by-line is appearing in person. This kind of commendation by the news organization, or the disciplinary act of removing the by-line privilege from a man who normally receives one, also signals to other journalists what priorities the news organization is stressing. Status is especially strongly communicated by changes between editions. The last editions are regarded as the most important, the early editions which go to outlying areas as least important. Consequently the status message is clear when a piece is cut down, or cut out, from its first edition prominence, and another late-arriving piece of copy is given prominence in the last edition.

Clearly the product is not the sole channel of communication within a news organization. In some newspapers the Editor's comments on yesterday's output appear on a notice-board. There are executive 'conferences' each day on a daily medium. There is a great deal of face-to-face casual conversation in the office – 'informal' interaction is 'formally' encouraged by the open-floor layout of the newsroom. There are also many memos, reminders, notes and circulars – and internal telephoning operates on a grand scale of frequency, speed, gossip and noise.

The speed and rigidity of edition times shape much of the other communication. Attending a conference inside a newspaper office, the outsider is at first startled that the entire business of the conference appears to consist of swapping headline-like sentences, each of a few words. At the midday (primarily newsgathering) meeting the biggest item of business is the News editor reading out a long list of stories his men are covering; the News editor is followed by the Features editor, Sports editor, Foreign editor and Picture editor. The Editor, or the man editing the paper for the day, says a few sentences, and the meeting is over.* The 'conference' is mainly a co-ordinating meeting at which shopping lists are exchanged, possible overlaps settled, and a rough sketch of the day's menu produced. Even at the late afternoon (primarily news-processing) conference it is perhaps four hours to the first edition, and such major decisions of the day as choice of splash story can be made later by the Editor and the executive concerned, in this case the Night editor.

Brief exchanges of headline-sounding sentences are also used when a reporter is assigned to a story by a News editor. This phenomenon has been noted elsewhere.[27] The details of the story are still uncertain, and the headline-like description summarizes the major news 'angle'. When one item has to pass many gatekeepers, and when processing executives have to pass or process many items, it can only be done at all by extreme brevity in oral and written references to separate stories, many of which will ultimately be rejected altogether.

'Executive' has no firm definition, but if we assume that an executive has 20 subordinates he cannot have much time to talk to each – especially since the intense activity of the executive is concentrated into perhaps two or three hours, during which he must also talk to his desk assistants, and his superior, as well as reading a large number of separate stories. A shallow hierarchy with a bulge in the middle allows even the most junior reporter or sub-editor to have direct personal access to his News editor or Night editor. But such personal communication is only possible if it remains extremely brief.

Outside observers, who see a newsroom in action, get an impres-

* Discussion is not inhibited by the presence of an outsider. The outsider is welcomed because little discussion occurs.

sion of some people shouting into telephones, others thumping type-writers, others gossiping or drinking tea, boys dropping piles of paper on desks, a general atmosphere of disorder. All this activity is, how-ever, pre-programmed by yesterday's edition, by fixed edition times, fixed pages assigned to various subjects, and the delegation of res-ponsibility for particular pages to specific 'desks'. The product itself talks to the journalists about status, rules and goals; the gathering and processing procedures require executives to address other jour-nalists in a language of headlines. Thus members of a non-routine occupation which values individuality, personality, and creativity are nevertheless programmed by organizational requirements to talk like precocious parrots swapping tomorrow's headlines.

Harold Wilensky (1967) describes *secrecy*, *rivalry* and *hierarchy* as three organizational pathologies which distract the effective flow of organizational intelligence; in governmental and other bureaucracies the performance of certain operations in *secret* severely inhibits the long-term upward flow of information. But in news organizations secrecy is inhibiting more frequently in the shorter term, and often horizontally rather than vertically. The common phenomenon of one individual journalist 'sitting on a story' for a day or two illustrates another of Wilensky's pathologies – namely *rivalry*. Where subject areas are in dispute, specialists are reluctant to pass on information to their rivals; knowledge which could have been pooled is not; news sources are not approached for information; the wrong man writes the story; two and two are not put together to make four.

But the main axis of conflict between the processors and the gatherers often channels rivalry into a form which is positively useful for the organization. The American newspaper in which the editorial staff were polarized along politically partisan lines was a paper in which the gatherer/processor divide had been abolished.[28] Moreover, rivalry will often not lead to secrecy but to competition for space, or to a jurisdictional dispute which will bring the potential news story to the notice of a senior executive or the Editor. In getting informa-tion to the top and getting quick decisions, news organizations appear more effective than most large organizations upon whose activities they report. However, this type of organizational flexibility, which is well suited to being 'first with the news', appears less successful in other ways – in producing stories which cannot be summed up in a single short sentence, stories which do not immediately seem strong in news value, stories which do not reach a peak of interest that can be communicated up and down the hierarchy in a few minutes on one particular night.

A substantial price is paid for the relative success with which the news organization evades the organizational pathologies of *secrecy*, *rivalry* and *hierarchy*. On certain night-desks the flow of paper is so voluminous and so fast that some rigidity must be introduced. On quality papers the tendency is to de-emphasize processing, to use a small processing staff and to pre-programme the operation by assigning spaces before the gatherers' copy arrives; this inevitably means that the 'wrong' stories occupy some prominent spaces. Popular papers tend to emphasize processing, to use a larger processing staff, and to assign spaces only after the copy has been received; this system involves especially severe time pressures, a rigid division of labour and fixing of responsibility for particular pages. One result is that the two senior processors (P.1 and P.2) may concentrate on the front page and one other news page, where they place the 'big' stories – especially those from the Political, Foreign, and Labour specialists. Another senior processor (P.4) may handle only the splash story, while another concentrates on a summary of Parliament (P.5). Two other senior men (P.6 and P.7) are copy-tasters. A very large share of the remaining burden falls on a single individual (P.3) – who may be a 'deputy chief sub-editor'. P.3 may supervise as much space as P.1, P.2, P.4 and P.5 put together. P.3 will tend to use the general reporters' stories which, because he is laying out so many stories, must be very quickly handled. Consequently while less 'important' stories, written by more junior journalists and carelessly processed, are commanding large spaces on the 'lesser' news pages, stories by Foreign correspondents and other senior specialists, after careful processing and appearing on the front page, may in later editions be rejected altogether.

The remedy would be more flexibility among the senior processors; a national political or foreign story squeezed off page one or page two might be transferred to a page lead or other largish space on one of the 'lesser' pages. But all the men involved are working flat out, only a few pages are changed at each edition, and the page from which the story was being removed might change on a different edition from the page which would otherwise be its most suitable new destination.

A relevant story relates to a time-and-motion man who was studying a night-desk. One journalist was sitting idle doing nothing. The time-and-motion men asked why, and was told: 'He's the splash sub-editor.' Whether this answer is utterly devastating depends upon whether a processor should sit idle for the first two hours of his shift waiting for the splash story to be chosen. Assessment of this question would depend upon stating explicitly certain organizational priorities, which are usually left unclear by both management and journalists.

The news organization provides quick personal communication between an individual journalist and a senior executive, which may allow a rapid focusing of organizational resources on a single story. But the same organization is also capable of first allocating a story to the front page and then – through time pressure and rigid division of labour – rejecting the story altogether in the next edition.

f. Routine and non-routine: audience and source orientation

Processing lends itself to a greater degree of routine than does gathering. Rules are more applicable in processing – it is the sub-editors who have a house 'style book' close at hand, not the gatherers. The sharper hierarchy is another bureaucratic element. Whereas the raw material of a processor is a typed story (or picture or film), the prime raw material of the gatherers is defined as being people. Confronted with a point to check, the processor can 'search' the style book or the library cuttings. But a gatherer with a dubious story engages in the search technique of 'standing the story up' (or alternatively 'knocking it down'). This often merely means telephoning another news source to get another opinion or another quote. Newsgathering can become more routinized by more reliance on certain well-tried sources, but news values put a limit on any such tendency. So long as the basic newsgathering technique consists of talking to people, newsgatherers will continue to be news source-oriented.

The gatherer/processor divide is so fundamental that only 7 per cent of journalists belong to neither category – these are general executives and their assistants (Table 2.3). 'General' here is defined as executives who are in control of both gatherers and processors. This includes the Editor, and his deputy, plus such departmental executives as the Foreign editor, Sports editor, Features editor and Financial editor. Within sports or features departments more flexibility between gathering and processing is possible because it takes place within a rigid departmentalization – represented at the processing end in the fixed allocation of certain pages as feature pages or sports pages. But sports writers still say that sports sub-editors are jealous because they never meet the famous sportsmen or see the big contests; Foreign correspondents, in some news organizations, complain that sub-editors are ignorant of the world outside Fleet Street. Sub-editors, of course, insist that gatherers become spokesmen for a particular sport, team or country and forget the interests of the ordinary reader.

In many departments either the gatherers or the processors are dominant. But a latent structural conflict exists – not merely between some people who work at a desk at night and other people who work 'outside' in the day. Nor is it merely a conflict between people with educational or career (or personality) differences. The conflict is about something more basic – between an audience orientation and a news source orientation. It is a continuing dispute about the overall goals and purposes of the news organization itself.

4. NEWS ORGANIZATIONS: GOALS AND GOAL BARGAINING

a. Publishers, editors and policy

> 'How can the editor, with responsibility for editorial content only – no responsibility for getting advertising, circulation management, buying newsprint and making deals – rate ahead of the manager? . . . The editor is no longer the top man in any viable newspaper. That is an old concept.'
>
> Lord Thomson (1967) [29]

Newspapers in the 18th century and early 19th century were mainly launched by printers, who exercised the predominant role. Sometimes the printers acted as their own Editors. *The Times* later seemed to have institutionalized the sovereign Editor. John Delane, Editor from 1841 to 1877, was, however, to some extent the beneficiary of a freakish set of circumstances. He was appointed Editor at the age of 23 while the youngest member of the staff. As in the case of some other very young appointments, this appears to have enabled John Walter II, the proprietor, to retain control. Five years later, in 1846, Delane was very nearly sacked following a financial scandal. However, the proprietor died next year, and the new proprietor, John Walter III, a friend and admirer of Delane, confirmed him in office for another 30 years. But not long after Delane's retirement in 1877 *The Times* was in serious financial trouble. The prestige London evening papers which carried on the tradition of the sovereign Editor (*Pall Mall Gazette*, *St James Gazette* and *Westminster Gazette*) were small circulation papers dependent on subsidy; these papers all eventually disappeared. In the case of *The Times* editorial independence resulted in dependence on financial saving operations in 1908 (Northcliffe), 1922 (Astor) and 1967 (Thomson); in the last case editorial freedom was openly limited by the appointment of an editor-in-chief.

Statements about the declining powers of Editors are misleading if one is comparing *The Times* as it was when Delane became Editor in 1841 – an expensive eight-page newspaper with a protected monopoly situation – and the quite different circumstances over a century later. All discussions as to the power of Editors are inclined to be speculative – since evidence on the power of an Editor within his own news organization is largely lacking.[30]

The editorial role can be seen as made up of three main constituent roles:

Firstly, the Editor interacts with business executives in charge of finance, advertising, circulation, production and promotion; if there is an active publisher* interaction with him may be important. On a day-to-day basis such matters as the amount and placing of advertising or any likely impact on circulation in specific local areas might be involved. On a somewhat longer-term basis, questions like the number of pages and the size of the editorial budget are important.

Secondly, the Editor may choose to perform some of the functions of the chief gatherer – such as directing specialists – or of the chief processor, which may include sitting at night with the backbench handling raw copy. Perhaps more common is to maintain an overview of both activities by presiding over morning and afternoon editorial conferences, choosing the front-page lead and taking a few other key decisions. National daily Editors, however, 'edit' in this detailed sense considerably less than the possible 14 hours a day six days a week. Some Editors concentrate on the early (gathering) or the later (processing) hours; another alternative is a full 12- to 14-hour stint of editing for perhaps three days a week. The personnel management decisions with a staff of 300 journalists are considerable – hiring and promoting a wide range of journalists, as well as controlling salaries and expenses of over £1 million a year.

Thirdly, there is the editorial role of relating the news organization to the general environment. Some of this is activity of a commercial and promotional kind – presenting prizes won in competitions or addressing advertising agency media planners. Other activities involve the maintenance of the news organization's respectability and legitimacy – for instance, sitting on the Press Council, and talking to politicians. This shades off into the direct exposure of an Editor to news sources – from the Prime Minister to show-business personalities.

It was noticeable when interviewing national Editors in late 1968 that about half of them had just visited, or were about to visit, the United States. Such visits could presumably be justified as first-hand exposure to the 1968 US Presidential Election, and as visiting the New York and Washington bureaux to check on provisions for additional news coverage. Nearly all the Editors seemed to personify some of the attributes which the particular news organization would probably prefer to regard as its authentic image. One had the impression† that

* In the late 1960's this American term began to be used in place of the traditional Fleet Street term 'Proprietor'.

† All of this section is inevitably impressionistic. However it is based in part on interviews in 1968 with 15 national Editors (average duration 65 minutes) – although these interviews were primarily about specialists. Also during the study seven ex-national Editors were interviewed, plus eight Editors of daily provincial newspapers.

the broad task of maintaining favourable relations with the external environment was a major part of the total editorial role – or was regarded as such by the people who appointed Editors.

One assistant editor of a national newspaper said that the only practical way to run a newspaper is 'to assume that the Editor is a genius'. Publishers, of course, have seldom favoured this conception of the editorial role. Although similar arrangements existed for other national newspapers the introduction of an Editor-in-chief to whom the Editors both of *The Times* and the *Sunday Times* would be responsible caused the members of the Monopolies Commission some anxiety in 1966:

> 'The roles of the editor and the editor-in-chief and their relationship with the proprietors were a matter of concern to most witnesses. Many were doubtful whether a satisfactory relationship could be established between an editor and editor-in-chief; experience elsewhere suggested that the editor-in-chief would emerge as the effective editor.'[31]

Such statements, of course, give little indication of how an 'effective Editor' could be recognized. If the previous Editor, Sir William Haley, was an effective Editor, it was in some non-profit sense. The Monopolies Commission reported on the Thomson concept of Editor-in-chief as follows:

> 'We were also told that the role of the editor-in-chief would be to allocate the editorial budget; to organize such joint projects, joint services and cross postings of staff as he might decide; to make senior staff appointments; and to recommend to the board the appointment of the two individual editors "and then in the words of Bagehot to advise, encourage and perhaps warn them". Each of the two editors, in consultation with the editor-in-chief, would be responsible for the day-to-day running of his newspaper.'[32]

The Monopolies Commission preferred the title 'editorial director' to 'editor-in-chief' but the significance of the role, however named, surely lies in the establishment of an additional level in the overall hierarchy interposed between the Editor and the chief executive. Indeed the prevailing tendency is for the Editor – after a trial period – to be made a director of the overall company; on this board he works alongside directors responsible for production, advertising, circulation and other business functions. This concept was explicitly welcomed by the EIU Report of 1966, which was followed by many appointments of new directors, including Editors, in Fleet Street.

A number of Editors explicitly stated that certain kinds of editorial content had a primary purpose of attracting revenue. More than one national Editor had extremely hostile things to say about advertising in the columns of his own newspaper. A common Editor's attitude was that more editorial coverage than he would ideally prefer must be given to certain fields for revenue purposes – in order that money would be available for such things as Foreign correspondence. Several Editors stated explicitly that the great expansion of financial coverage during the 1960's was primarily due to advertising and revenue considerations. Editors nevertheless approved in general of increased financial coverage. But business and financial news – whether located in separate sections or on separate pages – is under the control of a senior editorial executive. Inevitably a team of financial newsgatherers – attracting large sums in advertising revenue – must develop a substantial degree of autonomy. Moreover, financial journalists are both highly paid by Fleet Street standards and independent in the career sense that other job opportunities are available in the financial world.

Financial journalism (a major force in only a few news organizations) is an extreme example of another impediment to the sovereignty of Editors. Within the editorial department, increasing division of labour leads to increasing autonomy in certain limited areas. This tendency is backed by representatives of business functions within the overall organization, with whom the Editor is increasingly encouraged to see himself acting in coalition. Moreover a new level above the Editor in hierarchical terms is becoming established. The many available roles open to the Editor are, as a result, increasingly being played by others above, below, and to the side of the Editor.

The making of 'policy' inside a news organization probably has much in common with the formulation of policy in other companies and organizations; much of it is traditional. One *Daily Express* journalist said of that newspaper's politics: 'Most people here regard it as something you have to put up with – like the English climate.' On major political issues and at any one time the news organization's policy will be relatively fixed. In 1965 only one British national paper, *The Guardian*, devoted more of its space to British politics than to sport. The big circulation papers devoted between 11 and 14 per cent of domestic editorial space to British politics, and between 33 and 45 per cent to sport.[33]

A politically active publisher will himself set political policy; examples include most of the first-generation tycoon publishers and some of their sons. In other cases major political policy is made by a business director; Cecil King made *Daily Mirror* policy at a time when he was its advertisement director.[34] But the policy-maker can also be junior to the Editor; on some issues, perhaps involving major

sums of public money, the news organization's policy may be set by
a middle-level member of the editorial staff – such as a leader writer
or specialist.

Some members of the 1947–9 Royal Commission wondered how
the policy was transmitted to the ordinary journalists; was there an
internal memorandum system by which journalists were told that the
organization was for this and against that? This function is, however, performed in the columns of the paper itself. Senior executives
control the processing, where changes can be made to align stories
with policy; but any gathering journalist on the *Daily Express*, for
instance, has by experience and observation a fairly specific idea as
to what sorts of stories will be used by that paper. Journalists observed on stories discussing what they will send, what 'angle' they
will use, what the 'intro' will be, make only limited references to the
political policies of their organization. The political policy of the
news organization is relatively fixed – certainly by comparison with
the more uncertain and non-routine, characteristics of most potential
stories on the day in question.

The notion that policy appears, or can appear, only in 'leaders' is
too naïve to require discussion. Nevertheless the leader column does
play a special part in policy-making. Firstly, the popular papers had
one or two leader writers under the general direction of the Editor,
writing short, usually rhetorical, leaders. Secondly, the quality papers
– especially *The Times* and *Daily Telegraph* – had substantially larger
teams of specialized leader writers working under the direct super-
vision of the Editor. Readers have increasingly been encouraged to
regard unsigned pieces as of lesser importance. The senior leader
writer has tended to jump across the page to write large 'feature'
articles over his own name. This development can be seen as further
weakening the whole concept of editorial policy.

The author observed shortly before the 1966 General Election an
editorial decision being made in a national newspaper as to whether
a policy statement from the then Prime Minister, Harold Wilson,
should be made the splash story. After consultation between the
deputy editor, an assistant editor and the News editor (and checks
with the Labour and Lobby correspondents) the Editor changed the
splash story just before the first edition deadline – substituting a
story about a Conservative speech and demoting the Harold Wilson
story lower down the front page. Subsequently one news executive
said the decision was based on political opposition to Harold Wilson;
but another executive argued that the substituted story had greater
news value because it had been said 'on the record', whereas Harold
Wilson's statement had been made off the record and was consequently less 'hard'. Such debates as to where 'news values' end and

'policies' begin often cannot be resolved, because both are part of the same broader whole.

Editors say they must often decide whether a suggested line of argument, perhaps being put forward by the leader writer, can be reconciled with the broad character of the news organization. The problem thus is often seen by those making political policy as how to bring particular leader policies into line with the overall values of the newspaper. 'Tradition' must inevitably account for a major part of the news values and political policies of any news organization. Radical overnight changes usually only follow from attempts to arrest financial losses. Newspapers, as repeat purchase products depending on consumer habit, can more quickly alienate the existing audience than they can attract substantial numbers of new audience members. All newspapers aim to establish a reputation for taking certain sorts of positions, or providing certain sorts of services. These become the news organization's 'traditions'.

While the leading article committing the whole news organization to a possibly unpopular political position became less prominent, a more characteristic editorial development was the 'team investigation'. Such 'investigations' are attractive to the audience which receives an impression both of excitement and of journalists' integrity; investigations seldom bring the news organization into serious conflict with major news sources or advertisers – on the contrary they often develop from information first supplied by the police or by business men; investigations attract all journalists for whom relative anonymity is outweighed by involvement in journalism which seems to be strongly in line with the occupational ideology. Investigations provide a theme for promotional advertising. The heavy editorial expenses involved, however, justify executive control over the choice of subjects for investigation. Above all 'team investigations' typify the de-emphasis of partisan policies and a positive stress upon co-operation between journalists, Editor and business departments in pursuit of the coalition goal of sales.

National Editors,* in mid-1968, had a median age of 48, and had been appointed to their editorships at a median age of 42. Of the seven 'prestige' national newspapers (three Sunday, four daily) Editors, all were university graduates – four having been to Oxford and two to Cambridge. Editors in other national news organizations had predominantly *lower*-middle-class origins – leaving school around age 17 or 18 and not going to university. Nearly all Editors had come through one of four areas of journalism: processing, foreign, political, financial. Most had shown very rapid upward

* This is based on evidence about only 15 national Editors. Much of the data is from *Who's Who*, some from interviews with Editors themselves.

movement at some point in their career. Nearly all had done something 'unorthodox'. Robert Edwards was Editor of the socialist
weekly *Tribune* (1951–4) before becoming Editor of the *Daily Express*
(twice) and then *The People*. John Gold spent most of his journalist
career in New York before becoming Editor of the *Evening News*.
Harold Evans, the only national Editor to have edited a provincial
daily, went from it with only a very brief pause into a national
editorship – the *Sunday Times*.

Most Editors had had early experience of an executive post and
had held a *general* executive post (in charge of both gatherers and
processors) – such as Features editor or Foreign editor. Most had
also had a number two or three job which gave them a chance to
perform the Editor's role on a part-time basis. The preference for
relatively young but broadly experienced men with general executive
preparation suggests a good deal of business caution in editorial
appointments. Most Editors will inevitably know of some very long
and some very short Editorships – with the obvious implication of a
trial period. Some of his older rivals for the job will be still there in
senior positions; the Editor's most important decisions in his first
few years may be filling the gaps left by his own elevation, and subsequent moves (and resignations). After this first shuffle round he must
sit out a trial period. A new Editor will often be appointed as one of a
collection of measures designed to pursue some new business objective – a young Editor may be appointed as part of revenue policy of
attracting a younger audience. For his first years an Editor may find
himself committed to a basic strategy devised by others.

Collectively Editors are extremely weak. The provincial Editors'
Guild of British Newspaper Editors is an offshoot of the Proprietors'
Trade Association. National Editors have no organization of any
kind. One of the most surprising things to an outsider about national
Editors is that they know little about each other.

The Editor role is not defined as being primarily concerned with
those parts of the operation which attract either audiences or advertising. Not a single national Editor had a background in sports or
crime journalism. The majority of Editors have newsgathering backgrounds and the appropriate source orientations. One popular
Editor said he was bored by sport but fascinated by foreign affairs:
'Foreign news is more important, more interesting.' Selecting a man
to send to a revolution in Africa was something he liked to take a
hand in; selecting a man to cover a football match in Madrid was
something he preferred not to be bothered with. Even if an Editor
has a processing background, or if he edits a popular newspaper
which expects the Editor to play an active processing part, he is still
likely to concentrate on the big political stories.

Editors are encouraged not to be primarily concerned with revenue but to be responsible for maintaining the legitimacy of the news organization on the national scene – among politicians, civil servants, senior business men, and the best-educated sector of the audience. The Editor who adopts this non-revenue orientation may resist the plans of advertising, promotion and marketing personnel – but beyond a certain point they are bound to prevail. This is no less the case in quality news organizations, where the weakness of Editors is emphasized by the presence of editors-in-chief or editorial directors and the tendency for 'policy' to be of a kind which will be regarded as neutral by the audience in question.

b. News organization goals: a revenue classification

News organizations do not fit neatly into any of the established sociological goal classification systems. Talcott Parsons[35] suggests a fourfold classification: Adaptive, Implementive, Integrative and Pattern-Maintenance.

(1) Adaptive – this is the goal of economic production, with the business firm as the leading example. (2) Implementive – this means having a primarily political goal. (3) Integrative – this Parsonian goal has to do with maintaining the efficiency of the total society, for instance by adjusting conflicts. (4) Pattern-Maintenance – this goal lies in cultural, educational and expressive functions. The difficulty with Parsons' classification is that news organizations appear to include all of his major types of goal. One could argue that this is inevitable since they perform a function of surveillance of other organizations.

Etzioni says: 'Newspapers typically have a dual organizational structure, with a highly utilitarian wing in which the newspaper is actually produced, and a normative editorial wing in which it is written and edited.'[36] By describing the production side of a newspaper as '*utilitarian*' he is suggesting that printers have a 'remunerative-calculative' type of involvement. The editorial wing is described as *normative* – implying that the involvement of journalists in their newspapers compares with that of church members, political party members, or academics in universities. On the involvement of the journalists Etzioni quotes only the study of Warren Breed; but this study describes journalists as having a generally calculative and negative orientation to their employers' non-commercial goals – certainly not a positive ideological commitment or 'belief'.

Peter Blau and Richard Scott argue for a 'prime beneficiary' approach – organizations can be classified in terms of the type of person who benefits: (1) Members or rank and file participants; (2) Owners or managers; (3) Clients or public-in-contact; (4) The public-at-large or the whole society.[37] There are possible arguments for placing news organizations into each of these four categories.

The unsuitability of such classifications illustrates an important aspect of news organizations' goals. All organizations are unique in some way or other. No other type of organization has the news organization's dependence on *advertising* and *sales* revenue – plus their involvement in *non-revenue* activities, including contacts with a very wide environment upon which they report. A further complexity is that the connection between profit goal and non-revenue goal is so varied; a 'popular' newspaper can be losing large sums of money, while a 'prestige' paper is making huge profits. Types of coverage bearing such labels as 'foreign' or 'education' may vary so much from one news organization to the next as to be barely comparable.

News organizations should be seen not as *unitary*, nor as *dual* organizations, but as having *several* types of goal. A continual process of bargaining takes place as to which goals should be pursued. This process of goal bargaining adds one further element of flux and instability to news organizations. Internal debates as to the target audience, the balance between advertising and news, the ratio in the numbers of journalists covering foreign, women's, political or sports news – all these concern the overall direction of the news organization.

Yuchtman and Seashore[38] prefer the concept of 'bargaining position' in relation to the organization's environment, rather than any specific goal, as a criterion of effectiveness. However, they want to retain the goal concept:

'(1) as a specification of the means or strategies employed by members toward enhancing the bargaining position of the organization; and

'(2) as a specification of the personal goals of certain members or classes of member within the organization system.'

Robert Park wrote in 1922 that 'the sources of newspaper revenue are from subscription, advertising and subventions'. He suggested that the degree of control exercised by the supplier of subventions is greater than the control which can be exercised by subscribers or advertisers. One individual subsidizer would exercise greater control – because he could threaten to withdraw the entire subsidy.[39] With the decline in partisan political subsidy this kind of analysis can now be applied to few major publications. However, Park's emphasis on *revenue* remains important.

In the present study the concept of 'goal' will be used in the limited

sense proposed by Yuchtman and Seashore. Within this broad perspective, news organizations' goals will be classified in terms of
revenue. This produces three main types of goal as follows:

(1) Audience revenue goal.
(2) Advertising revenue goal.
(3) Non-revenue goal.

(1) *The audience revenue goal* exists because a news organization
operating on a commercial basis must have an audience. This is the
case with a newspaper sold daily or weekly to a public; it is equally
so with a broadcast news organization – whether financed by advertising or licence fee.

(2) *The advertising revenue goal* is obviously not present with a
licence-financed broadcast news organization–which gives the BBC (as
well as news agencies) some distinctive aspects. But in the predominant situation of national newspapers (and commercial broadcasting)
dependent on revenue from advertising, the maintenance (or increasing) of this form of revenue inevitably becomes *one* of the goals of
both news organizations and media organizations.

(3) *Non-revenue goals* are, however, also present in all news organizations. Both national Editors and ordinary journalists, to a
greater (newsgatherers) or lesser (news processors) extent, are oriented toward a non-revenue goal. Moreover non-revenue goals are also
pursued by the publishers, owners and senior managers of media (and
news) organizations; this may involve support for particular political
policies – which are likely to conflict with an unambiguous profit
goal. Even when political partisanship is de-emphasized there is still
some element of non-revenue goal; this may be greater in the case of
'quality' news organizations, but even 'popular' news organizations
are likely to involve some non-revenue goal element.

c. Goals, goal bargaining and mixed goals

Yuchtman and Seashore argue that the 'goal' and the 'effectiveness'
of an organization are often defined in terms of each other. Instead:

> 'We propose, accordingly, to define the effectiveness of an organi-
> zation in terms of its bargaining position, as reflected in the ability
> of the organization, in either absolute or relative terms, to exploit
> its environment in the acquisition of scarce and valued resources.'[40]

For a news organization, and its encompassing media organization,
these 'scarce and valued resources' include physical plant, sales

revenue and advertising revenue as well as 'prestige' and influence (or social legitimacy). Such resources involve the *loyalties* of audiences, advertisers, news sources, and employees. Yuchtman and Seashore regard human activity as a crucial organizational resource:

> 'We view members of an organization as an integral part of the organization with respect to their organizational role-defining and role-carrying activities, but as part of the environment of the organization with respect to their abilities, motives, other memberships, and other characteristics that are potentially useful but not utilized by the organization in role performance. An "effective" organization competes successfully for a relatively large share of the member's personality, engaging more of the personality in organizationally relevant ways, thus acquiring additional resources from its environment.'[41]

News organizations compete with other organizations for the loyalty of their journalist employees. A national news organization's leading journalists have independent reputations as 'stars' in their particular fields; consequently a news organization in search of prestige or social legitimacy, as well as of revenue 'success', must compete for the services of leading journalists. Thus it may have to let the goals of journalists become – to some extent – incorporated into the collective goals of the news organization. This will tend to emphasize the non-revenue goal.

Even those news organizations which place an unusually heavy reliance on revenue goals probably never try to *maximize* profits:

> 'The position taken here is that maximization of return, even if possible, is destructive from the viewpoint of the organization. . . . An organization that fully actualizes its exploitative potential may risk its own survival. . . . Furthermore, an organization that ruthlessly exploits its environment is more likely to incite a strong organized opposition that may weaken or even destroy the organization's bargaining position.'[42]

In the case of national news organizations any attempts to 'maximize' either audience or advertising revenue may produce a vigorous competitive response and accusations of 'irresponsibility' or 'letting the advertisers take charge' – which will immediately damage prestige and ultimately might antagonize both audience and advertisers.

The three-fold goal classification – audience revenue, advertising revenue, non-revenue – can be applied at a number of levels, for instance:

(1) 'Popular' and 'quality' media.
(2) News organizations and journalists as against media organizations and non-journalists.
(3) News processing and newsgathering journalists.
(4) Different specialist fields within newsgathering journalism.

Firstly, 'popular' and 'quality' media. In general the popular news organizations emphasize the revenue goal and the quality media emphasize the non-revenue goal. The 'qualities' rely more heavily on advertising revenue and the 'populars' rely more heavily on sales revenue.* British quality newspapers can charge very much higher advertising rates per thousand of their affluent readers. The advertising revenue and the non-revenue goals thus overlap in the case of affluent readers. The distinction between 'quality' and 'popular' national newspapers – long made in public discussion – has long been strongly supported by survey evidence, if one chooses to define 'quality' in terms of the proportion of the audience which has a relatively high income or educational level.

Secondly, the news organization and the journalists who work in it tend to stress non-revenue goals to a greater extent than does the media organization. The advertising department and the circulation department can be expected to emphasize their own particular types of revenue. Important groups within the media organization are likely to regard *profit* as more important than revenue. Furthermore, within the overall media organization, any constituent national news organization will be regarded as carrying prestige and thus allowed some non-revenue goal emphasis – to a greater extent, for instance, than a consumer or trade magazine.

Thirdly, while newsgatherers tend to emphasize the non-revenue goal, news processors tend to emphasize revenue goals – especially the audience goal.

Fourthly, some newsgathering fields in general emphasize a non-revenue goal (e.g. Foreign correspondence), some an advertising revenue goal (e.g. Motoring correspondence) and some an audience revenue goal (e.g. Crime correspondence). Even though Crime correspondence, for instance, may be classified as an audience goal field, Crime correspondents – like other newsgatherers – can be expected to try to push their field toward a non-revenue goal; and there clearly are strong non-revenue elements in this field.

A 'goal bargaining' approach emphasizes that no type of newsgathering is rigidly tied to just one type of goal. Crime correspondents

---

* For national daily newspapers in 1967, advertising produced 72 per cent of total 'quality' paper revenue, but only 34 per cent of total 'popular' paper revenue. See National Board for Prices and Incomes (1970), p. 4.

may try to redefine their field (perhaps as 'criminology' or 'legal affairs') in a more non-revenue direction. Similarly Motoring correspondents may try to de-emphasize their advertising goal by further stressing the existing audience goal element, or they may seek a more non-revenue goal (perhaps as 'transportation correspondents'). The huge costs of retaining staff Foreign correspondents abroad are not justified in revenue terms; despite this non-revenue goal, efforts may be made (for instance by processors) to emphasize the audience goal more; or the advertising department may try to emphasize its goal (which may be seen by the Foreign correspondent as an attempt to redefine him as a 'travel correspondent').

All specialist newsgathering fields include an element of each of the three goals, and some fields will lack a predominant goal. This gives us a *fourth* type of goal – namely a 'mixed goal'. This involves a mixture of the other three types of goal. An example is Aviation correspondence, which contains an element of advertising revenue goal – there is much aviation-related advertising; there is an element of audience revenue goal, since aviation stories are strong in news values (élite individuals, sudden events and 'volume' – in terms of speed, size, records, technological advance); aviation also has non-revenue elements of various kinds.

d. The coalition goal: audience revenue

Despite goal bargaining, the combination of goals pursued by a news organization will usually alter only a little from one year to the next. A coalition goal tends to develop; this is the audience revenue goal – which tends to receive the greatest support from the various bargaining (or conflicting) interests involved. This can be seen by returning to the four dichotomies:

Firstly, both popular and quality newspapers (as well as broadcast and agency) try to maintain or expand their current (or traditional type of) audience. *Secondly*, the conflict between news organizations and journalists on the one hand and media organizations and non-journalists on the other hand is a conflict primarily about advertising revenue. Whereas the media organization's commercial executives regard advertising as providing desirable revenue, journalists and Editors regard advertising as at best a necessary evil. But journalists give more support to the audience goal – which the media organization also supports as providing revenue in itself and as a *sine qua non* of advertising revenue.

Thirdly, the conflict among journalists between processors and gatherers is largely one of *interpretation* of the audience goal. Gatherers see the audience and non-revenue goals as more incompatible than do newsgatherers; the latter emphasize 'talking up' rather than 'talking down' to the audience. But both newsgatherers and news processors agree on the pursuit of an audience revenue goal – which consequently carries widespread legitimacy within journalism.

Fourthly, a related difference of interpretation of the audience revenue goal exists also between different sorts of newsgathering specialists. Foreign correspondents try to appeal to at least part of the news organization audience – just as do the Crime or Football correspondents.

The coalition audience revenue goal is opposed by some and not vigorously supported by others; but it is a common denominator to which most consent (with varying tactical reservations and interpretations) while bargaining about other goals continues. The 'audience revenue goal' is the other side of the 'news values' coin. News values – and competition, editionizing, headlining, élitism, personalization and preference for negative events – are pursued with vigour by most journalists because these values represent not merely a goal with which almost all journalists can more or less agree, but also a news organization coalition goal which can be agreed to by most of the disparate, bargaining and conflicting forces within its overall media organization. Great significance is attached to small changes in total audience size; the latter becomes accepted as the prime indicator of a news organization's success, because journalists, as well as advertising, circulation and marketing men, accountants and printers – and the national audience – are all broadly united in recognizing this as an acceptable indicator. Both news values and total audience size – which may appear to outsiders to receive an irrational and excessive emphasis – assume such importance because, while goal bargaining continues, the audience revenue goal is the only possible coalition goal.

5. CAREER UNCERTAINTY

a. Lack of a career structure

> 'Fleet Street and broadcasting almost invariably recruit only experienced journalists. So if you want to be a journalist, you must get your first job on a local paper. . . .'

These statements appear in *Careers in Journalism*, a leaflet aimed at young journalism recruits in the late 1960's.[43] The belief that the London news organizations should recruit young journalists from provincial papers was also held 50 years earlier by Northcliffe. Stress on competition, and concern with short-term objectives led all of the major newspapers (and later BBC news and ITN) to continue this predatory approach to recruitment. The weakness of the occupation of journalism in relation to the news organizations follows from the non-routine work and the indeterminate, segmented character of journalism. The general absence of coherent personnel policies made any long-term career planning unlikely.

Journalism in any country poses special problems of recruitment and training; and in Britain these problems appear in an extreme form because of a combination of peculiarities:

(1) The English amateur tradition.

(2) The low status of vocational education and training in British universities and society generally.

(3) The strong literary traditions of the British press.

(4) The unacknowledged derivation of most Fleet Street 'innovations' in the last 100 years from American experience – resulting in a false and strident insistence on the Britishness of Fleet Street traditions.

(5) The relatively long history of the British press, combined with the deep freeze newsprint rationing period of 1939–45 and after – both resulting in a reverence for traditions of all kinds.

(6) The unusually sharp distinction between '*quality*' newspapers which could attract educated gentlemen, when required, and the '*popular*' newspapers which favoured neither education nor gentlemen.

(7) The unusually sharp distinction between *national* and *provincial* press, the lack of major regional papers, and hence the lack of a well-developed high status regional career ladder.

The national news organizations look down on the provincial press as in every possible way inferior, yet this provincial press has been allowed to carry out the bulk, not only of the occupational socialization and training, but also the original recruitment. However, this predatory tradition could not last for ever.

The present study reports in the next chapter some data on the previous careers of national specialists, but there is little data for comparison with the occupation as a whole. American studies of journalists' careers concentrate on graduates of journalism schools or upon journalists in small local areas. In the absence of an adequate study of the whole occupation of journalism within any major Western nation, one can speculate that journalism careers will resemble white collar careers in industry and commerce (rather than career patterns typical of law or medicine graduates).

Meanwhile the only *national* study of a whole labour force of journalists, and their careers, is from the small country of Israel. Two surveys, based on the total membership of the Israeli Journalists Association, collected data about 370 and 400 Israeli journalists in 1955 and 1959.[44] In other countries national studies may well produce evidence similar to these findings from Israel:

(1) In Israel, newspaper journalism was predominantly a male occupation but there were more women in other branches.

(2) Journalists came from a broad range of social backgrounds, but the lower half of the population in socio-economic terms was very under represented.

(3) Journalists overall were older than one might expect in a 'young man's' occupation.

(4) There was a strong literary element in the occupation.

(5) Journalists, especially older ones, were rather sensitive about their educational qualifications.

(6) Broadcast journalists included more women, were younger, better educated, and of somewhat higher status background than press journalists.

Journalism lacks defined career timetables such as exist in medicine, the military, or the civil service – where maximum and minimum speeds for promotion can easily be discerned. As in the electronics industry,[45] however, the lack of bureaucratic structures, clearly defined career ladders, and established promotion criteria may increase – rather than diminish – the individual's anxiety and concern about the progress of his own career.

Asked about their future, many journalists specified ages by which they hoped to have reached certain points. Although the average age of around 40 years was higher than frequent references to a 'young man's trade' might suggest, in the late 1960's rapid promotion was going to some fairly young men. For instance, Editors of both *The Times* and the *Sunday Times* were appointed in 1967 and both were aged 38. Such appointments perhaps lent some substance to a belief among journalists that vertical movement was often completed by age 40. At the entry end of the career, age 24 had a special significance. At 24 the National Union of Journalists' 'Senior' rate began.

If the years between about 24 and about 40 were indeed the period in which any vertical mobility must be achieved, a journalist who wished to get to the top must be advancing up one of the promising career ladders around age 30. Those under the age of 26 made up 8·1 per cent of all national newspaper journalists in 1969; those under age 30 accounted for 20·9 per cent.[46] The key career ages mentioned by journalists were not necessarily the precise ages of 24, 30 and 40. Nevertheless some precise ages were frequently quoted spontaneously as having special importance.

b. Recruitment and training dilemmas

During the late 1960's most senior people in both national and provincial journalism in Britain were saying, privately and publicly, that a recruitment crisis had arisen: The traditional paths up the provincial newspaper and from the provinces to London had grown less attractive to many provincial journalists. Not only in Glasgow, Belfast and Manchester but also in other regional cities there has been a substantial increase in regional television, both BBC and ITV, and in regional public relations. Television and PR helped to raise the provincial NUJ minimum rates of pay, hence making moves to London less attractive. The younger marriage age now meant that whereas once the typical ambitious provincial journalist of 24 or so was still single by now he might be already married and less mobile.

Increasing division of labour had occurred in London news organizations; and although TV had provided better career opportunities in the provinces it had also seemed to lengthen the career ladder in national journalism – by introducing a small new high prestige level at the top of London journalism. Although information on such matters as the changing age of marriage or changing differentials in minimum pay is quite easy to obtain, British news organizations took little interest in even this kind of elementary social analysis and personnel planning.

As might be expected in British journalism, no person or organization had even a reliable estimate of the proportion of journalists who were university graduates. The present study in 1968 found that about 30 per cent of national specialists in selected fields were graduates. This compared with 51 per cent of Rosten's Washington correspondents in 1936.[47]

The Times has for over a century hired graduates straight into its London office, and *The Guardian* into its Manchester office. But before 1950 graduate entry appears to have involved primarily a small number of graduates entering a small number of news organizations.* The post-1939 paper freeze probably held back what would otherwise have been a more gradual development. In the 1950's a number of news organizations introduced graduates into the occupation with more sudden enthusiasm than careful thought. Some provincial news organizations with substantial proportions of young university graduates faced special dilemmas. Some national news organizations preferred not to employ inexperienced graduates; and the National Union of Journalists opposed direct graduate entry to Fleet Street. But the consequent attempts to combine the provincial and graduate career routes were thought in some news organizations to be ineffective because the most able and talented graduates might be unwilling to work on a small provincial paper with only uncertain prospects of a move to London. Television current affairs was not presented with this dilemma. From the early Reith days in the BBC, graduates were acceptable. There is little broadcast equivalent in Britain to the Fleet Street provincial tradition. The quality newspapers having always employed graduates, and being especially attractive to graduates, faced less of a problem. Consequently the serious newspapers saw no need to combine with the popular papers to institute any kind of overall graduate recruitment scheme.

In some countries, notably the United States, training *for* and/or *in* journalism has been institutionalized in universities. University courses also existed in a number of East and West European countries, and were extending from Japan and Latin America to other areas of the world. In Britain, however, nothing comparable existed. A great difficulty in training recruits for journalism lay in the lack of answers to basic questions, such as: What are recruits to be trained for? Who shall teach them? What shall be taught? How will recruits be motivated to learn? These questions worried the Royal Commission which reported in 1949. Belatedly and half-heartedly a very modest national training scheme was set up in 1953. This apprenticeship scheme emphasized shorthand and was entirely provincial. The second Royal Commission in 1962 again expressed concern. From 1965 onward there was indeed a rapid development of the National Council for the Training of Journalists under new leadership. A block-release system was introduced by which a recruit during a three-year apprenticeship spent two eight-week periods at a technical college. Educational qualifications of recruits improved somewhat and by 1968 thirty full-time journalism lecturers were in action.[48]

The introduction of an Industrial Training Board for the printing and newspaper industry in 1968 showed once again how journalism was tucked under a printing umbrella. It was also one more instance

* Notably the Kemsley (subsequently Thomson) and Westminster Press (subsequently Financial and General) chains of provincial newspapers.

of British journalism reacting to changes imposed on it from outside. Journalism training was advancing only just fast enough to maintain its backward position relative to many other white collar or semi-professional occupations. Many recruits were still entering journalism only after failing to enter other white-collar occupations. Educational standards were rising, mainly because journalism was benefiting from rising numbers and standards in the school system. The major training centre near London was at Harlow, a new town without several obvious requisites for practical instruction in journalism. The training given to apprentice journalists – shorthand, law, and practical exercises – defined journalism primarily in white-collar or clerical terms. The journalism teachers – experienced journalists, some of whom had held senior jobs on provincial dailies – found themselves in a difficult marginal role.

In 1970–1 the first British postgraduate course in journalism began at Cardiff. A two-year course at King's College, London University, in the inter-war years was not continued after 1945. One of its problems was indicated by Carr-Saunders: 'It is noteworthy that the University of London grants a diploma for journalism and not *in* journalism.'[49]

If in the future such courses become securely established the subject is likely to remain controversial. As Alfred Friendly, a former CBS news executive, has said:

> 'Of all academicians, the journalism professors are the most defensive breed, for the good reason that they are most constantly under attack.'[50]

Quite apart from the opposed occupational values of university teachers and journalists, there can never be a wholly satisfactory way of systematically training people to do non-routine work within an indeterminate occupation.

c. Entry, occupational socialization and careers

Most recruits to British newspaper journalism during the 1960's began on *weekly* provincial newspapers. 'Juniors' made up about two-fifths of the journalists on these small papers in each of the years 1964–7.* During the late 1960's the majority of recruits had academic qualifications below the usual university entrance requirements.†

---

* In 1967 Newspaper Society figures showed 1,404 juniors out of a total 3,450 journalists on weeklies.

† In 1967–8 of recruits to provincial newspaper journalism, 12·1 per cent were graduates, 11·5 per cent had three or more GCE 'A' levels, 17·6 per cent had two 'A' levels and 8·3 per cent one 'A' level.

Most came from middle- and lower-middle-class families,[51] and were indentured for three years on a newspaper near their parents' home. Most journalists started in the sort of places where the weeklies were strongest – namely in towns and suburbs too small to have a daily newspaper. Editors of small newspapers in such centres were thus front-line recruiters for all British newspapers.

Over half of the young journalist recruits in his study told Oliver Boyd-Barrett (1970) that they were writing, or intended to write, a novel. Perhaps most relevant to the young journalist recruit was a desire to escape from set routines. In addition to early rejection of routine, another career-long journalism theme was the importance of personal contacts. Personal contacts, alliances and recommendations play a part in most occupational careers. But in journalism they assume a special significance, because not only examinations, but any other impersonal criteria are widely regarded as poor guides to ability in journalism. Moreover, from the local Editor's point of view it might be quite rational to select recruits from candidates who approach him through personal contacts. Some journalists claimed that to be successful a journalist required ambition and determination to overcome obstacles, and consequently a little difficulty in getting into the occupation was no bad thing. But job opportunities were unevenly spread geographically; moreover, many young people still entered journalism without difficulty and without any special 'ambition' or noticeable attributes relevant to journalism.

In his first months and years a journalist learnt the role of the local journalist and the discipline of writing to order; he internalized news values. The technique most emphasized by small provincial papers in Britain was shorthand, which stresses accuracy, the spoken word, the formal statement, and personalization. The young journalist learnt the 'house style' and the art of the 'intro' – the riveting first sentence. He was socialized to unusually intense work in the hours before the main deadline. He was exposed to a wide variety of social areas including accidents, death and the social arrangements for dealing with them. He might interview famous entertainers on their appearance at the local theatre. Such small pieces of power and 'inside dope' were quoted to support the romantic-derisory judgement 'it's better than working'. In addition to his enthusiasm for the occupation of journalism in general, a young journalist was often aggressively disillusioned, for instance by the lack of criticism in the local paper – whether of local politicians or the films at the local cinema.

Within only a year or two of entry to the occupation, some journalists found themselves already earning substantial amounts of money beyond their ordinary pay by working for other news organizations.

Much of this activity was 'linage' – local news supplied on order to agencies or national news organizations. Often linage was 'owned' by one of the senior journalists such as the news editor, for whom the young recruit might find himself working in both his regular and irregular capacities. The young journalist learnt the practice of getting a foot into the doorway of another news organization in the interest of security; he also learnt the rules and available roles in another news organization for which he would like to work, by first working for it on an occasional freelance basis.

Almost all recruits to newspaper journalism started as general reporters. Photographers were the one type of journalist who specialized strongly from the start. The first chance for a young reporter to specialize was in sports reporting. On a typical provincial daily 5 per cent of the staff were sports reporters in the head office and a fair proportion of work done by the 28 per cent of total staff located in district offices was sport. Other specialist newsgathering was weakly developed on most provincial papers – apart from the odd rather senior industrial correspondent or other specialist responsible for a major local interest (e.g. agriculture). But the young reporter anxious for promotion must look elsewhere, in particular to sub-editing.

On a provincial daily of 60 staff there were about a dozen or so seniorish jobs. Any journalist who stayed on the paper, by the age of 40 could regard himself as having a fair chance of getting one of these jobs. Remembering the opportunities for extra earnings and the jobs available in regional television and public relations, there was no need to be too cynical about statements by some provincial journalists that they did not wish to go to London.

Preliminary interviews for the present study suggested that only a minority of all journalists on London papers had started their careers in the North of England or Scotland. This was consistent with the social processes by which journalists joined London national news organizations. National jobs were usually obtained through some kind of *personal* contact; news organizations with jobs to fill alerted relevant staff members to suggest suitable people. Secondly, another important aspect was *observation* of a journalist's work. This combination of printed (or broadcast) output plus personal contact reinforced the dominance of the South of England. Because most national journalists' beginnings were in the south, social contact networks were stronger in the south; news executives in London when studying the competition also studied mainly *London* (not Manchester or Glasgow) editions. Similarly, young journalists on local papers in the south sent stories to the London offices of national papers, whereas those working in the north sent them to the Manchester offices.

The 'traditional' emphasis given to provincial 'experience' was something of a myth if any kind of clearly pursued policy was indicated, although most journalists had worked outside (central) London previously. National news organizations avoided the short-term costs of a vigorous national recruitment policy and exploited provincial papers which in turn often exploited young journalists. Weak emphasis also was given to experience on one of the larger provincial news organizations; 'experience' primarily meant previous work on any news organization of almost any size or character – and thus experience mainly in avoiding elementary mistakes.

There were two polar extreme career paths to London: Firstly the *élite career* path straight into national journalism without previous 'experience'. Secondly the *provincial career* path – based on 'experience' on a weekly provincial newspaper, then a provincial daily, then some provincial/national job (such as in the London office of a provincial daily, or in the Manchester office of a national paper) and finally a post on a national news organization in London. But so lacking in an orderly career structure was journalism that only a minority of careers followed even this *provincial career* path at all closely. Moreover, the *élite career*, although followed only by very small numbers, was especially important in three high prestige specialist newsgathering fields – foreign, financial and political – fields from which national Editors were disproportionately drawn.

The lack of a career structure and the lack even of accurate information about the prevalent disorderly career processes reinforced the emphasis upon personal contacts, the forging of career alliances, the pursuit of promotion tactics and the prevailing sense of insecurity and anxiety on the issue of careers.

'On your 35th birthday they push you down the rubbish chute.' This statement was made by a journalist in a national newspaper newsroom where the majority of journalists looked past age 35. Indeed over 60 per cent of national journalists were past this age.* Nor was there any evidence for the often-repeated assertion that journalists die young. Alcoholism, mental illness, coronaries and suicide were claimed to be common; but a sociologist interested in occupations may come to believe that most occupations make such claims.

Apart from the closure of publications there was also little evidence to support assertions that many journalists were sacked. During 1965–8 only two examples could be discovered of sacking involving

---

* In January 1969, 62·5 per cent of all journalists in London offices of national newspapers were aged 35 and over. In Manchester offices the proportion was 61·7 per cent. The average ages were 41 and 39 respectively. See National Board for Prices and Incomes (1967), p. 22.

more than the occasional individual – both multiple cases followed from the sacking of Editors of popular daily newspapers.* But at least as common as sackings were examples of older men being kept on in a state of semi-retirement. Perhaps the latter type of case contributed more to the prevalent sense of unease.

In line with their rather dated personnel policies national newspapers combined a flamboyant organizational concern (e.g. free cruises) for seriously ill journalists with a reluctance to concede that pensions should be transferable. The 1947–9 Royal Commission on the Press (Report, p. 171) expressed concern on this topic, but twenty years later the situation was improving only slowly. The lack of transferable pensions schemes was one factor in the sharp contrast between rapid job mobility in the early part of most national careers followed by rigid immobility in the later years. It was probably one factor also in the sharp divorce between most provincial and national careers in the later years, and the segmented nature of the whole occupation. It contributed to the paradoxical position in which to an outsider older journalists on national news organizations *looked* fairly secure, but still felt insecure. One new executive said: 'Older journalists get steadily more paranoid.'

Older men knew that journalists of some seniority were seldom fired outright; but 'encouragement' was more common, such as promoting men's juniors over their heads, making new appointments in border areas, and also giving some people roving commissions – seen by others as a licence to trespass. Many small events from day to day connected with the coverage of this story, the arrangements for that man's day off, the preferences of a newly promoted executive – each of these could be read by an insecure journalist as evidence of intrigue. Hence the prevalence of gallows humour, talk of rubbish chutes, and the *Daily Mirror*'s local pub familiarly known as 'the-stab-in-the-back'.

6. JOURNALISM AS OCCUPATION

a. External orientations and timetables

'Performers' are the stars of politics, entertainment, sport and any other activities with which journalism deals. Learning to be a journal-

---

* In the case of 12 national daily newspapers (including two London evenings) each of 12 senior news executive posts was held during the 15-year period, 1954–68, by an average of 2·9 men. In view of the prevalence of changes between executive jobs within the same news organization this seems a lowish rate of turnover; the evidence is taken from World's Press News, *Directory of Newspaper and Magazine Personnel*, 1954–68 (annual).

ist involves absorbing the perspective that 'People make news', more specifically which people make news. Journalists are continually ranking individuals in terms of more or less news value. Part of this performer-orientation consists of deciding who are the declining stars in the relevant field and who are the rising stars. There are more politicians who were in the cabinet, actresses who once won awards, pop singers who at one time topped the charts, athletes who once held the title, compared with the much smaller numbers of current stars in each field. Whether they be specialist newsgatherers eager to establish personal relationships with the stars of their field, or sub-editors whose task is to present the current stars to the audience, journalists are conscious of a seemingly inevitable insecurity in that part of the outside world upon which their occupation focuses its attention.

Journalism is a 'bridging' occupation – it provides, through work experience, the conditions and opportunities for movement from one occupation to another.[52] One attribute which makes journalism a bridging occupation is *access* to people in other occupations, and to helpful knowledge. The move from journalism into politics is one of the most visible and traditional forms of bridging. Max Weber noted the connection between social democratic journalism and politics in Germany before 1914. A similar connection has frequently been noted in the United States with the Democratic party, and in Britain with the Labour party. These two non-routine types of work may fit neatly together. But much more numerous than the journalists who become full-time politicians are those who move into jobs in public relations. This is probably the one occupation for which there is a strong preference for previous experience as a journalist.*

Specialist newsgatherers often move into the field they previously covered. Why should specialist newsgatherers often find employment outside journalism, in the field they have covered, while a newspaper specialist seldom moves to a specialist magazine in the same field? A journalist is led into social contact with news sources and competitors on media of similar frequency and type. These orientations over time become cemented by job moves and a propensity to regard both sources and competitors as 'colleagues'. The role of competitor and the role of source allow for colleagueship because they involve people-oriented journalists with personal contacts, and these can only be developed with people who operate on similar frequency and deadline timetables.

Journalists work odd hours; any one journalist tends to work different hours from other journalists. Rigid deadlines involve inten-

---

* Forty-one per cent of IPR members worked previously as journalists. *Public Relations* (Institute of Public Relations), January 1964, pp. i–xv.

sive work shortly before the deadline. Periods of alternating intense activity and slackness come in different combinations within different types of news organization. For instance, Sunday-paper journalists have their busiest day, Saturday, when all daily men have the day off. Within the news organization the processors have their easiest time while the gatherers are writing against deadlines; while the processors approach the first edition times, most gatherers will have gone home. Timetables in television have an extreme segmenting impact.

In journalism these timetables carry the impact of work into the domestic sphere. The reverse tendency is for the leisure sphere to permeate work, and for journalists to indulge in a good deal of eating, drinking, gossip and entertainment with 'colleague' journalists in and around their places of work. These 'colleagues' may often be opposite numbers on directly competing organizations.

Rigid timetabling introduces an extra element of competition into work relationships within the same news organization. A daily newspaper's six-day week means that most people have one day off plus Saturdays. On his day off the News editor's job will be done by his deputy. But the News editor may also be deputizing for his superior – perhaps the assistant editor in charge of all news and features. This makes two days out of five in which the deputy does the job. Annual holidays, illness and special crises may mean that for fully half of his working time a man may be doing the job of his boss. There thus can be little in journalism of one's 'own' desk, office, secretary, files – less of a sense of being the only incumbent of one clearly defined work role. Moreover, in journalism there are few compensating devices – such as graded salary structures, job-tenure, codified qualifications. Instead there is a constant sense among journalists that the curtain will always go up on time – and one day it may go up on your understudy playing your part.

b. Profession or trade?

'It has often proved difficult to describe the whole range of activities falling within the scope of a profession; more often than not they are many and various. But a connecting link can usually be found between them because it appears on analysis that these activities take the form of applying a particular technique in different spheres of practice. This cannot be said of journalists. They are employed in reporting, writing up, interviewing, sub-editing and though these are not jobs which any one can do without a considerable amount of experience, no specialized intellectual training is an indispensable preliminary. . . .

'This onerous and responsible task of ascertaining the truth about current events, and of commenting upon them in the light of "the fixed and true principles of justice, humanity and law" has fallen under the sway of men with the manners and morals of vendors of quack medicines. . . .

'It seems that somehow or other the regard for the honour of the profession has never found effective means of expression through associations. Perhaps the impossibility of controlling the main lines of development makes journalists feel so much at the mercy of powers beyond their reach that they have never taken up problems where their influence might be of some effect.'

A. M. Carr-Saunders & P. A. Wilson, *The Professions* (1933)

In their analysis of journalism professionalization Carr-Saunders and Wilson referred to the appearance of a body in British journalism which had professional aims. The National Association of Journalists, founded in 1884, led to the Institute of Journalists, incorporated by Royal Charter in 1890. The Institute (IOJ) had a primary impulse to copy the established professions. Editors were allowed to become members and the aims were of a lofty type, with little emphasis on pay and conditions of work.

In 1907 there was a breakaway of young men who founded the National Union of Journalists in Manchester. The NUJ's primary aim was to improve the pay and conditions of underpaid and overworked provincial journalists. Pay and conditions improved rapidly after 1907, and the NUJ soon passed the Institute in membership. By the early 1930's the trade union, NUJ, had 5,000 members against the professional IOJ's 2,000 members. The NUJ had about 19,000 members and the Institute perhaps 2,000 in 1966 when both bodies agreed upon a 'trial marriage' with a view to an ultimate merger. This was 50 years after the first of several attempts at such a merger.

Long before 1966 the Institute of Journalists had ceased to be an effective force. Among specialist newsgatherers on national media – the kind of fairly senior journalists whose support a 'professional' body would presumably require – only 8 per cent belonged to the Institute; in contrast 87 per cent of London-based specialists (and 50 per cent of Foreign correspondents) belong to the National Union of Journalists. The detailed figures in Table 2.5 should be cautiously interpreted,* but there is considerable indifference to all three bodies. The overwhelming majority of specialists thought that the Institute 'has on my work situation no impact'. The most positive response was to the NUJ – and the overall response even here fell short of a 'little beneficial impact'.

---

* The numbers of 'no answers' varied considerably. There were 15 for the NUJ but 63 specialists gave no answer on the IOJ. One specialist claimed not to have heard of the IOJ. Moreover under the terms of the NUJ/IOJ 'trial marriage', any member of one organization officially acquired membership of the other.

TABLE 2.5

SPECIALIST NEWSGATHERERS' ATTITUDES TO
TRADE UNION AND 'PROFESSIONAL' BODIES
IN BRITISH JOURNALISM

	Foreign Washington, New York, Bonn, Rome	*Political* Lobby	*Mixed* Labour Education Aviation	*Audience* Crime Football	*Advertising* Motoring Fashion	*All* Selected specialists
National Union of Journalists	0·53	0·84	0·87	0·92	1·08	0·82
Institute of Journalists	0·03	0·00	0·09	0·04	0·09	0·06
The Press Council	0·28	0·58	0·55	0·68	0·32	0·49

Q. Do you think the NUJ or IOJ or the Press Council have any beneficial or harmful
impact?
Scoring: Very beneficial $= +2$; a little beneficial $= +1$; no impact $= 0$; a little
harmful $= -1$; very harmful $= -2$.

Many journalists claim an absolute professional right to protect
the confidences of news sources. An IPI report in 1962 noted that professional secrecy for journalists was largely protected in Sweden,
Norway, West Germany, Switzerland, the Philippines and 12 of the
United States. In the United Kingdom no such principle as professional secrecy for any profession is known to British law.[53] However,
such privilege is nevertheless usually accorded to doctors and priests,
and it can at least be argued that the exceptional event of the Vassall
Tribunal[54] underlined that on the issue of professional secrecy,
journalists in Britain are accorded at least semi-professional
status.

This 'peculiarly British' quality is also attributed to the British
Press Council:

'It is trite but true: the Press Council is a uniquely British Institution. It was set up in 1953 by the press itself, at the instigation of a
Royal Commission, and it has no statutory powers. Yet for thir-
teen years it has investigated complaints against the press, held
private hearings and given reasoned rulings. In doing so it has
established a moral authority which is probably more soundly
based than that of a statutory authority would have been.'[55]

It may be trite but it isn't true. The British Press Council set up in 1953 follows quite closely the Swedish Press Fair Practices Commission set up in 1916. Norway, Switzerland and the Netherlands are three other countries which had Press Councils long before 1953.[56] The Royal Commission which first called for a Press Council did not mention these precedents,[57] nor does the approved history.[58] Perhaps this is one more example of Fleet Street mythology.

It is widely agreed that after 1953, when the Press Council was set up, the newspapers used less intrusion, less sadistic crime stories, murderers' memoirs and the like. However, there is no reliable evidence of any causal relationship between the rise of the Press Council and the decline of certain types of story. Press Council decisions often involved photographers and reporters, but much less frequently specialist newsgatherers. The main exception to this statement concerns the Crime correspondents, who in the present study were the single specialist group most in favour of the Press Council.

Perhaps in the context of a discussion on professionalism, however, the most noticeable point about the Press Council is that the idea in Britain came from an outside body, namely the 1947–9 Royal Commission. The major changes in 1964 also came from an outside body, namely the second Royal Commission. The journalists themselves were almost unanimously opposed to the idea. Sir Linton Andrews, Editor of the *Yorkshire Post* (and later chairman of the Press Council), told the 1947–9 Royal Commission:

'Whatever slight reform was achieved by the Press Council intervention would be as nothing to the blow to freedom.'[59]

Regardless of the significance or otherwise of the Press Council, can a non-routine, indeterminate and segmented occupation like journalism ever be a profession? One sociologist has suggested that any profession must have five attributes: (1) systematic theory, (2) authority, (3) community sanction, (4) ethical codes and (5) a culture.[60]

It is extremely improbable that journalism could ever acquire these professional attributes to the extent of, for instance, medicine. A more realistic objective, if the occupation wished to pursue it, would be to make journalism into a semi-profession – in the way that teaching, for instance, is a semi-profession. Something of this kind seems to have been going on in Sweden – where apart from the Commission founded in 1916, entry to journalism is carefully controlled and certain categories of, for instance, crime news are completely excluded from publication. It could also be argued that some sectors of journalism in the United States have moved some way along some of the dimensions of professionalization – although whether journalism has altered its position on such dimensions relative to semi-professions like teaching or non-professions like business management is perhaps less certain.

Meanwhile the predominantly white collar and non-professional character of British journalism – whatever Delane may have said in 1850 and others since – was emphasized by the decline of the 'professional' Institute of Journalists, the rise of the National Union of Journalists, and their mutual decision to have a trial marriage in a new body one-tenth professional and nine-tenths white-collar trade union.

When the new union began in Manchester in 1907 its title, National Union of Journalism, was modelled on that of the National Union of Teachers, its rules were borrowed from the Engineers' Society,[61] but its general demeanour followed that of various recently-formed clerical unions. In the United States the Newspaper Guild threw in its lot with straightforward clerical workers in non-editorial departments. In France and West Germany the white collar versus professional issue has been especially salient. In Britain the National Union of Journalists developed a non-professional white-collar approach, with the support of the printing unions. The white-collar strategy of the NUJ involved furthering the interests of provincial journalists, with London journalists being relatively ignored. The National Union of Journalists concentrated on one major issue – raising the *minimum* pay of *provincial* newspapermen who made up roughly half of all British journalists. It was quickly successful in this, and in time pursued other related aims, such as acquiring some control over the entry of young journalists.

Under British conditions it was perhaps inevitable that a journalists' Union should concentrate on provincial newspapermen – the only sub-group with sufficiently large numbers and uniform interests to be able to dominate such a Union:

'Where we have a visibly higher status group, it is often the cadre from which the organization's officials are recruited and on which the administrative machine is based.'[62]

The centre which fulfilled these criteria was obviously the major sub-national centre of Manchester. The NUJ began in Manchester and has drawn much of its leadership from there.[63]

During the post-1945 period the minimum wage agreements of journalists failed to keep pace with those of some comparable occupations. Another trend was the narrowing of differentials between the bigger and smaller centres. (Both of these are familiar themes in white-collar Unionism.) At the end of the 1960's some journalists in London offices began a campaign for major increases in differentials. Once again this new 'militant' strategy was openly borrowed from other white-collar trade unions. The NUJ has also aligned itself with the printing workers – which caused great internal dissension in the NUJ during the General Strike of 1926 and the national printing strike of 1959. On each occasion substantial numbers of journalists left the NUJ on 'professional' grounds. Printing workers have long been an élite among manual workers, while journalism as an occupation has been low down in the pecking order of occupations with some element of professional orientation. Many changes in printing in the 1960's made some journalists think that they were falling behind the manual workers. Moreover, the NUJ by the late 1960's had an increasingly large minority of its membership, not in the traditional field of press journalism, but in fields like television, book publishing and public relations (both government and commercial). The indeterminate nature of the occupation lay at the heart of the National Union of Journalists' problems; and as that indeterminacy increased, the internal conflicts within a broadly defined '*Journalists*'' trade union were likely also to increase.

c. Ideology and façades

Public relations personnel are merely a new 20th-century development in the much older business of arranging façades. The journalist knows that most news 'events' such as speeches, openings, closings, prizegivings and even many contests and debates do not happen quite spontaneously. Thus journalists' news values stress events which are genuinely unplanned, or disastrous.

Long before the institutionalization of 'public relations', the state tried to control, manage, or shape the news. In the 17th century various English regimes – both Republican and Royalist – rigidly controlled the press. And three centuries later journalists every year or two accuse their governments of having sunk to new depths in news management and control. When John Delane, Editor of *The Times*, made some of his most ringing statements about journalistic freedom, some of the 'taxes on knowledge' were still in force. Perhaps his two most famous statements were these in 1852 and 1854:

'The press lives by disclosures . . . it is daily and for ever appealing to the enlightened force of public opinion – anticipating, if possible, the march of events. . . .

'To accuse this or any other journal of publishing early or correct intelligence, when there is no possibility of proving that such intelligence has been obtained by unfair or improper means, is to pay us one of the highest compliments we can hope to deserve. . . . We hold ourselves responsible, not to Lord Derby or the House of Lords, but to the people of England, for the accuracy and fitness of that which we think proper to publish.'

Perhaps for our present purposes the most interesting points are firstly the vagueness of such words as 'unfair' and 'improper'; secondly, the emphasis on accuracy and speed ('anticipating if possible'); and thirdly the emphasis on *disclosing* information for the people of England.

The emphasis on disclosure inevitably implies a political position – namely that journalists must align themselves on the side of the 'people' and against those in power. This ideology of permanent opposition often leads to an expectation that most journalists will vote left in politics. Delane's statements also include a mixture of the declamatory, the pompous, the self-congratulatory and the sentimental – all qualities present in many American discussions of that rather ambiguous term, the 'Fourth Estate'. Morris Janowitz studying the American military officer was reminded of journalistic ideology:

'. . . Military honor and the pursuit of glory are often a mixture of toughness and sentimentality. . . . The parallel with the professional journalist is most striking. Both professions attract men who have rejected prosaic routines and who have strong motives which seem to them to be idealistic. The pressures of these professions require that personal idealism be submerged under a façade of realism. But the emotions which produced this idealism persist in the form of sentimentality.'[64]

The 'heroic tradition', as Janowitz calls it, or the British Navy's 'fighter spirit', has its equivalent in the journalists' ideology of disclosure and revelation. Both occupations reject the nine to five routine and the values of the business world in particular. Both occupations are dissatisfied with what they see as the low motives of their ultimate bosses, yet both occupations nevertheless exhibit great loyalty to these bosses. Both soldiers and journalists work under rigid time pressures. Both think themselves above crass commercialism, but resent what they see as their low salary level and high insecurity level. Both occupations show occasional respect for the odd conspicuous political leader, but tend to contrast such leaders with the general fraudulence and unworthiness of most politicians. In both occupations, too, traditional ideology tends to lose touch with present occupational reality. Janowitz notes that only a few soldiers bear the main brunt of the fighting, while the heroic leader figure has long been less important than the 'military manager' with his interpersonal and political skills.[65]

The main public impression of journalism is produced by relatively few journalists – and probably fewer still ever disclose serious skulduggery or expose major public figures. The heroic figure of the disclosure and scoop journalist is less important in the overall occupation than the 'journalist manager'. The journalist, however, as a professional searcher behind façades is often eager to deride the ideology of his own occupation. Fleet Street's self-image as a Street of Adventure jostles with its other self-image as Grub Street.

Here are some representative answers from specialists as to what a journalist *should* be doing for society and his audience, and what function was *in fact* performed by British journalists.

Should 'Educating them through knowledge, style and wit'

In Fact 'The above to the best of their ability'

Should 'Informing and educating'

In Fact 'Inform, entertain, annoy'

Should 'Educating and entertaining them'

In Fact 'Entertaining and educating them'

The lack of complete fit between the disclosure ideology and the work situation is illustrated each week in the journalism trade press, where groups of journalists are seen boarding aircraft and grinning happily at the camera. These expeditions are variously known as 'press visits', 'facility trips', or 'junkets'. Such trips are merely the most visible sign that the journalist's style of life is often rather higher than his salary would seem to allow.

The reporter who commutes in each day from his heavily mortgaged house in the London suburbs can, as he awaits the News editor's instructions, expect a certain amount of luxury thrown in with his squalor – a dock-gate strike meeting, but also perhaps a champagne reception on the same day. He can also look longingly forward to covering a war – partly footslogging through the bush, partly over the bar at the local Hilton Hotel. In such ways his non-routine work spreads over into his leisure hours and dominates his style of life.

3

Specialist correspondents: goals, careers, roles

1. SPECIALIST CORRESPONDENTS IN JOURNALISM

The total *numbers* of specialists have increased rapidly in recent decades. Between the late 1930's and the late 1960's the number of British journalists doubled and the number of national newspapers declined, but the number of specialist newsgatherers per national newspaper probably at least trebled. But whether the *proportion* of specialists among journalists changed very much is less clear. Certainly specialist reporting as such is not a recent development in journalism. It dates back to the earliest days of the press. Indeed, 18th-century English newspapers carried material from 'foreign correspondents' – people living abroad who wrote letters to the publication in question. This raises the problem of the definition of 'specialist'.

a. The internal division of labour in specialist reporting

Just over half of all journalists on a national newspaper are *news-gatherers*. But only about 16 per cent of all journalists on a national newspaper are *specialist* newsgatherers (Table 2.3). These specialists can again be subdivided into two categories:

(1) Those who specialize in gallery, court, or grandstand reporting.

(2) Those who specialize in the behind-the-scenes of politics crime, sport or whatever the topic may be.

The present study focuses only upon the second type, the *behind-the-scenes* specialist who concentrates on the personal pursuit and gathering of news.

During the 19th century in Britain the development of specialist journalism involved primarily the coverage of set-piece events – the stock market, the criminal courts, sporting events as seen from the grandstand, and politics as seen from the press gallery. Only during the 20th century in Britain did behind-the-scenes specialist reporting gradually come to be regarded within journalism as more important than the gallery/law court/grandstand approach. At Westminster the gallery reporters of Parliamentary Debates and the sketchwriters (the drama critics of politics) slowly yielded pre-eminence to the Lobby correspondents[1] who specialize in the behind-the-scenes of British national politics. The reporters of the criminal courts yielded pre-eminence to the 'crime correspondents' – who cover crime before it reaches the courts. This tendency was strengthened by the appearance of television – which by making many 'events' directly visible to the domestic viewing public pushed the specialist journalists more and more into before-the-event, after-the-event and behind-the-event reporting.*

By the late 1960's this division between the gallery reporter and the behind-the-scenes specialist was clearly visible in fields such as Politics and Crime. But other fields of specialist coverage – such as the mixed-goal fields of Aviation, Labour and Education – carried a primarily behind-the-scenes personal gathering emphasis from the beginning.

b. *Selection of specialist fields by news organizations*

Why do some areas of human activity and some kinds of events receive regular coverage by specialist correspondents, while other areas and events receive only irregular coverage by general reporters – or indeed no coverage at all? The aspects of news referred to by Galtung and Ruge[2] are relevant to the selection of fields for specialist coverage – such aspects as personalization, conflict, cultural proximity, unexpectedness-within-predictability, élite individuals and nations.

In Foreign news (which Galtung and Ruge studied) these criteria are involved in the selection of countries to which staff Foreign correspondents are posted. British resident staff correspondents are stationed mainly in the United States and Western Europe (cultural proximity, élite nations). The other major form of Foreign news is war coverage (conflict, and unexpectedness-within-predictability) – which also emphasizes East-West rivalry (conflict between élite nations).

In Foreign coverage, news organizations emphasize the non-revenue goal, but Foreign news coverage is also heavily coloured by the news organization's coalition audience goal. Some other fields of specialist news coverage are more closely aligned with one of the two kinds of revenue goal (or customer demand). In the more 'consumer'

---

* Of course for a tiny handful of commentators and TV personalities (often not working for 'news' departments) television coverage of 'events' brought high pay and status.

fields of news (e.g. Motoring, Fashion, Travel, Real Estate, Gardening) the advertising goal is predominant – and a major criterion for deciding whether or not to allocate a full-time specialist to cover such areas is the likelihood of attracting related advertising. However, the possibility of attracting advertising is by no means the only criterion; the allocation of specialist journalists to cover advertising goal subjects is also strongly influenced by general news values and the news organization's coalition audience goal.

Before 1939 Shipping was an important field – strong in personalization, élite individual passengers, conflict between élite nations, and decisive changes (arrivals, departures). After 1945 Aviation was deemed to be stronger in all of these characteristics. While Shipping correspondence has declined, there have been more examples of fresh specialist fields emerging in the general news media. There is a common pattern of development – first a small number of correspondents with little competition, followed by a 'precipitating event'. In the case of Science correspondence this was the atomic bomb in 1945. For Education correspondence in Britain the precipitating event was a series of government enquiries, especially the Robbins Committee on Higher Education which reported in 1963.

c. Selection of specialist fields for present study

In designing a comparative sociological study about specialist journalism the selection of particular specialist fields for study poses several problems. Printed lists of specialists are unreliable, incomplete or (as for the Lobby) not publicly available. After the first interviewing stage of the present study the following definition was adopted:

A specialist journalist must:

(1) Work full-time for one of the 23 national news organizations.

(2) Be assigned at the time in question (23.5.1968) on a permanent basis to the field in question.

(3) Devote over half of his working time to the field in question.*

But what is the 'field in question'? Some news organizations have separate 'Aviation' and 'Defence' correspondents; other news organizations have a man or men covering both. In almost all fields at least some of the specialists spend at least some time on coverage of other subjects. As Table 3.1 shows, however, in the selected fields the

* Some of the non-response may have been due to some 'specialists' not fulfilling this criterion. It is also possible that in a few cases specialists who did fulfil these criteria were not approached.

specialists devoted the great majority of their time to the prime topic. In selecting these fields three additional criteria were deliberately introduced:

(1) A preference for fields with clearly defined boundaries.

(2) A preference for fields with a goal which appeared to fit fairly clearly into one of the four categories of goal.

(3) There was also a 'composition' criterion – that is fields were selected to span the four main categories.

There may have been a slight tendency to weight the selection in favour of the non-revenue field of Foreign correspondence. There may also have been some 'prestige' tendency, as in the choice of mixed goal fields – which included the political Lobby correspondents, plus Labour and Aviation; but on the other hand Diplomatic and Defence specialists were not included.

TABLE 3.1

PROPORTION OF TOTAL TIME DEVOTED TO
PRIME SPECIALIST SUBJECT

Field	Average proportion of time on prime subject %	Other subjects covered by some of specialists
Foreign		
United States (NY & Washington)	80	{ Latin America, Caribbean, Canada – United Nations
Italy (Rome)	90	Greece
W. Germany (Bonn)	85	Eastern Europe
Political		
Lobby	90	Diplomatic
Mixed		
Aviation	75	Defence
Education	90	—
Labour	75	Economic Planning
Audience		
Crime	95	—
Football	90	Other sport
Advertising		
Fashion	85	Other 'women's'
Motoring	90	Other 'transport'

There is a strong circular element in the definition of 'specialist' and the selection of fields. The fields were selected in terms of goal categories for which most of the supporting data (presented in the next section) is from specialists in the selected fields. But if fields which lacked clearly defined boundaries (e.g. medicine, or some of the lesser sub-specialisms within sport or financial journalism) had

TABLE 3.2

NUMBER OF SPECIALIST JOURNALISTS IN PRESENT STUDY: BY TYPE OF NEWS ORGANIZATIONS

	Goal of Specialist Field					
Type of news organization	*Foreign* Bonn, Rome New York, Washington	*Political* Lobby	*Mixed* Aviation Education Labour	*Audience* Crime Football	*Advertising* Fashion Motoring	*All* Selected specialists
'Quality' Newspapers	35	28	40	24	52	35
'Popular' Newspapers*	38	51	44	71	44	49
Agencies and Broadcast	27	21	17	5	4	16
TOTAL	100	100	100	100	100	100
N	55	39	48	38	27	207

* Includes the London evening newspapers.

been included, the social scientist would have been arbitrarily defining a 'field' which the individuals involved did not recognize. Secondly, the selection of fields which appeared to fit clearly into one of the categories of goal does not destroy the relevance of the categories – since the perspective stresses goal bargaining and coalition goals, and the selection specifically includes a 'mixed goal' category. Thirdly, the 'composition' criterion appears justified in a study which avoids random sampling and which seeks to develop a system for classifying the goals of specialist news.

Table 3.2 shows how different types of news organization allocate different proportions of their specialists to particular sorts of news coverage. In the audience-goal fields (Crime and Football) popular newspaper specialists outnumber by three to one those of quality newspapers; in the advertising-goal fields (Fashion and Motoring) the quality paper correspondents outnumber those of popular papers. This is consistent with the popular newspapers obtaining more of their revenue from circulation, whereas quality newspapers rely more heavily on advertising revenue. Compared with specialists overall both Foreign correspondents and mixed-goal specialists are relatively more numerous on the quality newspapers. Only the political Lobby is surprising – here the quality newspapers have a lower proportion than of specialists overall. This follows from restricted access to the Lobby – one of the unique aspects[3] which justifies the analysis of the political Lobby separately from the other 'mixed' fields.

2. THE GOALS OF PARTICULAR NEWSGATHERING FIELDS

How does one operationalize the concept of goal? It would be inconsistent to assume that there could be any single unambiguous way of operationalizing the concept. Since the perspective adopted here sees different individuals and groups within the organization as emphasizing different goals, it is necessary to examine the views of differing groups within the news organization, and then to consider them as a whole. The following sorts of evidence will be considered: the views of other specialists about those in particular fields; the self-image of groups of specialists in particular fields; the views of senior executives in charge of different departments within news and media organizations – namely Editors, circulation managers and advertising managers; other sorts of evidence – such as the editionizing phenomenon, the practice of juxtaposing editorial and related advertising, and historical evidence.

a. Specialists: *views of other specialists, and self-image*

The assumption that other specialists are likely to provide the most reliable single set of data about the goals of particular specialist fields, other than their own, rests on these points: the other specialists themselves operate within a similar tripartite set of roles as competitor-colleague, newsgatherer and employee; within the employee role most specialists work for news organizations where that other tripartite arrangement – editorial, circulation, advertising – is also present; in addition specialists have some opportunity to talk to other specialists at work and can also see their end product.

Table 3.3 broadly confirms the unsystematic findings obtained from unstructured interviews with specialists (upon which the preliminary goal classification was based). Football and Crime emerge with the largest proportions of other specialists attributing circulation interest; Motoring gets the largest vote for advertising interest.*

* Unfortunately Fashion was not included in the questionnaire.

TABLE 3.3

ACTIVE COMMERCIAL INTEREST IN SPECIALIST
FIELDS AS SEEN BY OTHER SPECIALISTS

'*I think in national journalism generally that an active
interest is taken in specialist fields as follows.*' (Questionnaire)

By Circulation Departments	By Advertising Departments
Football (60% said Yes)	Motoring (59% said Yes)
Crime (49%)	Finance (49%)
Motoring (37%)	Aviation (29%)
Finance (35%)	Football (22%)
Labour (32%)	Labour (15%)
Political Lobby (28%)	Education (13%)
Aviation (14%)	Political Lobby (12%)
Diplomatic (13%)	Crime (8%)
Education (12%)	Foreign (5%)
Foreign (11%)	Diplomatic (4%)

Note: Since the opinion of the specialists in the field in question are excluded, the
effective base numbers vary – from 125 to 159.

The numbers answering 'Don't know', 'Does not apply' and those who did not
answer varied from 30 to 48. Prominent amongst these were the newsagency and
BBC correspondents – who, of course, work for news organizations which have no
advertising revenue element. Respondents were offered only two alternatives in
the case of each field – 'active interest' or 'no active interest'.

At the other extreme Foreign correspondence scores very low on
both circulation and advertising. This comes out more clearly when
both the circulation and advertising columns in Table 3.3 are added
together:

	%	
Motoring	96	(Advertising)
Finance	84	
Football	82 ⎫	(Audience)
Crime	57 ⎬	
Labour	47 ⎫	
Aviation	43 ⎪	(Mixed)
Political lobby	40 ⎬	
Education	25 ⎭	

Diplomatic	17	
Foreign	16	(non-revenue)

Here Foreign correspondence achieves the lowest revenue score. Motoring emerges with the high revenue score; next (after Finance) come the two audience fields; followed by the 'mixed' fields including the political Lobby. Thus the preliminary classification is broadly supported by specialists' views about other specialist fields.

The self-image of the members of specialist groups is shown in Table 3.4. The fields which in the preliminary classification came under one goal heading are shown together under this heading; the

TABLE 3.4

ACTIVE COMMERCIAL INTEREST IN OWN FIELD
AS SEEN BY SPECIALISTS

	Foreign Bonn, Rome New York, Washington	*Political* Lobby	*Mixed* Aviation Education Labour	*Audience* Crime Football	*Advertising* Motoring (only)	*All* Selected specialists
% seeing active *Circulation* interest	22	18	30	90	79	42
% seeing active *Advertising* interest	11	6	19	29	43	18
N =	37	34	37	31	14	153

Note: 'Don't knows', no answers, 'Does not apply' etc. = 43.

procedure seems desirable in view of the very small numbers in some single fields and the high level of no answers. (A full third of Foreign correspondents gave no answers – some indicating that they never had any contact with any commercial department.) The advertising field data is only for Motoring. Nevertheless 90 per cent of the audience goal field specialists see their fields as having audience interests. Motoring also has the highest proportion seeing the field as having advertising interest (although more of them acknowledge an *audience* interest).

While only 18 per cent of all selected specialists see their own field as having advertising interest, 42 per cent acknowledge circulation/audience interest. This indicates the greater legitimacy within journalism of audience interest and is in line with the *coalition audience goal*.

Specialists were also asked: 'Are you aware of any advertising pressure on yourself at present?' 84 per cent of all specialists (N = 193) answered in the negative. But the following proportions of specialists said they were aware of at least 'a little' advertising pressure:

Foreign	16%
Political	9%
Mixed	11%
Audience	11%
Advertising	42%

The advertising goal fields (which in this case includes both Fashion and Motoring) stand out sharply from all other fields in the fairly high proportion acknowledging advertising pressure.

b. Other evidence on specialist newsgathering goals

During unstructured interviews with Editors and circulation and advertising managers (or directors) the revenue-based goal classification system was offered for comment. The response from the national news organization commercial executives was generally positive, while that of Editors was more varied.

The views of *Editors* fell into three roughly equal-sized groups: One third of national Editors denied that such a classification contained any element of reality. A third of the Editors thought the classification was not applicable to their own news organization but was broadly applicable to most other news organizations. A third of Editors thought the classification broadly realistic in relation to all or most news organizations, including their own. In this group were Editors of both prestige and popular national news organizations. Thus two-thirds denied that the classification applied to their own news organization; but two-thirds of national Editors agreed with the application of the classification to national news organizations in general.

The *advertising* executives were in general agreement with the contention that news organizations had advertising, audience and non-revenue goals. While making the point that the overall character of the audience of a news organization was what most appealed to advertisers, nevertheless advertising managers spontaneously quoted types of news coverage which attracted advertising. They quoted financial news as attracting financial display advertising and also pointed out the connection between editorial features and certain types of classified advertising – such as property and jobs. In these cases – and in display advertising for cars, travel or gardening – they saw a connection between advertising and editorial.

Circulation managers were somewhat more inclined to qualify their general approval of the tripartite goal classification by stressing 'balance'. There was general agreement that political and foreign stories would almost never increase the sales of a popular newspaper. A General Election in France, for instance, would have no impact at all on a popular newspaper's sales, although it might sell several thousand extra copies of a quality newspaper. Only a very exceptional political event, such as the assassination of President Kennedy in 1963, would sell extra copies of a popular British newspaper. Sport was the type of news which circulation executives quoted as most often boosting sales. There were nationally spread sales increases for major horse racing or football events. When a team reached the final stages of one of the major football competitions, there were usually extra sales in the team's home city. Crime was mentioned by some circulation executives as selling extra copies – but only in the case of exceptionally dramatic crimes.

In most organizations both advertising and circulation managers had regular contact with the Editor. Advertising managers or directors consulted with the Editor on most days about positioning of advertisements and page layouts. In some organizations the number of printing editions varied from night to night according to the day's news. In two important types of editorial decision both advertising and circulation managers expected to be consulted. Firstly, in the case of 'supplements', special consumer 'features', and giveaway 'colour magazines', it was common to assume that a balance of audience and advertiser interest should be maintained. Secondly, advertising and circulation executives in most cases expected to be consulted in decisions to develop entirely new specialist newsgathering fields. They did not expect that their advice would necessarily shape the decision, but their stress on a 'balance' between sales, advertising and other factors (such as 'integrity'), pointed to the kind of goal outlined above as 'mixed'.

Further, impressionistic evidence relates to the phenomena of *editionizing* and of *juxtapositioning* of editorial matter and related advertising. The first appears related to the audience goal, the second to the advertising goal. *Editionizing* is the practice common to press and broadcast news organizations of producing several editions each containing 'later' news than the previous edition. (With news agencies the process is one of more continuous updating.) By providing

late editions of updated news, news organizations incur major additional costs. In the case of newspapers there is also a strong *regional*
element in the editionizing phenomenon. The first editions of national newspapers typically go to areas 100 miles away from the printing
centre. The next edition may go to places 50–100 miles away, and so
on. An element of local news is put into each edition. Since this expensive process can only be justified in terms of trying to increase
audience interest, the news organization concentrates its editionizing
upon including those types of news believed to have the strongest
audience appeal. Impressionistically, it seems that Sport and Crime
news take up a disproportionate amount of the content changes.
This line of argument could be used as a central hypothesis in a study
relating content changes to costs.*

The *juxtapositioning* of editorial news and related advertising is
widely regarded within journalism as indicating a lack of integrity.
Indeed, in British commercial television the relevant legislation explicitly prohibits the placing of advertisements in time slots adjacent
to programmes of similar subject-matter. This legislation presumably reflects scepticism on the part of at least some members of the
general public. News organizations thus are unlikely to place 'editorial' matter alongside related advertising unless there is strong
reason to suppose that such juxtapositioning does indeed attract
advertising revenue. Here again a separate study could test this
hypothesis.† Meanwhile impressionistically such juxtapositioning of
editorial and advertising appears to include motoring and fashion –
as well as travel, gardening, real estate and job-'news'.

c. Non-revenue goal: Foreign correspondence

In classifying *Foreign correspondence* as having a non-revenue goal,
the most vital point is the *cost of having staff Foreign correspondents
permanently posted abroad*. A news organization can of course acquire foreign news relatively cheaply from the great international
news agencies. A good deal of foreign news used by British news
organizations comes from Reuters, which has a much bigger staff
of Foreign correspondents than does any newspaper. It is the high
cost of each individual staff correspondent, especially compared with
the comprehensive and respected service provided by the great international agencies, which marks this specialist field off from all others.

---

* One problem which such a study would have to confront: Crime and mid-week
sport may both happen in the late evening more often than do other categories of
event.
† Which would be much more complex than may at first appear.

The major cost is not in salaries, but in expenses. Whereas the total expenses of employing a journalist within Britain are very roughly equal to his salary, in the case of a Foreign correspondent total expenses are several or many times as high as his salary. A Foreign correspondent communicates with his office usually several times a day – by telephone, telex, cable or by radio. One has only to compare the cost of a half-hour phone call from Los Angeles to London with the cost of phone calls within Britain to realize that the costs of daily Foreign correspondence are on a quite different scale from those of British-based specialisms. There is also office rental in the centre of a foreign capital. Bringing the correspondent (and family) home on leave is expensive. Another less obvious but highly expensive item is the cost of travel from the foreign base – for instance sending a New York-based man to California or a Rome-based man to Athens for a few days; this involves air fares, expensive hotels, and still higher transmission charges. It is difficult to obtain reliable estimates of costs – partly because these vary greatly from posting to posting; partly because some costs are recouped by selling a foreign news service to other newspapers (provincial or overseas); partly out of organizational caution; and partly because some foreign news departments appear not to operate on a fixed budget.

Foreign correspondents' stories also take up a disproportionate share of the time and energy devoted by printers and journalists to late news, as well as the time of senior executives including Editors. These stories (along with audience goal news) receive an undue share of edition changes; this is especially true of news from the heavily staffed New York and Washington offices, covering events which are five hours earlier than London time. (Foreign correspondence could also be accused of channelling some of the outstanding journalistic talent away from the revenue-producing fields.)

In 1965 three news organizations – *The Times, The Daily Telegraph* and the BBC – had half the total of 141 staff Foreign correspondents for all British news organizations (excluding Reuters).* Clearly there had been a big change since 1870 when Paris was the sole established centre for British resident Foreign correspondents. Despite a substantial increase during the 1930's, numbers of full-time resident correspondents in major centres roughly doubled between 1937 and 1968:

* Dailies: *The Financial Times*, 8; *The Times*, 26; *The Guardian*, 6; *The Daily Telegraph*, 30; *Daily Mail*, 13; *Daily Express*, 13; *The Sun*, 4; *Daily Mirror*, 11; *Daily Sketch*, 0; *Evening Standard*, 2; *Evening News*, 2. Sundays: *The Observer*, 6; *Sunday Times*, 3; *Sunday Telegraph*, 1; *Sunday Mirror*, 1. Broadcast: BBC, 16; ITN, 1.
This list excludes Reuters. Sources: Economist Intelligence Unit (1966); BBC Handbook.

	1937		1968	
New York	20	25	34	61
Washington	5		27	
Germany – Berlin	20		—	
Bonn	—		18	
Rome	5	45	18	73
Paris	20		37	
TOTAL*	70		134	

* These figures include Reuters. Sources for 1937: PEP *The British Press* (1938) pp. 161–3, 292–3. *Royal Commission on the Press – 1947–49*. Evidence. Sources for 1968: Lists supplied by British Embassies in relevant countries.

Between 1937 and 1968 Paris became the major European centre for British correspondents. In the United States, Washington, which in 1937 had been a relatively minor interest to British media, became more heavily covered – despite the appearance of the United Nations in New York.

There was little change between 1937 and 1968 in the concentration on a few rich northern nations. Whereas in 1937 Shanghai had ten British staff journalists, by 1968 Hong Kong, Singapore and Delhi were the main Asian centres. In 1968 Saigon was the most important semi-permanent centre – playing a part similar to Spain in 1937.

But in the smaller Foreign correspondence centres in the poorer countries the definition of 'staff correspondent' is much more difficult; these centres expand and contract according to the political situation – wars and civil wars, which attract the interest of major powers, acting as a magnet. These centres have a high proportion of 'stringers' who work for several news organizations. A further definitional problem is the Reuters correspondent of non-British nationality. Fairly standard features are centres like Hong Kong and Beirut which are used as 'listening posts' and jumping-off points for covering China and South East Asia, and the Middle East respectively.

But the basic division involves devoting approximately equal resources to each of three areas: (1) North America. (2) Europe. (3) The rest of the world. This division of labour is often criticized in terms of devoting excessive attention to Europe and North America. The image presented of Africa, Asia and Latin America, it is said, is one of civil war, assassinations, coups, earthquakes and other natural disasters. But such images may also be presented when one rich nation reports on another. The complaint that British media in the late 1960's portrayed the United States as violent merely echoes this complaint of 1938:

'America is depicted to England as a territory of crazy politics, gangsters and law breaking, divorce and fierce warfare between capital and labour. . . .'[4]

News organizations, journalists and outside critics all seem agreed that Foreign correspondence should have a primarily non-revenue goal. The dispute, however, concerns the weight which should be given to this primary goal.

d. Political (Lobby) correspondence

Political (Lobby) correspondence in Britain exhibits a number of unique characteristics; it has long been shrouded in secrecy; the number of journalists covering the field is controlled by the news source. A British national newspaper may have five – or any other number of Foreign correspondents – covering Washington; but it cannot have as many as five in the Lobby at Westminster. A new Lobby correspondent is merely allocated to the job by his Editor, and the Serjeant-at-Arms at Westminster puts his name on the 'Lobby List'. The journalist also compulsorily joins a 'voluntary' Lobby grouping which involves a nominal subscription. He is now free:

(1) To use the members' Lobby of the House of Commons and mingle with MPs.

(2) To attend off-the-record briefings given every day by the Prime Minister's press staff, and less frequently by other Ministers and senior politicians.

(3) To acquire 'proof' copies of all public documents before the official time of publication – that is before Members of Parliament themselves.

The present study is only concerned with one type of political journalist – the Lobby correspondent; but there are two other types. The first type of political journalist to arrive on the Westminster scene was the *debate reporter*; this was the job Charles Dickens was doing in the 1830's – working as one of a team taking down, in relay, a complete shorthand record of debates. This function is now performed by an official Hansard team; by the Press Association; and in a slightly more limited form by *The Times* and *The Daily Telegraph*. Secondly there are the *'sketch' writers* – journalists who produce short commentaries and criticisms of the formal debates in the Chamber. The third category, the *Lobby correspondents*, gradually during the 20th century emerged as clearly the senior of the three categories. The Lobby correspondent has become 'Our Political Correspondent'.

It is no accident that the term by which they are known both in journalism and politics is a physical place – the members' lobby, or entrance, to the Chamber of the House of Commons. Moreover most of the major changes in the history of British political correspondence have derived from changes in the physical accommodation and arrangements. Political journalists have long suffered from a dual squeezing process – the breadth of Parliamentary privilege and the narrowness of Parliamentary physical space.

By 1852 the Editor of *The Times* had acquired a special position in British politics – in effect as the first, part-time, Lobby correspondent. *The Daily Telegraph* emerged after 1855 as the second most respectable paper. By the 1870's the *Telegraph* also had a regular Lobby correspondent – the father of the Editor (Edward Levy Lawson). A critic wrote at the time:

> 'His son is the Editor. He may be seen every day in the lobby of the House of Commons during the session button-holing members, and when he is not thus occupied he is sneaking up official back stairs to pick up scraps of news.'

Lawson of the *Telegraph* and Delane of *The Times* established the personal privilege – possessed also by members of the Commons – of standing at the bar of the House of Lords during debates.[5]

During the 1870's other newspapers were acquiring substantial circulations and inevitably other journalists had frequent personal access to politicians. Often these were alliances based on the partisan policies of the paper. Some provincial morning newspapers wanted access to the gallery. This was granted by the Commons, and a gallery Committee was formed. At the same time the access to the lobby was put on a more formal basis. National and provincial daily men gained approved access. Some Members of Parliament for a number of years found it hard to regard journalists as other than partisan agents of partisan newpapers. But the 'professional' image steadily strengthened.[6] In the 1930's even major provincial *evening* newspapers – like the *Manchester Evening News* – had no more access to the Commons than did members of the general public. In 1941 the Commons was again physically destroyed – by Hitler's bombs – and the new chamber opened in 1950 provided enlarged space for the press. The provincial evening papers were admitted for the first time – to both gallery and Lobby. (A special gallery was also built for foreign and Commonwealth journalists who were granted limited lobby access on one day per week.)

During the 1950's the numbers of Lobby correspondents increased somewhat. Additional 'deputy' Lobby correspondents were allowed to larger organizations – these deputies in practice having virtually the same access as their seniors. In 1961 the arrival of the *Sunday Telegraph* led to all the Sunday national newspapers acquiring full week-long Lobby access. A further change after 1950 was the emergence of broadcast Lobby correspondents. At the end of 1967 the names on the lobby list numbered 109. However, this study concerns only the 47* national Lobby correspondents; they are primarily *newspaper* journalists. The Lobby correspondents base themselves on Westminster and visit Fleet Street much less frequently. The 'briefings' – which many other journalists regard with suspicion – take place twice a day; there is a late morning briefing at 10 Downing Street – mainly for evening paper journalists, and a late afternoon one in a special room at Westminster overlooking the Thames.

Since a separate publication (*The Westminster Lobby Correspondents*) exists which is also based on the present study, this introduction has been brief. But enough has already been said of the Lobby's unique characteristics to illustrate the difficulty of classification. The prestige (non-revenue) element in covering national politics more seriously than commercial considerations might justify is obvious. There is an element of audience goal; the popular newspapers heavily stress personalization and conflict in their political coverage. Thirdly, despite little directly related advertising, the political coverage of a news organization influences its general image and atmosphere – to which advertisers and their advertising agencies have long attached some emphasis. Nevertheless, despite this strong 'mixed goal' (generally supported by the data presented at the beginning of this chapter) the unique characteristics of this field argue that the Lobby correspondents should be analysed as a separate category.

e. *Mixed goals: Aviation, Education, Labour*

The 'mixed' goal fields of Aviation, Education and Labour lie in territory where not only the goals are mixed. So is the history, and so especially are the definitions. *Education* is perhaps the main exception here – its definition is fairly standard between news organizations and its history is short, mainly confined to the 1960's.

Aviation is a field which despite the great interest of Northcliffe has never been sharply defined. *The Daily Telegraph* has given Aviation consistently full coverage, always using an ex-service officer;[7] there was a tendency elsewhere for a news organization to have a

---

* 48 to be more precise but in one case our definition differs from that of the Serjeant-at-Arms.

J.A.W.—D

single 'Aviation and Defence' correspondent. Aviation correspondents overlapped with a number of other specialists – not only Defence, but also Science (for space stories), Diplomatic (for NATO stories) and Technology (for Aviation production).

Labour correspondents, with similar overlapping characteristics, have long been called 'Industrial' correspondents; but, especially since the General Strike of 1926, they found British trade unions and strikes better material for news stories than were management and policy. By the 1960's there was an increasing tendency for the field to split into Industrial (Labour) and Industrial (Industry); Industrial (Labour) correspondents covered the Labour party, primarily due to the dominance of trade unionists in the origins of that party, which meant some overlapping with the Political (Lobby) correspondents. During the early 1960's Labour correspondence expanded to include several new national economic planning agencies; here obviously there was overlapping with financial journalists.

How is the mix in a 'mixed' goal field composed? One sign that a non-revenue goal is expected by outsiders are 'enlightened' appeals to the effect that the public good would be better served if a particular field were more seriously and responsibly covered.

Education expanded faster than the other mixed fields in the 1960's. But Education had a strong element of audience goal; circulation managers wanted to reach affluent young students, teachers, and the booming education industry in general; there was also a series of official reports on all aspects of British education, and the emergence of the Minister of Education as an important political figure.

When during the 1960's most national daily newspapers first decided to have full time Education correspondents, the *Labour* field was acquiring teams of two, three or four. While even quite small American newspapers had Education writers, the specialist 'Labour Editor' was disappearing by the late 1960's. There might be a temptation to explain such a difference in terms of the ideology of American newspaper owners. But three contrasts provide a much simpler explanation.

(1) Only one-fifth of US workers belonged to a trade union, against two-fifths in the UK.

(2) A much higher proportion of young US adults were receiving full-time education than in the UK.

(3) American newspapers, with their local monopoly positions aimed at the middle market, appealed less to manual workers than did the popular British papers operating in a class-stratified national market.

A British popular newspaper would thus have several times as many trade union readers in relation to students, compared with an American newspaper. Hence the greater seniority of Labour correspondents in Britain seems to have a simple audience/sales basis.

Each of the mixed goal fields includes an element of advertising goal. After Motoring and Finance, Aviation is seen by specialists as the next most advertising oriented of our fields (Table 3.3). Specialist journalists appear to think primarily of *display* advertising in this connection, ignoring the importance of *classified* advertising; much of the latter is for jobs, which provides at least some element of advertising backing for Labour correspondents; more particularly there are several types of job advertisement closely connected with Education.

The development of mixed goal fields requires, within some easily recognizable field, a frequent supply of events and an adequate supply of persons apparently strong in 'news values' – plus elements of non-revenue, advertising, and audience appeal. The development of further mixed goal specialist fields is extremely probable, given the prevalent tendency for decisions through consultation between Editors, and market research, circulation and advertising managers.

f. Audience goal: Crime and Football

Specialists in general believe that Football and Crime correspondence has a strong audience goal (Table 3.3); the advertising goal is weak in both fields, and both tend to be regarded negatively from the point of view of non-revenue goals. During the 1960's a popular paper like the *Daily Mirror* which was pursuing an 'up-market' strategy deliberately reduced its emphasis on crime news in general. In the last century newspapers which had non-revenue goals were already using crime news with a vigorous audience goal emphasis. In 1886 *The Daily Telegraph* devoted 62 columns to a single divorce case – which included a Duke and a General.[8] Lord Burnham, a member of the family which founded *The Daily Telegraph*, justifies such coverage:

'They were very clear-minded about their intention for their content, a wider field of home news with a human touch, a literary quality generally inconspicuous in the Press of their day, provision for the cultural interests of newly educated public, and an extensive and efficient foreign service through their own correspondents. . . .

'The circulation to pay for these ambitious and praiseworthy aims had to be achieved somehow, and if "human interest" had to be hotted up a bit to finance long-term programmes of perfection they were not going to be foolishly narrow-minded about it. . . . The end may or may not have justified the means, which anyway were not very improper. Family pride, however, does not justify humbug.'[9]

In 1900 Crime reporting was primarily a matter of reporting Court cases and 'human interest':

'Crime was much more prominently featured in the newspapers than it is today, and I would often come across energetic free-lances who specialized in murderers' last letters, pathetic interviews with relatives of notorious criminals, etc.'[10]

The vigorous *gathering* of crime news was a more recent phenomenon. In the 1930's Scotland Yard viewed with considerable suspicion journalists who wanted to report crime before it reached the courts.

Football reporting was also well established in 1900, but confined largely to the matches. By the 1950's Football journalism paid much more attention to personalities, tactics, transfers. In the 1960's Football often led the sports pages of popular dailies six days a week – although the matches were concentrated on only two days a week.

In both Football and Crime the *newsgathering* specialist emerged as the dominant figure. Many Football match reports were the work of part-timers, freelances, stringers and sub-editors. Football *correspondents* report on Football first, and Football matches only second. Similarly, Crime correspondents report Crime; they move over to the Courts only to cover the especially dramatic case – rather as for the big occasions Lobby correspondents move into the House of Commons Gallery.

The usual two, three or four Football correspondents in the London office concentrate on the London clubs. The audience goal ensures that much Football reporting is carried on from Manchester, Glasgow, and the regional offices. The frequent televising of Football did little damage to the news reporting of the subject. It was, however, an additional pressure towards behind-the-scenes newsgathering – rather than event reporting.

g. *Advertising goal: Motoring and Fashion*

The majority of other correspondents believe that an advertising goal is served by Motoring correspondents (Table 3.3); the latter rather less eagerly admit a connection with advertising. The advertising goal involves various kinds of pressure upon the journalists concerned. This may come in the form of memos from the advertising manager inside the news organization: 'Could you possibly give x a mention?' Pressures to be non-critical may come from processors; sub-editors if presented with an unusually critical piece may consult the 'rule book' of the cuttings, and trim the criticism back to the usual low level.

Other pressures are external. Both Fashion and Motoring journalists' *news sources* tend also to be *advertisers*. A criticized politician cannot withdraw advertising, but a criticized car manufacturer or a criticized fabric manufacturer can. These organizations can also stop supplying some sorts of news information to the journalist. In advertising goal fields of journalism, major news sources acquire considerable control over the newsgathering arrangements. The journalist was given full access to the information, but only for a *limited period of time* – a few hours or at most days for test driving a new car, seeing a fashion collection, or visiting – out of season – a foreign holiday centre. Another aspect of such newsgathering was the common occurrence of a long time gap between gathering the information and the appearance of the full story. A car might be tested in North Africa but the story would be 'embargoed' for a fortnight – meaning it would not be used, even if the same information is obtained from another source. Fashion shows were held in Paris one week, but only partially reported; full coverage was embargoed for several weeks (to allow manufacturers to produce cheap versions for the ordinary consumer). There was a boom period for travel journalists making visits abroad in the autumn – in preparation for the Christmas travel advertising supplements. Embargoes of a day or two are accepted, and even welcomed, by journalists in other fields – as allowing for more considered coverage. But the gap of weeks or even months between acquiring the information and writing the story would not be tolerated outside advertising goal fields. Journalists would refuse to accept such information on the grounds that they could acquire it elsewhere in the meantime. But these advertising goal journalists – at least when dealing with specific models, or fashions (or holiday services) – did not feel sufficiently strong. The traditions of these fields are such that neither their competitor-colleagues, nor their employing news organizations, would support them.

For advertising goal specialists work is made easy. Pictures tend to be important (cars, dresses, beaches) and are provided – or good facilities provided for getting them. Another aspect is much free travel. Fashion correspondents get trips to Paris, and Motoring correspondents to places like North Africa:

'No self-respecting manufacturer nowadays launches his latest model in the country of manufacture. Instead correspondents are flown on a two-, three- or four-day binge to somewhere glamorous like Outer Patagonia and entertained with belly dancers and lots and lots and lots of alcohol. As a way of trying out new cars this is not ideal, for the Patagonian roads are usually straight for mile upon mile and dry for three hundred and sixty-four days of the year – making comparisons with British conditions peculiarly difficult. The effort and expense from the manufacturer's point of view is usually worth while, however, in terms of the amount of extra space that newspapers feel obliged to give – their correspondent having been away for so long.'[11]

Classification of these fields as having a predominant advertising goal does not imply any absolutely fixed subservience to advertising. Motoring correspondents cover not only new cars, but also motor racing, the motoring organizations, and the Ministry of Transport; Fashion writers cover areas of the fashion industry which do no general national advertising. Moreover even in areas where advertising is important some journalists working for some news organizations maintain some independence. The classification does imply, however, that the *predominant* goal of these fields is to attract advertising. The coalition audience goal also remains important; even if they did not attract advertising these fields would still be covered – but probably with less space and much more critically.

3. THE CAREERS OF SPECIALIST JOURNALISTS

a. The stages of a specialist's career

There is a sharp contrast in most specialist journalists' early careers between rapid job mobility before specialization, followed by a pattern of job *immobility* after specialization. Despite appearing secure in his job within his chosen occupation, the specialist journalist often exhibits a strong sense of disillusion and unease – of subjective, if not objective, insecurity. Nevertheless there is no other kind of work which would appeal to most specialists. It is still 'better than working'.

The median specialist in this study was aged 40 (in 1968); there were almost equal proportions aged under 35, aged 35 to 44, and aged 45 and over. Taking the ratio of those under 35 to those over 45, the political (Lobby) correspondents were the oldest and the advertising goal specialists the youngest:

	Percentage under 35	Percentage over 45
Political (Lobby)	22	44
Foreign	26	42
Audience	30	41
Mixed	44	22
Advertising	36	16
All selected specialists	32	34

There is considerable divergence in median age within the mixed goal fields (Aviation 41, Labour 37, Education 30) and within the audience goal fields (Crime 47 and Football 37). The youngest field, Education, is itself young and growing. The field with the oldest specialists, Crime, is itself old and in decline.

TABLE 3.5

AGE SPECIALISTS STARTED NATIONAL SPECIALIZATION

Age	*Foreign* Bonn, Rome, New York, Washington	*Political* Lobby	*Mixed* Aviation Education Labour	*Audience* Crime Football	*Advertising* Fashion Motoring	*All* Selected specialists (N=174)
	%	%	%	%	%	%
22 and under	13	6	8	21	10	11
23–26	26	27	18	26	19	24
27–30	32	27	34	23	38	30
31–35	15	24	13	21	24	18
36 and over	15	18	27	9	10	16

Almost half started national specialization between the ages of 27 and 35. But over a third started by the age of 26, and 16 per cent started after their thirty-sixth birthday. Clearly there is no sharply structured specialist career pattern. But the median age within each separate field is much more uniform. In most cases the median for all specialists in the field is a starting age around 30. For all selected specialists, average ages for a typical career were roughly as follows:

Entered journalism	age 18
Entered national journalism	age 26
First national specialization	age 30
Began present specialization	age 33
Present age	age 40

The median age of
specialization for
specialists by field
was as follows:

Crime	32 years
Motoring	31
Aviation	31
Labour	30
Washington	29
Bonn/Rome	28
Political lobby	28
New York	27
Education	27
Football	25
Fashion	24

There are big differences in the length of specialist careers – varying from the median Education correspondent who has been in that specialist field for only three years to the Crime man who has been covering crime for fifteen years.

b. *How specialists had entered journalism*

Twelve per cent of the specialists were themselves sons of journalists. Most specialists' fathers had been in non-manual occupations – with a substantial bulge in the Registrar-General's social class two. 'Schoolteacher' was the single commonest father's occupation – after journalist, which also falls in class two. But a third of fathers were in manual occupations – with printing trades the most frequent. At the other end of the scale, 11 per cent of fathers were in social class one – here ministers of religion and university teachers were the most-quoted fathers' occupations. Overall the occupations of the specialists' fathers were heavily weighted towards administrative, educational and service occupations, with little representation of manufacturing or heavy industry.

The field with the highest class background is Foreign correspondence; the mixed fields are second. The Political Lobby journalists exhibit an unusually wide range of social class background – with a higher proportion than the other fields in either the top or the bottom social classes; this reflects the wide variety of paths by which journalists reach the Political Lobby. The New York correspondents, in keeping with their precocious flavour, are overall of the highest social class parental backgrounds. The Football correspondents, on the other hand, have the most working class backgrounds.

Predictably Table 3.6 shows the field with the most education to be Foreign correspondence. And again the Political Lobby correspondents show an unusually large spread. 54 per cent of all specialists finished full-time education at age 17 or earlier. Only 33 per cent continued education to age twenty or beyond – almost all of them to university first degrees. The field with the oldest average, Crime, was

TABLE 3.6

AGE OF FINISHING FULL-TIME EDUCATION

Age	Foreign	Political	Mixed	Audience	Advertising	All (N = 196)
	%	%	%	%	%	%
14–15	8	14	13	17	0	11
16–17	23	54	31	67	58	43
18–19	17	3	13	11	23	13
20+	52	30	42	6	19	33

the least educated. The Education correspondents were both the youngest and the most highly educated.

The majority attended a Grammar School. About a quarter went to a fee-paying 'Public School', and these bulked large among the university graduates. Two-thirds of the graduates had attended Oxford, Cambridge or London universities. The most commonly quoted degree is a second class in Politics, Philosophy and Economics at Oxford; English and History are the other preferred subjects. Nine-tenths said they would advise a young relative to obtain a degree before entering journalism today. The opinion that British journalism would become an all-graduate occupation was often expressed, which inevitably made education a sensitive topic. The range in education was much wider than merely between graduate and nongraduate. Over half of the specialists had not achieved the minimum educational level required for university entrance, while 11 per cent left school at age 14 or 15. By contrast most of the graduates had attended élite South of England universities.

On average there was a gap in these specialists' pasts of two to three years between finishing education and entering journalism; the gap was primarily due to military service. Entry to journalism at age 21 or later was obviously most common in the most educated fields – Foreign and mixed. In only one field, Washington, did any substantial proportion start journalism in their late twenties; a third began at age 26 or later – mainly due to a combination of war service and university.

TABLE 3.7

SPECIALISTS' FIRST JOB IN JOURNALISM:
TYPE OF NEWS ORGANIZATION

	Foreign	Political	Mixed	Audience	Advertising	All (N=195)
	%	%	%	%	%	%
Weekly newspaper	22	47	49	44	35	39
Provincial Evening newspaper	10	26	16	17	4	15
Provincial Morning newspaper	10	13	9	3	0	8
News agency	16	3	9	14	15	11
Magazine	2	3	7	8	19	7
National newspaper	16	5	7	14	15	11
Broadcast, radio/TV	6	0	2	0	4	3
Overseas News organization	18	3	2	0	8	7

The most common type of news organization for a specialist's first job was a weekly newspaper. The figure for weeklies and provincial dailies combined is 62 per cent (Table 3.7). At first there seems to be a good deal of support for the belief that most national journalists have previously taken the 'traditional' provincial route to London.

But Table 3.8 throws much more general doubt upon the 'provincial route'. 27 per cent actually had their first journalism job in central London; not only some of the news agency starts, but also some of those on provincial daily newspapers were in the London offices of these organizations (e.g. *Yorkshire Post* London office). 18 per cent of subsequent specialists began their careers on weekly newspapers in the London suburbs; since 10 per cent of the starts were overseas, *of those who started in Britain exactly half began in greater London.* Another 22 per cent started elsewhere in the South – especially on small daily newspapers in places like Exeter, Oxford, Cambridge, Bristol, Cardiff and Portsmouth. But since the biggest centres for employing journalists outside London are Birmingham, Manchester, Leeds, Liverpool and Glasgow it is remarkable that only 23 per cent of specialists began to the north of Birmingham (inclusive).

TABLE 3.8

SPECIALISTS' FIRST JOB IN JOURNALISM:
LOCATION OF NEWS ORGANIZATION

	Foreign	Political	Mixed	Audience	Advertising	All (N=193)
	%	%	%	%	%	%
London Central*	32	18	23	28	40	27
London Suburban	12	18	27	22	8	18
Elsewhere in South	12	18	25	31	28	22
North of Birmingham (inclusive)	18	42	20	19	12	23
Overseas	26	3	5	0	12	10

* Includes Fleet Street newsagencies and magazines, and London offices of provincial daily newspapers and broadcasting organizations.

Again Foreign correspondents are a deviant group. 70 per cent began in London or overseas (either in a foreign-owned organization or an overseas office of a British organization). The audience fields are the most overwhelmingly London and South of England in entry pattern; in both Crime and Football there is a strong tradition of entry through small papers outside London or specialized Fleet Street news agencies. The Political Lobby correspondents, by contrast, have a much stronger Northern entry pattern. Moves from home to first job in journalism cancel out, with the exception of a tendency for those living in the South to have moved to work in London. But the most usual pattern was of a young man who had left school at about 17 and entered journalism within the locality where he was already living.

139194

EMORY & HENRY LIBRARY

When asked: 'Could you say briefly what made you enter journalism?' specialists replied:

'It was the work in which I was most interested – it seemed like being paid for what I most wanted to do for enjoyment.'

'I wanted to write and I wanted to see life at first hand.'

'Desire to use a talent for English and a desire for a more exciting life than my schoolfellows.'

'Always had attracted me in a romantic way and apart from teaching seemed one of the few things you can use an Arts degree for.'

For young men wishing to write, journalism appeared to offer not only a salary, experience in writing, but also dramatic material to write about. Another repeated theme is the explicit rejection of more routine jobs; this varies from the 16-year-old school leaver who did not want to work in a bank or an insurance office to university graduates who had rejected job offers in large companies or government departments. Specialists recall having balanced the 'romantic' choice of journalism against some more 'sensible' and more ordered career.

About 30 per cent of specialists did work other than military service before entering journalism. 12 per cent of specialists did humble non-journalist work in news organizations. Most of the other non-journalist work had been of a lower white collar kind. The specialists were asked what they would have done if they had not become journalists. The most quoted other occupation was Schoolteaching, followed by Architect (especially Foreign correspondents) and business management. A third said they didn't know or had never considered anything else. These answers give an impression that as a group these specialists had a very strong commitment to journalism – some for reasons of romantic enthusiasm, some because they saw it as the last acceptable fall-back choice.

Although an apprenticeship approach is sometimes regarded as traditional in British journalism, four-fifths of the specialists had not been indentured. Seven-tenths denied having received any training. Certainly training had long been quite actively pursued within some groups of provincial papers, such as Kemsley (later Thomson). But only 23 per cent of specialists began on a provincial daily (Table 3.7); probably the weekly papers were too small, and the other organizations too national, to take training very seriously. The specialists were asked: 'Looking back, what was the most useful thing you learnt during the first full-time job in journalism?'

'Working to a deadline.'

'Brevity and accuracy.'

'How to spot an essential news point and put it into the first paragraph.'

'That the world is different from the impression I had from my mother.'

'That people are only rarely certain about anything.'

'Being trained (by being told to go out and do it) to write fast for numerous different papers (from *Times* to *Mirror*) on one event.'

They emphasize two main kinds of learning. Firstly, they learnt the *discipline* of writing to order – speed, accuracy, length, the appealing first paragraph. Secondly they claim to have learnt about *people* – especially news sources and other journalists.

c. Journalist careers: before and after national specialization

The varied pattern of entry to journalism is matched by an equally varied patterning of careers between entry and national specialization. Before becoming a national specialist a journalist is about equally likely to have worked for either one, or two, or three, or four plus news organizations. The advertising goal fields show the greatest extremes – with Motoring correspondents likely to have had five jobs before specialization and Fashion correspondents likely to have specialized in their very first job. Another field in which specialists in general had worked for few separate employers was Foreign correspondence. This again emphasized the élite entry and sometimes overseas starting points of Foreign correspondents – as against the mobile provincial early careers of the Lobby men.

Since 44 per cent of all specialists worked for three or more news organizations before specialization (Table 3.9) the predominantly South of England starting points (Table 3.8) might be misleading; journalists could start on a small southern weekly newspaper, then move to a daily in a large northern city, before moving to London and subsequent specialization. But only 20 per cent of all these specialists had *ever* worked in either Manchester or Glasgow – the two major provincial centres and satellite printing centres for national newspapers; this only equals the proportion who started in the London suburbs.

Nearly all these careers involve moves from smaller to larger news organizations. Secondly, most moves occur within one region of the country; this is based on personal contact networks and supported by the larger news organization's surveillance of the output of smaller local news organizations. A third aspect is the operation of this process within greater London and the South of England; 27 per cent of all specialists started in central London and another 40 per cent started in the London suburbs or elsewhere in the South.

Between arriving in London and becoming a specialist, two points recur: most have worked in London as general reporters before becoming specialists. Secondly, once chosen as specialists most remain

TABLE 3.9

NUMBER OF NEWS ORGANIZATIONS WORKED
FOR BEFORE SPECIALIZATION

	Foreign	Political	Mixed	Audience	Advertising	All (N = 186)
	%	%	%	%	%	%
None*	16	0	3	9	33	11
One or two	56	45	49	46	17	45
Three or four	20	47	36	31	21	31
Five plus	8	8	13	14	29	13

* If a journalist started in a news organization as a specialist this is not counted as working for a news organization before specialization.

in the same specialist field. Only a quarter of current specialists previously specialized in another field in national journalism; this is most common among political Lobby correspondents, nearly half of whom have previously specialized (usually in a semi-political field such as Foreign correspondence or Labour).

Once in a national specialist field a journalist is likely to remain both within that field and in the employment of the same news organization (Table 3.10). The most mobility since specialization is among national Lobby correspondents (having first been a *provincial* Lobby correspondent was common) and Football correspondents.

Two-fifths of specialists have been in their present specialist field under five years; but another two-fifths have been in it for ten years or more (Table 3.11). In a team of three specialists typical length of experience in the field might be as follows:

Number One man	15 years
Number Two man	7 years
Number Three man	2 years

But any such picture is again misleading; some number twos have more experience than their number one. There are also some bulges around certain ages – such as around 20 to 23 years' experience (began specialization 1945–8), with a gap before and afterwards.

TABLE 3.10

JOB SWITCHES BETWEEN NEWS ORGANIZATIONS
SINCE SPECIALIZATION IN PRESENT FIELD

(*Whether national or provincial specialization*)

No. of job switches	Foreign	Political	Mixed	Audience	Advertising	All (N = 187)
	%	%	%	%	%	%
None	71	47	71	56	58	61
One	15	32	29	19	17	22
Two or more	15	21	0	25	25	16

TABLE 3.11

YEARS IN PRESENT SPECIALIZATION

	Foreign	Political	Mixed	Audience	Advertising	All (N = 179)
	%	%	%	%	%	%
Under 5 years	34	34	57	18	58	40
5–9 years	17	26	17	33	17	22
10 years or more	49	40	25	48	25	39

Does the seven years' median duration in present national specialization indicate job insecurity? Some specialists move to another specialist field.* There is little evidence of specialist newsgathering being a 'young man's job' from which older men are ruthlessly

* Which raises the median length of time since *first* specialization to ten years.

ejected. Some specialists enter public relations, or newspaper management, or become news executives; but the median seven years in the present specialism reflects the rapidly increasing numbers of specialist newsgathering jobs in the 1960's. A man aged 50 in 1968 probably entered journalism in the late 1930's since when the total number of journalists in Britain had doubled. The involuntary loss of experienced men has often forced news executives to bring in younger men. Moreover the age bulge among specialists is about equal in the thirties and forties – and the numbers only fall off substantially for specialists aged 50 to 59 (and hence who entered journalism between 1925 and 1939).

Increasing age brings higher status to some specialists but not to others (Table 3.12). Specialists aged under 30 were precocious

TABLE 3.12

SPECIALISTS' SALARIES BY AGE IN 1968

Specialists aged:	under 30 years of age	in their 30's	in their 40's	50 and over	All ages (N = 173)
	%	%	%	%	%
Less than £2,500	81	32	12	19	31
£2,500–£2,999	8	23	22	18	19
£3,000–£3,999	8	35	41	29	32
£4,000 & over	4	9	25	35	18

anyway and 89 per cent were paid under £3,000. The majority of those in their 30's also received salaries under £3,000. The very wide range of salaries paid to specialists over 40 illustrates the lack of a clearly defined career pattern or seniority structure. Some older men clearly see their own salaries relatively frozen – while the pay of age equals continues to increase – and men with frozen salaries may see this as an attempt to freeze them out altogether.

d. Later career prospects

Most specialists said there was another job they would like in the future. Some merely wanted promotion within their present job – number twos wanted to be number one; Foreign correspondents wanted to be posted from the USA to Europe and *vice versa*. But more quoted a job which was on a different career ladder or involved a different function; an Education or Aviation correspondent might want to be News editor. Other job wishes included becoming a columnist (especially Sport or Political); running a specialist magazine programme on television; having a 'quieter life' on a Sunday. Several still hoped to earn their living from book writing alone. Outside journalism the main job wish was in management (newspaper, broadcast, or in industry). Not a single specialist volunteered an ambition in the direction of public relations.

When asked what they *expected* to be doing in five years' time there was more mention of public relations. In Aviation and Motoring there is an established tradition of specialist correspondents moving into PR jobs for the major manufacturing companies in those fields; several Labour correspondents have gone into Governmental-Industrial public relations; ex-Lobby correspondents were working in PR jobs both for the Prime Minister and the leader of the Opposition. But the most common specialist's expectation was that in five years' time he would be in the same job. A sense of being locked into a static career situation was seen as aggravating the long-term insecurity of certain employing news organizations. More anxiety about the possibility of their news organization going out of business was expressed by specialists on 'popular' papers.

Most specialists said that their pensions could not be transferred to another organization. But differences in salary – as well as in expenses and opportunities for extra earnings – are often so great between apparently comparable jobs as to outweigh any loss of pension rights.*

Most national Editors saw specialist careers as a 'problem'; a minority believed that specialists should stay in the same field as long as possible – since 'experience' was the vital factor in specialist newsgathering. The majority view among national Editors was that, despite the importance of 'experience', at some point diminishing returns either might, or usually did, set in. In the short term Editors tend to be plugging gaps. Even Editors who believe that specialists should in general not be left too long in one specialist field still quote the odd exception – 'Of course, there's X who has made that field his own, and would not be willing to move. Nor would we want to move him.' Several Editors replied that a 'tour of duty' scheme was desirable ideally, but the overwhelming Editorial view was that in practice it was not workable. The specialists themselves would become extremely insecure as the appointed time for transfer approached, while the news organization would be reluctant to lose a man's years

---

* Many specialists were extremely vague about their pensions. For instance, in some news organizations where compromise forms of transferability had been negotiated this appeared to be unknown to the specialist. There was often similar vagueness about contracts; but most said theirs was a 3-month contract.

of experience in a specific field. Most Editors thought they had to adopt an *ad hoc* approach.

Some patterns, then, do exist in the past careers of specialists; but there are always many exceptions, and within one field exceptions may include the majority of careers. This relative lack of career pattern accompanies a good deal of insecurity and anxiety. Despite complaining about their specific case, specialists still tend to believe that no more firm planning of careers is possible – and national Editors tend to agree.

4. ROLES AND GOALS: AUTONOMY AND CONTROL

a. Work roles, status and tension

A number of factors already discussed might be expected to produce differences in self-perceived status – not only as between the work role and life outside work, but also between different roles within the specialist's working life. Firstly, career insecurity is likely to differ between fields. Secondly, the different goals predominating within different specialist fields can be expected to carry strong status implications. Thirdly, each specialist operates at work within a tripartite division of work roles. Each specialist is:

(1) An *employee* (of an organization which itself has advertising, audience and non-revenue goals).

(2) A *specialist gatherer* of news from news sources.

(3) A *competitor-colleague* within a group of specialists covering the same field for other news organizations.

When specialists are asked about their own status, they do recognize differences between their status in different work roles. All the selected specialists collectively say they see themselves as having their highest status (2·24 or just above 'fairly high') in the specialist newsgatherer role; they see their next highest status in the role of employee of their own news organization (1·97); next comes their status within British national journalism (1·87); and lowest by a substantial margin is their status as a private citizen (1·53). There is also a remarkable consistency through nearly all the fields in seeing the specialist *newsgatherer role* as conferring the highest status, and the private *citizen role* as the lowest.*

* These are means for all selected specialists (N=192) based on this scoring system: Low status=0; medium=1; fairly high=2; high=3.

Specialists say that they experience only fairly low levels of tension; the main finding for all fields combined is:

(1) Most tension is experienced by specialists in dealings with *news executives* and desks* (0·85).

(2) Second, come dealings with *sources and contacts* (0·62).

(3) Least tension is experienced in dealing with *competitor-colleagues* in the same field (0·46).

The specialists indicate that the strongest tensions come not from dealings with important news sources, and not from face-to-face and day-to-day competition with competitor-colleagues, but from the way in which competitive and other pressures are channelled through the news organization. Some of these are normal news pressures of time and space; others depend on personalities and processing:

'Very few middle range executives have any useful recent practical experience.'

'There is an alarming lack of team-work inside newspaper offices in the Street. Everybody seems too concerned with protecting his own interests all the time.'

'Tension with news executives results from an indeterminate power structure and different news interests; with sources and contacts because one's interests are different and sometimes opposed.'

'The answer here clearly depends upon which executive one is dealing with. I have no problems (and therefore no tension) with some; but with less competent executives tension arises depending on their rank.'

'The Editor is a fascist bastard.'

All three roles potentially involve specialists in conflict. Loyalty to a news executive may involve a specialist in conflict with a news source or a competitor-colleague; loyalty to a news source may involve conflict with the news desk – and so on. However, within the competitor-colleague role specialists may be able, to some extent, to

---

* These are means for all specialists (N=190) based on this scoring system: None=0; a little=1; a certain amount=2; much tension=3.

defend themselves from, and to cushion themselves against, the conflicting interests of news executives and news sources.

Specialists were asked whether they regarded themselves 'primarily as a specialist covering this field' or 'primarily as a journalist working for my present organization'. The following percentages chose the *specialist* alternative:

Foreign	%
specialists	28
Political	66
Mixed	42
Audience	54
Advertising	46
All selected	
specialists	46
(N=192)	

The Foreign correspondents tended to interpret the question in terms of their present foreign posting rather than of Foreign correspondence in general. But between other fields there are noticeable differences; in particular the high status political Lobby correspondents are especially likely to see themselves as *political* first and journalists second.

b. Status of particular specialist fields

The occupational pecking order is inversely related to the revenue goal emphasis in particular fields. When specialists are asked about other specialist fields, they do indeed have the lowest opinion of Motoring specialists (Table 3.13). Labour correspondents come out well above the other mixed goal fields; below these in the opinion of other specialists are the audience goal fields. Here (using the same scoring system as in Table 3.13) are the opinions of the field in capital letters about the other fields listed below:

WASHINGTON		NEW YORK		BONN/ROME	
Pol. Lobby	(1·9)	*Foreign*	(2·3)	Pol. Lobby	(2·2)
Education	(1·9)	Pol. Lobby	(2·2)	*Foreign*	(2·0)
Labour	(1·9)	Labour	(2·2)	Labour	(2·0)
Foreign	(1·7)	Crime	(1·8)	Crime	(1·6)
Aviation	(1·5)	Aviation	(1·7)	Aviation	(1·5)
Football	(1·5)	Education	(1·7)	Education	(1·5)
Crime	(1·3)	Football	(1·7)	Football	(1·5)
Motoring	(0·9)	Motoring	(1·4)	Motoring	(1·2)

POL. LOBBY

Pol. Lobby	(2·4)
{ Labour	(2·2)
{ Foreign	(2·2)
Aviation	(1·5)
Education	(1·3)
{ Crime	(1·2)
{ Football	(1·2)
Motoring	(0·8)

AVIATION

Pol. Lobby	(2·4)
Labour	(2·2)
Aviation	(2·0)
{ Foreign	(1·9)
{ Education	(1·9)
Crime	(1·4)
Football	(1·2)
Motoring	(0·8)

EDUCATION

Foreign	(2·3)
{ Pol. Lobby	(2·2)
{ *Education*	(2·2)
Labour	(2·0)
Aviation	(1·8)
Crime	(1·3)
Football	(1·2)
Motoring	(0·6)

LABOUR

Labour	(2·6)
Pol. Lobby	(2·3)
{ Foreign	(2·2)
{ Crime	(2·2)
{ Football	(2·2)
Education	(2·0)
Aviation	(1·9)
Motoring	(1·0)

CRIME

Crime	(2·6)
Pol. Lobby	(2·5)
{ Foreign	(2·4)
{ Labour	(2·4)
Aviation	(1·7)
Education	(1·6)
Football	(1·5)
Motoring	(1·0)

FOOTBALL

Foreign	(2·5)
Pol. Lobby	(2·1)
{ Labour	(2·0)
{ Crime	(2·0)
Football	(1·9)
Education	(1·6)
Aviation	(1·5)
Motoring	(1·0)

FASHION

{ Foreign	(2·7)
{ Education	(2·7)
{ Pol. Lobby	(2·0)
{ Crime	(2·0)
Football	(1·8)
Labour	(1·6)
Aviation	(1·5)
Motoring	(1·2)

MOTORING

{ Foreign	(2·1)
{ Pol. Lobby	(2·1)
{ Labour	(2·1)
{ Aviation	(1·9)
{ Education	(1·9)
Motoring	(1·8)
{ Crime	(1·6)
{ Football	(1·6)

There is great consistency in the Foreign and Political correspondents being most highly thought of; moreover, Motoring correspondents are the least highly thought of by every other specialist field.

The specialists in general push their own fields up a few places in the pecking order. Motoring and Football correspondents push themselves up two places; Crime correspondents immodestly push themselves up five places; Labour and Education both up two places; Aviation goes up from fourth equal to third; Political Lobby up one place. The Washington men are unusual in placing Foreign correspondents in only fourth place (possibly on the assumption that they themselves are superior to the general run of Foreign correspondents); but all the Foreign correspondents collectively place themselves second to the political Lobby men.

Despite a certain amount of immodesty about themselves, the specialists still acknowledge a status order which accords the highest status to non-revenue Foreign correspondence, followed by the

TABLE 3.13

SPECIALISTS' OPINIONS ABOUT OTHER SPECIALIST FIELDS

Opinion held about these fields	Opinion held by these specialists					
	Foreign	*Political*	*Mixed*	*Audience*	*Advertising*	*All*
Foreign	—	2·2	2·1	2·5	2·2	2·27
Political *Lobby*	2·1	—	2·3	2·2	2·1	2·20
Mixed:						
Aviation	1·6	1·5	—	1·6	1·8	1·61
Education	1·7	1·3	—	1·6	2·1	1·61
Labour	2·0	2·4	—	2·1	2·0	2·14
Audience:						
Crime	1·6	1·2	1·3	—	1·7	1·44
Football	1·6	1·2	1·2	—	1·7	1·40
Advertising:						
Motoring*	1·2	0·8	0·8	1·0	—	0·96 (N=171)

* Unfortunately no question about Fashion correspondents was included in the questionnaire.

Note: This table is based on the mean for each field using this scoring system:

Low opinion	0
Medium opinion	1
Fairly high opinion	2
High opinion	3

political Lobby, the mixed fields, then the audience fields; the Motoring correspondents have a lower relative opinion of themselves than does any other field about itself.

c. Fields by goal type

The non-revenue goal of Foreign correspondence is reflected in the opinion of other specialists – who see this field as very low on both advertising and audience interest. Foreign correspondents are concentrated in the newsagency (Reuters) and quality newspapers. This field provides both the longest career ladder of all the selected fields, and also the most precocious careers; Foreign correspondents have finished formal education later and started national specialization earlier. They have also worked for unusually few news organizations both before and after specialization. A Foreign correspondent's career often started by his being sent in his mid- or late-twenties to cover a war. Next a typical posting is to a junior job in one of the bigger bureaux, such as New York or Paris.

Foreign correspondents in general were highly thought of by other specialists. They seem securely entrenched in their careers. There is a definite career ladder leading from one capital to another and there are jobs in London on the Foreign desk. Yet the very presence of a career ladder induces insecurity among Foreign correspondents – because moves on the ladder mean moving house, wife, children's schools, local language, and entire way of life. The risk of marriage breakdown was quoted by many Foreign correspondents. The danger of losing touch with the British audience is known to be discussed by news executives in London. Some Foreign correspondents seem slightly forlorn, aware that they are in a much desired job, which can be another source of insecurity – a sense that able younger men are waiting in the wings. The approach of retirement may also present special problems for Foreign correspondents who have lived most of their adult lives abroad.

The Political Lobby correspondents are similar to the Foreign specialists in present age, long duration in the field and high esteem in the eyes of other specialists; but Lobby men overall differ in having had substantially shorter formal education, much more provincial newspaper and non-London early careers, and much higher job mobility both before and after specialization. Lobby correspondents are the only specialists to see their status as equally high in the *newsgatherer* and *employee* roles; also reflecting the unusual status and delicacy of Lobby correspondence, these specialists emphasize that they are *political* correspondents first and journalists only second. Two types of contrasted Lobby careers might be: (1) The non-privileged career: leave school at 15; messenger boy; reporter on provincial daily; Press Association debate notetaker, and then number three national Lobby correspondent. (2) The privileged career: Oxford degree; reporter on national; Foreign correspondent; and then number one national Lobby correspondent. In practice many Lobby careers are a mixture of the two types.

The Lobby is unusual in that its high status and the value placed by Editors on scarce access to the Lobby lead to a high proportion of correspondents having had other previous specialist experience. It is also unusual in providing a relatively long career ladder – from Lobby man on a small provincial to the chief Political correspondent of a national news organization. Lobby men see their work as especially demanding in terms of energy and the long late hours at Westminster. It is the great volume of detail and the pace of Lobby work which produces unease – and leads some Lobby men to think that almost any other sort of journalism including television work, with its much shorter stories and less detail, would be less demanding.

Consistent with the classification of *Aviation, Education and Labour as mixed goal fields*, the background characteristics of correspondents in these three fields exhibit overall a pattern similar to that of all the selected specialists combined. *Aviation* correspondence is seen by other specialists as having a stronger element of advertising goal than the other mixed fields. Aviation correspondents, indeed, are similar to the Motoring men in lowish formal education, and an unusually long time-gap between entry to journalism and ultimate national specialization. *Education* correspondents are much younger and have had more precocious careers. More Education correspondents are university educated and more started on *daily* newspapers; in the shorter period of time they also made more job moves before specialization. Education is extreme in the short average duration of specialists in the field; the field is relatively new and of lowish status. Some young Education correspondents see this field as a stepping stone to higher things. *Labour* correspondents are another relatively highly educated group. They also have a solid background on weekly papers – but some jumped straight from this to a much bigger news organization. Labour is a youngish field, but a third of the specialists have specialized in another field previously – a further indication of the fairly high status of this field.

Collectively these fields in the estimation of specialists in general occupy an intermediate level of status, below Foreign and Political correspondents but superior in esteem to the revenue fields. Of the three mixed goal fields Labour is held in the highest esteem. Among the mixed goal fields, Education, the most junior, is also the one with the most secure and comfortable feeling of riding on a growing wave. The highest status of the mixed fields, Labour, whilst believed to be a passport to higher things in journalism, is regarded by the specialists in it (as well as by some news executives) as the physically most demanding and uncomfortable of all the specialist fields. There is a widespread attitude among Labour correspondents that this is not something to make a lifetime's work.

Audience goal: Crime and Football. Among *Football* correspondents a few have previously been professional footballers. Three sorts of journalism experience are found to a greater extent here than in any other specialist field; these are experience as news executives – often as sports editor of a London suburban paper; secondly experience in a news agency; thirdly these specialists often have had national sub-editing experience. Just as Football correspondents have had an especially close connection with their subject-matter, so

also have *Crime* correspondents; it is not unusual for a Crime specialist to have a close relative who is a policeman. In the careers of both
Crime and Football men specialized Fleet Street news agencies have
been especially important. Both are extreme in low formal education;
both were especially likely to have started in the South of England.
Both Crime and Football specialisms are unlikely to lead on to any
other kind of specialist journalism. Both Crime and Football are
held in low esteem by specialists in other fields.

Both fields regard their news sources as exceptionally unhelpful
and both are pessimistic about the future. Football correspondents
worry about growing older and out of touch with the young players,
they believe that a number of the previous generation of Football
writers became alcoholics, and they do not welcome the prospect of
sports executive jobs. The Crime correspondents also profess much
gloom about the decline of Crime news, the difficulty of getting
young men into the field, and the lack of graduate Crime correspondents.

Advertising goal: Fashion and Motoring. The representative
Fashion correspondent is a woman, who started extremely young in
Fashion specialization and has never worked in the British provinces.
In contrast to all other specialists in the present study, the Fashion
correspondent typically not only started her career in London but
also in a specialized job. The career beginnings of the Motoring
correspondents could scarcely have been more different. Most
Motoring correspondents had followed a very non-precocious provincial career route – low formal education and early age of entry to
journalism, usually on a weekly paper; Motoring correspondents had
also experienced considerable job mobility before unusually late
specialization.

Nevertheless the two fields have much else in common. They both,
at least partially, acknowledged the existence of the advertising goal.
Both sets of specialists report unusually low levels of tension with
news sources. In both cases the general view of their future prospects
is much different from the audience goal fields. Both Fashion and
Motoring correspondents have been in their fields for an unusually
brief time, and both have the prospect of being offered public relations jobs with former news sources.

d. Implications for autonomy and control

Four general points emerge from this chapter. Firstly one cannot
assume all specialists to be working under the same constraints.
Secondly career patterns and previous experience of specialist
journalists differ considerably between individuals and between

fields. Thirdly a specialist journalist operates within three distinct work roles. Fourthly, specialists are attributed differing status according to their field, and specialists see themselves as having differing statuses within their different work roles.

'Autonomy' and 'control' will be discussed at greater length below. But no matter how such terms are defined these four points all have important implications for the autonomy of, and control of, specialist journalists. Firstly, autonomy and control will differ according to the predominant type of goal under which a specialist operates. To take two extreme examples, a Foreign correspondent based in Bonn, Rome or Washington may feel free to write critical stories about British cars; but a Motoring correspondent, based in London, may not feel free to write such stories, because the car companies are advertisers and he is working under an advertising goal.

Secondly, a brief look at some data on the previous careers of specialists shows that (to take another extreme contrast) Education correspondents are a very different collection of people from Crime correspondents. The typical Crime correspondent was (in 1968) aged 47; his education had finished at age 16 in 1937. The typical Education correspondent was aged 30; his education had finished at age 21 in 1959. Quite apart from the different goals and the different news sources in these two fields – the Education correspondent was clearly in a much stronger position from a career point of view.

Thirdly, each specialist newsgathering correspondent operates within three separate work roles:

(1) Employee in relation to news organization.
(2) Specialist newsgatherer in relation to news sources.
(3) Competitor-colleague in relation to other national specialists covering the same field.

These three roles are the subject of the next three chapters. But already it seems probable that these roles will have implications for autonomy and control – especially in view of prevalent 'news value' emphasis on conflict and competition.

Fourthly, data has been presented to show that specialists accord other specialist fields differing statuses – broadly with an inverse correlation between the strength of revenue goal and occupational esteem. This status ranking itself is in line with the strongly non-revenue orientations of journalists in general; it seems likely to carry implications for autonomy and control within different fields.

4

Specialist correspondent
as employee

Fred E. Katz argues that the issue of autonomy within organizations[1] can best be looked at in terms of four types of autonomy:

(1) Autonomy internal to organizational roles and enacted *inside* the organization. (This type of autonomy would presumably be at issue if the News editor in the news organization requested a correspondent against his own wishes to cover a particular story.)

(2) Autonomy internal to organizational roles but enacted *outside* the organization. (Such autonomy would be exercised when a correspondent decided to interview a news source of his own choice.)

(3) Autonomy external to organizational roles but enacted *within* the organization. (An example here would be a correspondent using his news organization's office facilities while engaging in freelance journalism for another news organization.)

(4) Autonomy external to organizational roles and enacted *outside* the organization. (This could involve political, social or freelance activity carried on by the correspondent on his days off work.)

But clearly the correspondent does not fit easily into these categories. His work roles are not clearly defined. Nor is the difference between activity inside and outside the news organization.

Nevertheless, Katz's general proposition that 'restraints placed upon the expert must inevitably be balanced against a degree of autonomy' is applicable to specialist journalists. Katz himself continues:

'The proposition that follows from recognition of this balance is that the *greater the degree of specialized knowledge and skills required of the occupant of a position, the greater the degree of autonomy that accrues to the position.*'[2]

a. Specialization and the occupational/organizational balance

When he is designated as a specialist by his Editor the journalist becomes if not an instant expert, at least an instant specialist. The specialist is given his specialist platform by a stroke of the Editor's pen. And what the Editor can thus give, he can also take away. The specialist, then, lacks the kind of recognized or 'rational' basis for his specialization which is possessed by the professional who studies for an examination qualification and is backed by the supports of an established profession such as law or medicine.

Nevertheless when a journalist has been a specialist for even a year or two, the news organization's scope for exercising arbitrary control over him is already limited. The news organization by now has an investment in the man; and the specialist has some element of reputation in the specialist field, quite independent of whether the same news organization continues to want to employ him. When specialist expertise is defined largely in terms of *experience*, the specialist with even a year or two of experience may well be able to sell this experience to competing employers.

Specialists in general belong to an occupational élite of the 1,000 or so senior British journalists. The dividing line between specialists and executives is unclear – and this occupational élite can hire journalists as well as fire them. Editors and other senior executives come from, and have more in common with, these 1,000 journalists than with business executives in media organizations. Opinion within this occupational élite is a major restraint upon arbitrary news organization power. Reputation in the occupation, status within the news organization, and autonomy, are likely to be closely related. If a specialist is highly thought of within the occupation, other news organizations will make him offers of employment. His current news organization will often recognize the specialist's market strength by conceding him more autonomy than most journalists obtain. His high occupational reputation and his high organizational autonomy will earn him high status.

The extent of this autonomy depends on the balance of power between journalists and news organizations in the relevant specialist area. But certain organizational controls are broadly regarded as legitimate by journalists and certain kinds of journalist autonomy are regarded as legitimate by news organizations. For instance all journalists concede to the news organization the legitimacy of establishing rigid edition deadlines, whereas all news organizations will concede the legitimacy of specialist correspondents cultivating *personal* relationships with news sources.

Individual journalists tend to see themselves as being free, while other journalists are in chains:

'Some reporters are quick to point to the personal freedom but view their cases as unique. Recurrent among Washington correspondents is the view that the press generally is not free but that they, as individuals, are very independent.'[3]

This follows partly from specialists comparing the autonomy of specialists and of other journalists; also relevant are differing definitions of which are, and which are not, legitimate news organization controls. To a journalist working for another newspaper, it may seem that anyone who works for the *Daily Express* has submitted to unjustified organizational restraints. However, the man who works for the *Daily Express*, by doing so, concedes a degree of legitimacy to that newspaper's organizational control. Specialists tend to feel, or claim that they feel, relatively free because occupational norms stress that once a journalist works for a particular news organization he should regard most of its requirements as legitimate.

b. Outside affiliations

'... the distribution of autonomy indicates to what extent outside affiliations are permitted and how tightly members are incorporated into organizations. The organization's bargain with its environment becomes revealed.'
Fred E. Katz, *Autonomy and Organization*

To the extent that outside affiliations permitted to members are an indicator of organizational strength, news organizations are weak in relation to specialists. In the case of specialist newsgatherers (but not all journalists) there are three obviously relevant sorts of outside affiliation: Firstly, the basic definition of the specialist newsgathering role requires the correspondent to engage in close and frequent interaction with news sources. Secondly, the news organization defines the specialist's role in terms of effective competition with other correspondents covering the same news source area but employed by competing news organizations; this effective competition involves close and frequent interaction with the competitor-colleagues. Thirdly, the specialist journalist, as he acquires a reputation in his field, tends to be offered opportunities for freelance writing and broadcasting.

The news organization lacks clear rules to cover all three sorts of outside affiliation. What different individuals within the news organization require of specialists lacks consistency. Firstly, the news organization wants specialists to be friendly with news sources – but not so friendly as to become mouthpieces for news sources. Secondly, the news organization wants its specialists to pursue the same news stories as the competing specialists – and to make use of certain sorts of information from these competitor-colleagues – but the news organization does not want its specialists to become too loyal to competitor-colleagues groups. Thirdly, news organizations also have ambiguous requirements and policies on freelance earnings; these earnings help to keep specialists happy, but also may enable them to become very independent and to devote much of their time to other news organizations. However, such outside work may bring prestige to both the journalist and the news organization.

c. Uncertainty and differing goals

In addition to unclear occupational norms three other important areas of uncertainty can be listed. Firstly, uncertainty in the organizational control structure; secondly, in the nature of news; thirdly, career uncertainty. Firstly, in a news organization the *control structure* itself is uncertain. Gathering and processing control structures overlap as do such areas as news and features, and most specialists do not report to one superior alone. A broad shallow structure allows rapid communication with the top; but time scarcity always blocks detailed understanding. Unclear organizational goals make the controls exerted by the organization still more uncertain. In such circumstances the degree of autonomy must also be uncertain; Katz suggests (p. 24) that 'autonomy may be clearest by contrast, when rules for compliance are most clearly stated'.

Secondly, since *news* is defined in terms of the unusual, it is impossible to lay down firm rules for gathering and processing it. News is also defined in terms of speed and competition. Speed prevents full information about organizational requirements from being available. Competition to some extent reduces the strength both of organizational control and of specialist autonomy – since both become subject to 'news values' broadly held within the occupation of journalism. But in many particular instances news values also are uncertain.

Thirdly, *career* uncertainty is of great importance to autonomy. In any trial of strength between organizational control and specialist autonomy, the specialist's job security and future career prospects are relevant. But here again, there is uncertainty – the familiar contrast between lack of legal security of tenure combined with a substantial degree of *de facto* security. Nevertheless, if a particular specialist is trying to expand his autonomy against news organization control pressures, there is likely to be uncertainty as to how far he can safely go.

All of these kinds of uncertainty are, of course, related to individualistic values within journalism. Even though general norms exist, the strength of such norms will differ between individuals. Some individuals in apparently similar jobs acquire quite different levels of autonomy, status and reputation. An individual's autonomy may vary sharply over quite short time-spans. For any specialist journalist there is some level of *ascribed* autonomy implied in his appointment to cultivate relevant news sources. But there is also substantial additional room for *achieved* autonomy. This basic situation of uncertainty produces among journalists – as among many other kinds of employees – a drive towards expanding autonomy. This drive towards autonomy is answered by counterdrives towards organizational control.

Differing goals between, for instance, Foreign correspondence and Football journalism lead to different combinations of autonomy and control. Some differences follow from the work situations – whether a journalist is snooping around the State Department and the British Embassy in Washington or whether he is snooping around Tottenham Hotspur and Chelsea in London. Other differences in autonomy and control may arise not from the intrinsic structure of the specialist fields but from the social characteristics of the journalists who come to work in the particular field.

Advertising specialists are likely to experience some controls from prominent advertisers, or from the advertising department within the employing media organization. Where prominent advertisers are also prominent news sources this control may be especially strong. However, being subject to such external controls, Fashion and Motoring correspondents may acquire compensating autonomy – for instance in relation to certain news executives.

Audience goal specialists are likely to experience some control from the audience sales/marketing area. Since an audience goal is only possible in a field where large-scale public interest already obtains, this may place the relevant news sources in a powerful position. However, this dependence upon public interest and control by news sources may allow Crime and Football correspondents compensating autonomy of other sorts.

Non-revenue goal specialists may be relatively free of direct pressures of the audience and advertising kind. But although Foreign correspondents will thus have greater autonomy in relation to news sources, they may be placed in a weak position in other ways; an element of audience goal remains and the organizational requirement that foreign news be of at least some interest to British audiences will exercise an important negative control.

Mixed goal specialists will be subjected to a more even balance of the previous three sorts of controls. A specialist may find himself reacting to the lowest common denominator of audience, advertising and non-revenue control pressures. But a specialist may also – by skilfully responding to the conflicting controls – be able to achieve an extremely autonomous position.

Obviously, the overall mixture of a particular news organization's goals will also be important. A specialist on a 'quality' newspaper can be expected to have more autonomy – because such a news organization tends to require more detailed knowledge and is, therefore, more dependent on specialist expertise and experience. However, expectations as to what is legitimate in autonomy and control may differ; specialists on quality media may not acquire as much additional autonomy as they consider justified. Clearly also the partisan political element in a news organization's non-revenue goal component will be important for specialist autonomy. Moreover, the 'neutral' policies of newsagencies and broadcast news organizations will also be an important control element.

d. Spheres of autonomy and spheres of control

A specialist cannot extravagantly praise a news source or an advertiser, nor can he write word-for-word the same story as a competitor-colleague from a competing news organization, without this being observable to other journalists. What a specialist writes in a newspaper or says on television is very much more observable than how the same specialist interacts with his news sources; less observable still is a specialist's personal interaction with his competitor-colleagues. What is most easily observable to the news organization is also most easily controlled; the content of a story written by a specialist can be controlled by the processors. But the newsgathering activities of a specialist are both less observable and less easily controlled. And in his personal interaction with competitor-colleagues the specialist is least observed and most autonomous.

The observability of content, the internal communication within a news organization and the lateness of the relevant news are all closely related to autonomy and to status. If a story arrives near a deadline, little internal communication can occur before a decision to include or reject the item is made. Lower status specialists will have less chance of getting material into the content the closer they leave it to the relevant deadline. Thus correspondents who frequently produce material very near to a deadline will tend to be correspondents either of high status or with an audience goal.

Since observability so shapes the opportunities for organizational control, struggles for more autonomy will take the form partly of struggles to escape surveillance by the news organization. Hence specialists tend to be hostile to processing – the point at which their output is most subject to negative controls; specialists emphasize the importance of newsgathering, where they are more autonomous. Finally it is in his role as competitor-colleague that the specialist is least subject to organizational control.

The general approach of this chapter will be to indicate a compromise between some spheres of specialist autonomy and other spheres of news organization control. The news organization exercises control by defining the field and its goal, by appointing the specialist, and by its daily exercise of news processing. The specialist maintains a degree of autonomy by emphasizing his *newsgathering* role, by cultivating personal contacts and personal knowledge which can be shielded from the news organization. But the continuing struggle between journalists and news organizations, the uncertainty both of occupational norms and of news itself, the differing goals and imperfect communication within the news organization, combined with the *personal* status and reputation of individual journalists – all these make autonomy and control an issue in continuing dispute.

2. THE CASE OF POLITICAL PARTISANSHIP

Do right-wing news organizations succeed in controlling and curbing the autonomy of left-wing journalists? Table 4.1 appears to indicate an affirmative answer. Of specialists on Conservative quality papers 54 per cent are to the left of the news organization (while only 4 per cent are to the right); on Conservative popular papers 59 per cent are to the left (while only 11 per cent are to the right).

44 per cent are to the left overall; but an equal proportion say their politics are 'about the same' or 'it depends on the issue', and 12 per cent are to the right. Moreover in the case of both the 'neutral' broadcast and agency news organizations and the pro-Labour news organizations there is a roughly even balance between left and right, with the majority in general agreement. The phenomenon of journalists being to the left is confined mainly to the pro-Conservative papers, and even here only a quarter are 'well to the left'. Of the third who are 'somewhat to the left', some are themselves Conservative voters. Rather than showing any huge gap between journalists and organizations, then, perhaps the most important finding of Table 4.1 is that 81 per cent of specialists are either in broad agreement with their news organization or only 'somewhat' to the left or right.

Moreover even for the 19 per cent who are well to the left or right, partisan political control may still not impinge seriously on specialist autonomy: firstly, the sphere of interest of any one specialist is much narrower than that of the news organization overall; although a

TABLE 4.1

SPECIALISTS' POLITICS IN RELATION
TO POLITICS OF NEWS ORGANIZATION,* 1968

Specialists' politics in relation to politics of news organization	Conservative quality newspapers	Conservative popular newspapers	Neutrals (broadcast & agency)	Labour quality & popular newspapers	All
	%	%	%	%	%
'I am well to the LEFT of my organization'	23	24	5	2	16
'Somewhat to LEFT'	31	35	26	19	28
'About the same'	23	15	47	35	26
'Depends on issue'	19	16	16	19	18
'Somewhat to RIGHT'	2	9	5	19	9
'Well to RIGHT'	2	2	0	6	3
N	57	55	19	48	179

* Conservative qualities: *The Times, Financial Times, The Daily Telegraph, Sunday Times, Sunday Times.*
Conservative populars: *Daily Express, Daily Mail, Daily Sketch, Evening News, Evening Standard, Sunday Express, News of the World.*
Neutrals: BBC, ITN, Press Association, Reuters.
Labour qualities: *The Guardian, The Observer.*
Labour populars: *The Daily Mirror, The Sun, The People, Sunday Mirror, Morning Star.*

Football specialist may disagree strongly with his newspaper's politics he may agree strongly with its Football policy. The same may be equally true in more political fields. Secondly, news organizations and their executives sometimes deliberately prefer to employ journalists of 'deviant' politics; a Conservative newspaper's Editor may believe that pro-Labour journalists get on better with trade union leaders. Or it may be thought that the political balance of the audience requires political 'balance' among journalists. In some cases there may be a preference within a three-man specialist team for balance. Thirdly, news values tend to override political values both for news organizations and for news correspondents; news organizations as well as specialists are usually keen to run a story which will reflect badly on their 'own' party – if they think the story strong in the usual ingredients of news. Fourthly, when a specialist is first appointed he knows from the overt content of the news organization (and from friends who work there) what its policies are; so also the news organization executives are confronted with a journalist whose propensity to submit to organizational policies can be ascertained from his previous output and career. Extreme cases of incompatibility are thus often avoided.

Obviously, any journalist submits to some extent to the policy controls of his news organization; but most journalists when producing stories manage to avoid the sharpest conflicts with their own political beliefs. In relation to the *audience*, journalists differ as to the legitimacy of 'giving the audience what it wants' politically. Up to a point all journalists support the coalition audience goal – and in the case of a newspaper the majority of whose readers are known to be Conservative, this gives legitimacy to a certain amount of pro-Conservative slanting. But most journalists also favour a strongish element of *non-revenue* goal, which lends some legitimacy to giving the audience what it does not want – including doses of unwelcome political propaganda.

While 67 per cent of advertising goal specialists voted Conservative in 1968, only 19 per cent of mixed goal specialists did so (Table 4.2). Overall there was a small Conservative majority in 1968 – which had changed from a Labour majority in 1966. This change was

TABLE 4.2

VOTING INTENTIONS IN 1968
(WITH HOW VOTED AT 1966 GENERAL ELECTION IN BRACKETS)

	Foreign	Political	Mixed	Audience	Advertising	All
	%	%	%	%	%	%
Communist	0 (0)	3 (0)	7 (2)	0 (0)	4 (0)	3 (1)
Conservative	32 (11)	34 (31)	19 (19)	54 (35)	67 (48)	39 (27)
Labour	38 (22)	31 (34)	55 (58)	31 (44)	13 (13)	36 (36)
Liberal	6 (3)	11 (23)	7 (14)	6 (9)	4 (13)	7 (12)
Other, and would/did not vote	24 (64)	20 (11)	12 (7)	9 (12)	13 (26)	15 (23)
N	34	35	42	35	24	170

broadly in line with the changing opinions of the British electorate. But the heaviest switches in party preferences between 1966 and 1968 were in the least political fields such as Football.

The non-revenue goal Foreign correspondents had mostly failed to go to the trouble in 1966 of getting postal votes. The fairly even balance of Labour and Conservative preferences among Foreign correspondents was similar to that among political Lobby correspondents. In one other semi-political field, namely Aviation, there was a balance. But in the two other mixed goal fields, Education and Labour, combined Labour party preferences outnumbered Conservative preferences by four to one. In contrast to these two fields, both the advertising goal fields, Fashion and Motoring, were heavily Conservative in 1968, and the Crime correspondents were even more strongly Conservative. In these three fields in 1968 Conservative preferences outnumbered Labour by no less than eight to one.

Looked at in single specialist fields the correspondents' 1968 political opinions stand out sharply:

> *Equally balanced*:   Foreign, Lobby, Aviation, Football
> *Strongly Labour*:   Education, Labour
> *Strongly Conservative*: Crime, Fashion, Motoring

These clearcut differences immediately point away from news organization control and focus attention on particular fields and the relevant news sources. Lobby correspondents confronted by the two main parties at Westminster are evenly balanced. Labour correspondents have similar politics to their mainly trade union news sources. Crime correspondents are strongly Conservative – presumably in line with the politics of their news sources among the police.

In the strongly pro-Conservative specialist fields – Crime, Fashion, Motoring – partisan politics are probably of little salience. A different kind of example is provided by the Labour field, where the mainly trade union news sources probably attract journalists of similar Labour party loyalty. Yet it is by no means clear that the resulting coverage – of industrial relations and strikes – is favourable to the Labour party. Nor is there any evidence that Conservative news organizations deliberately employ pro-Labour correspondents and encourage them to exaggerate the frequency of strikes in British industry. News coverage of strikes mainly derives from the broad news supply and demand situation in Britain.

Nevertheless, there are some signs that specialist journalists are selected – partly by themselves and partly by news organizations – with likely inter-personal sympathy with news sources in the relevant field as one important criterion. This inter-personal sympathy is then strengthened in some cases by an increase in political sympathy. For instance between 1966 and 1968 the Education correspondents became more pro-Labour – partly because they approved of the Labour government's schools policy.

Various sorts of anticipation tend to avoid outright political conflict. News organizations are not concerned to force their politics on individual specialists. The specialists in turn are able to preserve much tactical autonomy – including the production of news stories few of which are sharply in contrast with their own political views. Since there is a broad expectation among British journalists that newspapers in general will lean to the right, specialists on Conservative papers may be aware of less political control. Some Conservative specialists working for pro-Labour newspapers feel very constrained. But the greatest political control may well be exercised in 'neutral' news organizations; any right-wing or left-wing news organization experiences at least some pressures from its audience and its news sources to include some material from the opposite partisan wing, but the neutral news organizations tend to aim for 'neutrality' in all stories.

3. NEWS ORGANIZATION CONTROLS AND SPECIALISTS' DEFENCES

a. Specialist job definition

In established newsgathering fields the specialist job exists before the correspondent moves into it. The news organization defines the broad shape of the specialist job, firstly in relation to some established news source area, secondly in terms of competition with other news organizations, and thirdly in relation to an existing group of competitor-colleague specialists. The newly appointed Aviation correspondent, for example, is in effect told to go and compete with the other national Aviation correspondents.

But the novitiate specialist has no formal qualification, membership or loyalty in the relevant specialist field. He cannot be a specialist in the relevant field until a national news organization has so designated him. Moreover, there are various different ways of defining any particular specialist role. Some news organizations ask their Aviation man to cover space as well; others leave space to a Science correspondent. Some ask the Aviation man to cover the defence; others leave it to a Defence correspondent. All this, the new specialist may not regard as impinging on his autonomy. But the definition of the specialist's job by the news organization goes much further – to an extent which may indeed make a specialist believe that he is subject to arbitrary control. A Foreign correspondent may wish to cover regional developments, but will be told to stay in the capital – because 'our readers only want to hear about the big names and events'. A Labour correspondent may want to cover a story about industrial health, but will be told that a current strike has more news 'strength'. A Lobby correspondent may wish to trace the development of a new policy only to be told that the Minister handling the policy is 'not news'. A broadcast specialist may be told that a story will be no good for television unless a certain kind of film is obtained.

Such executive rulings on specific stories may appear arbitrary to the relevant specialist. In the longer run as he ceases to be an instant specialist and becomes an 'experienced' specialist, he will gradually play a larger part in defining his own specialist role. But the experienced specialist may clash less often with organizational controls, partly because he has already internalized them. Much of this kind of 'experience' is gained through his experience of how the news organization executives regard, and how processors handle, his stories.

b. News organization surveillance

Any newsgathering specialist journalist will spend time physically outside his news organization; he is then shielded from observation by his news organization executives. 46 per cent of specialists spend only half or less of their working time actually inside their employing news organization's office (Table 4.3). The great majority of political Lobby correspondents spend nearly all their time outside the office;

TABLE 4.3

PROPORTION OF WORKING TIME SPENT BY
SPECIALISTS IN NEWS ORGANIZATION OFFICE

	Foreign	Political	Mixed	Audience	Advertising	All (N = 194)
	%	%	%	%	%	%
Three-quarters plus	30	0	4	11	4	12
Half to three-quarters	51	3	59	39	61	43
Quarter to half	13	8	28	28	30	21
Quarter or less	6	89	9	22	4	25

the Lobby correspondents use the Press Gallery at Westminster as their base,[4] and some visit their employer's office only once a week or less. When almost all communication between a specialist and his news executives is confined to the telephone, little attempt is being made to exert control over the details of newsgathering.

The Foreign correspondents spend much more time in their employer's office – 81 per cent spend at least half their working time there, but they are referring to an office in Washington, New York, Bonn or Rome which is rented for them by their employers. The Foreign correspondents normally spend all of their time hundreds or thousands of miles removed from their Foreign editor; but Foreign correspondents in the four foreign cities in this study can probably be reached quickly by phone for a larger proportion of their working day than can most specialists stationed in London.

The audience goal specialists spend the most time outside their offices. Some Crime correspondents work mostly at Scotland Yard (where they can be quickly reached on the phone); Football correspondents do a fair amount, for instance, of watching training sessions at football grounds. But the amount of time spent in the employing organization's office is only a crude indicator of opportunities for organizational surveillance or specialist secrecy. The telephone, which allows the news organization to exert some control over a remote specialist, also allows the specialist, even when he is sitting physically inside the news organization office, to carry on conversations (with news sources, competitor-colleagues, and others), which are shielded from surveillance by news executives.

To what extent can the specialist block information within his employing news organization? The public nature of the product, the high frequency of output and the prevalance of competition usually prevent a specialist from blocking information about major news events, which inevitably appear in the competing media. But detailed information about news sources, or the tactics of newsgathering, can be blocked by a specialist who may thus know of developing events before news executives, and may have advance warning about stories in the competing media.

Wilensky, in his *Organizational Intelligence*, notes:

'It is likely that staff experts communicate most freely with colleagues in the same specialty, second with colleagues in the same unit of the workplace, then to subordinates, and last – with greatest blockage and distortion – to superiors and rival agencies.'[5]

Wilensky differentiates between two different sorts of 'colleagues' – those (a) 'in the same specialty', and (b) 'in the same unit of the workplace'. Among specialist journalists the term 'colleague' is often used to refer to journalists in *the same specialist field but working for competing organizations*. This question is dealt with more fully in chapter 6; here we can merely note that the specialist *may* communicate and co-operate more fully with his overt competing opposite number rather than with colleagues within his own news organization. In the case of *superiors* within the news organization, the possibility of a communication block is obvious.

A common aspect of failures in organizational intelligence is the preference for 'covert' data collection and secret operations. Wilensky suggests that, even in military intelligence, *open* sources of information – including daily newspapers – are often superior. Specialist journalism differs from military espionage and intelligence in many ways; but within journalism the preference for relatively secret sources is widespread. The news organization wants a general confidence that its journalists can be trusted to protect anonymity. But by reinforcing this norm of source anonymity the news organization cedes substantial autonomy to specialists.

Sometimes news executives ask a specialist for the name of his news source. The Lobby correspondents have a resolution covering this situation:

'That it is consistent with Lobby practice that members of the Lobby may tell their editors, or acting editors, the sources of their information at Lobby meetings on the rare occasions that this may be vital, but must, on every occasion that such information is passed on, explain to their editors, or acting editors, that the source is strictly confidential.'[6]

The point that only the Editor, and only on 'rare occasions', will be told the identity of sources, emphasizes the norm that relevant news executives will in general not be told the identity of Lobby news sources.

Although other specialist fields are not able to adopt such an uncompromising attitude, claims to protect the anonymity of sources even from news executives are recognized as normal. Combined with the general scarcity of time and the complexity of specific cases, such claims ensure that on even such a simple point as the identity of particular news sources, news executives have very incomplete information. This secrecy and anonymity of news sources – even if only relative rather than absolute – enables a specialist to hide much of his newsgathering activities from news executives. The specialist's desire for autonomy and protection from observability is best met by his concentrating on the more secret, more anonymous and least observable types of news source. But a deliberate pursuit of secret, 'personal', and behind-the-façades information is also in line with basic occupational ideology and occupational suspicions about news management and the techniques of the *fait accompli*. Moreover the competitive situation stresses the pursuit of exclusive news, the personal contact, the anonymous source, and hence supports specialist autonomy.

A superior often makes no attempt to observe a subordinate's *behaviour*, but concentrates on getting a more limited kind of conformity.[7] News executives can seek to direct a specialist's performance either by comment on his output or by more indirect instructions as to how he should behave in relation to the opposition. The specialist's output is highly observable to his superiors, to his competitors, and also to himself. Unlike some workers the specialist newsgatherer is very soon exposed to the ultimate product. This final link in the process is, however, on occasion disrupted. A common example is of the correspondent on a difficult overseas assignment who files material for several days without knowing how it is being used. Correspondents say this quickly induces low morale and a sense of disorientation. The challenge and excitement of long hours and difficult conditions in a remote part of a foreign country are soon experienced not as autonomy but as alienation and isolation – which can be dismissed by a single message from the home office to the effect that the material is being given prominent treatment.

c. Processing control

That a specialist correspondent can become demoralized and disorientated merely through not being aware of the use of his material in the news organization's output emphasizes once again the crucial importance of this final output. No matter how free of surveillance he may be in his dealings with news sources, a specialist lacks autonomy if his material is being heavily cut or completely rejected. Table 4.4 shows 71 per cent of the selected specialists claiming that four-fifths of their material is used in at least one edition. This is a very high figure by the general standards of British journalism. Nevertheless, even among specialists, one man in ten claims that under 60 per cent of his material is used even in one edition. Here then is strong evidence of day-to-day control over at least some specialists.

The political Lobby is close to the overall figure. The audience revenue and the advertising revenue goal specialists claim a very high proportion of material being used. Both the advertising goal fields – Fashion and Motoring – tend to be allotted fixed spaces, often adjacent to related advertising matter; the specialist knows in advance the number of words required. Every single Football special-ist claimed that at least 80 per cent of his copy was used, which again follows from fixed spaces. In these fields – and to a somewhat lesser extent in Crime – control is exercised in other ways than through processing.

TABLE 4.4

PROPORTION OF SPECIALISTS' ORIGINAL
MATERIAL APPEARING

(*in at least one edition of the medium*)

	Foreign	Political	Mixed	Audience	Advertising	All (N=159)
	%	%	%	%	%	%
80 to 100 per cent	57	73	56	97	87	71
60 to 79 per cent	30	20	24	0	12	19
Under 60 per cent	13	6	21	3	0	10

In mixed goal fields, however, stories have to 'fight their way in' on the basis of news value 'strength' and in competition with other stories on the day. What is true of mixed goal fields in relation to the space available for 'home' news is equally true of Foreign correspon-dents' stories in relation to the space available for foreign news. These two are the types of specialist claiming to get the lowest pro-portions of their material accepted.

Since sound, film and videotape recordings are all more or less awkward and/or expensive to cut, broadcast specialists usually only do items when a slot is already available. A BBC man may do several versions of the same story – perhaps a one-minute TV piece, and a two-minute British radio piece, plus a different two-minute radio piece for one of the BBC Overseas Services. But, even if a specialist gets 80 or 90 per cent of his material accepted, he is still far from fully autonomous.

Journalism may be extreme in the frequency and detail with which subtle controls can be exercised. A specialist may write two or three stories a day; one story may run intact through all editions, another story in the first two editions only, while perhaps a third story will be used but heavily sub-edited with a new 'intro' and somewhat different emphasis. With very many such light touches on the reins and tappings with the stick a new specialist may feel himself being ridden relentlessly by organizational policy. But an 'experienced' specialist may be aware of little such control. After some years in the specialist field, he may choose his own stories, suffer almost no sub-editing, and know by 'instinct' the number of words required. What is the difference between having internalized the organization's news values on the one hand, as against having shaped the news organization's values to the specialist's own approach? This is a difficult question to answer, especially in an occupation where the internalization of the organization's news values is regarded as not only legitimate but commendable.

d. Attitudes towards autonomy

When confronted with the question: 'Do you have much freedom NOT to report stories if for any reason you wanted this?' only 8 per cent of all specialists said they lacked this freedom. When asked, 'Are there many stories you feel you would like to write but cannot because of your editorial organization's attitude?' only 14 per cent said they were thus restricted.

A rather different response was received to a question which asked: 'Do you consider the coverage given to your field by your editorial organization in terms of space and importance is satisfactory?' Only a third said the space and importance accorded them is 'very satisfactory' (Table 4.5). However, the low proportion saying

TABLE 4.5

SATISFACTION WITH COVERAGE NEWS ORGANIZATION GIVES
TO SPECIALISTS' OWN FIELD

	Foreign	Political	Mixed	Audience	Advertising	All (N = 201)
	%	%	%	%	%	%
Very satisfactory	38	54	23	29	22	34
Satisfactory	49	43	67	61	70	57
Unsatisfactory	13	3	10	11	9	9

'unsatisfactory' is consistent with the general lack of strong resentment against news organizations. (The political Lobby correspondents stand out as most satisfied with space and importance – consistent with the restriction of Lobby correspondents' numbers.) Specialists, it seems, see their autonomy threatened not by being forced to cover, or prevented from covering, particular stories; rather they see the overall approach of their news organizations as threatening specialist autonomy. This is especially the case on the more popular media – where processing is more restrictive and the overall news organization goal runs more strongly counter to the predominantly non-revenue orientation of journalists. Most specialists are satisfied with the seriousness of their news organizations (Table 4.6). But those on popular newspapers stand out from all other specialists – with 35 per cent thinking their popular newspaper is 'not serious

TABLE 4.6

SERIOUSNESS OF CONTENT: SPECIALISTS' VIEW
OF OWN NEWS ORGANIZATION'S OUTPUT

'I think our overall output is':	Quality newspapers	Popular newspapers	Agency & broadcast	All selected specialists
	%	%	%	%
Too serious	9	4	12	7
About right	83	61	76	71
Not serious enough	9	35	12	22
N	69	98	34	201

enough'. Popular newspaper specialists have had less education (Table 4.7), which is relevant to their opinions about seriousness. But educational level may also be directly related to autonomy – since it influences opportunities for employment elsewhere.

TABLE 4.7

AGE OF FINISHING FULL-TIME EDUCATION AND TYPE
OF NEWS ORGANIZATION

Specialists' age on finishing full-time education	Quality newspapers	Popular newspapers	Agency & broadcast	All selected specialists
	%	%	%	%
14–16	24	50	28	38
17–19	23	33	34	30
20+	53	17	37	33
N	66	98	32	196

e. Specialist defences: newsgathering

In the choice of stories to cover, the specialist is in a radically different position from the general reporter. The reporter must go to the
News editor (or other news executive) each day for his assignment.
A specialist, however, has already been assigned to a specialist area –
and within this area he is acknowledged to have more expertise than
does the news executive. All specialists were asked about the choice
of stories and the median reply was as follows:

75 per cent of stories 'are my idea (or my number one's)'

15 per cent of stories 'are thought of by both desk and specialist'

10 per cent of stories 'are the idea of executive (or desk)'.

The highest level of autonomy in choice of stories is claimed by the
advertising goal specialists (Table 4.8); in these fields more control
is exercised by advertisers and news sources and hence less by news

TABLE 4.8

PROPORTION OF STORIES WHICH ARE SPECIALISTS'
OWN IDEA

*(or of his number one, in the case of a number
two, three or four specialist)*

Percentage of stories specialists' own idea	Foreign	Political	Mixed	Audience	Advertising	All (N = 191)
	%	%	%	%	%	%
80 to 100 per cent	41	51	40	36	60	45
60 to 79 per cent	22	27	19	31	36	26
Under 60 per cent	37	22	40	33	4	30

executives. The next highest claim to autonomy in choice of stories
is made by the political Lobby correspondents; control over Lobby
correspondents is exercised partly at a higher level within the news
organization (in conversation with the Editor) and on some types of
stories – for instance stories about the Prime Minister's plans –

control may be exercised by a monopoly news source. But the special newsgathering circumstances of the Lobby enable Lobby men to acquire an unusually high level of autonomy in the choice of many types of story within national politics.

Here the fields are arranged in order of claimed autonomy (defined in terms of number of specialists claiming over 80 per cent story choice against the number claiming under 60 per cent).

Highest claimed autonomy in story choice: Fashion
Motoring
Aviation
Political Lobby
Bonn/Rome
Labour
Washington
Football
Crime
New York
Lowest claimed autonomy in story choice: Education

The two advertising goal fields claim the most autonomy in story choice. And the Political Lobby comes in fourth place. Near the bottom in claimed autonomy come the two audience goal fields – Football and Crime. In these fields, where news organizations emphasize audience interest, specialists are vulnerable to accusations of being 'too close to the story' or too sympathetic to news sources – whereas news executives can claim to judge the likely appeal to the general audience member, and hence the right to decide which stories shall be covered.

New York correspondents make low claims for autonomy. New York (in comparison with Washington) is emphasized more by *popular* newspapers; much New York coverage is about the entertainment business – and news executives in London will claim to know what entertainment stories will appeal to British audiences. One might expect Bonn and Rome correspondents to claim lower autonomy than those in Washington – especially since Rome coverage also focuses heavily on entertainment. But the lower autonomy claimed by Washington specialists probably follows from three factors: firstly, time and distance place Bonn and Rome men in closer touch with London – for instance they listen to more BBC radio news; correspondents in the United States, because of time difference, have deadlines very early in their day and this may result in more stories done 'to order'. Secondly, many news developments in the United States are more easily accessible to Foreign editors in London; two of the four international news agencies are American (whereas none are German or Italian) and these provide a very full and fast news service on ticker tapes in Fleet Street; the speedy availability of American news magazines and other American publications in London and in England may be another influence. A third relevant factor is that more foreign news executives have themselves previously been stationed as Foreign correspondents in the United States than in Bonn or Rome.

The mixed goal fields again reveal a scattered pattern. Aviation correspondents make high claims for autonomy in story choice – consistent with the higher importance of an advertising goal element in Aviation journalism. Labour comes in the middle of the order. But Education correspondents made the lowest claim for story choice autonomy. This is in line with the tendency to regard the field as a 'feature' rather than a 'hard news' one; moreover emphasis on parents' interest in Education news defines the field in such a general way as to qualify news executives to make story choices.

According to all selected specialists it is more common for the specialist and the executive (or desk) both to choose the story together than for the executives alone to choose. Another way of seeing such joint choices is that neither desk nor specialist makes the choice.

> 'This is unanswerable. News stories are largely dictated by events outside the mind of me and the desk.' (Foreign correspondent)

Press releases or invitations are usually sent to both desk and specialist. Both desk and specialist, as well as the news source organization and the competing specialists, often all know that a particular event is certain to be widely reported. The specialist will tell the newsdesk that he will be covering the story. Should the specialist decline to cover such a story, the news organization may still use a news agency version. Sometimes a specialist may himself ask the newsdesk to assign a reporter.

Although it would be misleading to see story choice as a running battle between executive control and specialist autonomy, there is conflict in many specific cases. Specialist autonomy in story choice, while not unlimited, is still substantial. But the choice of some stories is virtually dictated by the processors; in the case of a story which he has failed to cover, but which competing specialists have in their first editions, the processors will ask him (usually by telephone) to dictate a story on the same subject. In other cases he has much more autonomy – when the deadline is still hours away, when the story is not a set-piece event but depends upon personal contact, and when there is uncertainty as to the story's likely authenticity, likely 'weight' or probable development.

f. Specialist defences: extra-organizational activity.

Clearly, the news organization does *positively* impinge on specialists' autonomy away from work. Occupational values require that a journalist must be willing to cover 'news' at the cost of leisure. Specialists expect to be telephoned at home, and expect to schedule their 'days off' to fit in with news developments.

On the other hand the news organization makes little attempt to control autonomy external to organizational roles. News organizations (at least British national ones) do little to discourage any political, voluntary, or other leisure activities in which a journalist may choose to participate; the news organization lacks sanctions and the specialist journalist usually lacks both the time and the inclination for vigorous external activity. The case most relevant to specialist autonomy is freelance journalism. Whether such freelance journalism is internal or external to a specialist's organizational role is unclear – in view of the '24 hours a day if necessary' definition. It is also unclear whether freelance journalism is being carried on *within* the organization. But his freelance journalism usually has some connection with a specialist's news organization role.

Some specialists claim to have no time available for additional freelance writing. Some individuals claim under 40 hours and others say they work over 60 hours per week. Table 4.9 shows broadly that two-thirds earned under £500 per annum from extra work, while a fifth of specialists earned £1,000 or over. Audience goal specialists have the *highest* extra earnings; but Crime and Football are also the *lowest* paid fields in terms of salary (apart from Education). This is again consistent with the audience goal – which implies a low status within the news organizations but also reflects strong demand from the public; the demand manifests itself in various forms of 'extra' writing, including the writing of books. Football and Crime specialists had published collectively more than one book a head (46 books from 38 correspondents); all the other specialists had published books at less than one-third this rate (61 books from 169 correspondents). Some of the Crime correspondents' books had been about famous crimes; the Football journalists tended to ghost 'as told to' books by famous players.

Freelance work enables low status specialists somewhat to improve upon their lowly position. In general, freelance earnings help a journalist to become less dependent upon his news organization. Instead he may become more dependent upon a news source; a number of specialists listed earnings from freelance work of a public relations nature. More commonly freelance work includes employment by another news organization. It increases the specialist's over-all autonomy.

Most news executives discourage public relations work – partly because it may compromise the news organization's reputation for independence. Some newspapers have a blanket prohibition against outside work on the grounds that it detracts from the journalist's prime loyalty; but this prohibition tends to be withdrawn if the out-

TABLE 4.9

ANNUAL SALARY, EXPENSES AND EXTRA EARNINGS BY FIELD

Annual salary	Foreign	Political	Mixed	Audience	Advertising	All (N=176)
	%	%	%	%	%	%
Less than £2,500	23	21	44	44	35	32
£2,500–£2,999	12	12	26	25	26	19
£3,000–£3,999	27	38	26	25	30	29
£4,000 and over	37	29	5	6	9	19

Annual expenses	Foreign	Political	Mixed	Audience	Advertising	All (N=156)
	%	%	%	%	%	%
Less than £500	12	36	40	4	35	25
£500–£999	37	42	46	43	50	43
£1,000 and over	50	21	14	54	15	32

Annual extra earnings	Foreign	Political	Mixed	Audience	Advertising	All (N=140)
	%	%	%	%	%	%
Less than £500	64	70	69	58	65	66
£500–£999	10	13	17	21	20	16
£1,000 and over	26	17	14	21	15	19

side work is likely – as in the case of prominent television appearances by columnists – to bring prestige to the newspaper. Moreover the news organization does not necessarily wish to reduce specialist autonomy. Outside work may enable the news organization to pay lower salaries or may improve a specialist's knowledge of his field. Freelance work in general provides a safety valve and morale booster.

Of all fields in the present study the Labour correspondents had the lowest level of outside earnings – because the offers of extra writing come mainly from impoverished trade union publications. This lack of extra earnings is one factor in the high rate of turnover among Labour correspondents.

The whole question of extra earnings among specialist journalists is a sensitive one – and the tension is duly marked by a stock of anecdotes. One story is as follows: Smith works for the *Daily X* which disapproves of freelancing; Smith's talents are, however, admired elsewhere – in particular by the Editor of the *Weekly Q* for whom Smith writes regular pieces under a pseudonym. Back at the *Daily X*, Smith's news executive boss is a reader of the *Weekly Q* and draws Smith's attention to pieces which appear there regularly. Smith dutifully writes stories 'following up' pieces he has himself written under the pseudonym. This illustrates the central argument that newsgathering offers more potentiality for autonomy than does news-processing. Specialists have to submit to processing, but they *are* newsgatherers. News organization surveillance cannot cover much specialist newsgathering, which involves personal contact, personal experience, personal choice of stories. It provides opportunities for forming loyalties and obtaining extra work outside the news organization. The gathering of news strengthens specialist autonomy, and is emphasized by specialists; emphasis on the gathering of news weakens the control of, and is resisted by, news organization executives and processors.

4. Status and interaction within news organizations

a. *Specialist status and autonomy within news organizations*

Status and autonomy are very closely related within news organizations as elsewhere:

> 'At high levels the very prescriptions regarding expected behaviour leave greater scope for autonomy within the formally structured role than they do at lower levels.'[8]

Within news organizations 'prescriptions regarding expected behaviour' are less clear than in many other organizations – expecially in relation to newsgathering specialists. The personal element is emphasized, and the predominant goal differs from field to field; since there is a continuing process of goal bargaining and a tendency towards coalition goals, the goal itself may be influenced by status. Thus any discussion of autonomy is also about status. With this warning in mind, we can look at six possible indicators of status which are also possible indicators of autonomy:

1. Salary
2. Volume and prominence of coverage
3. By-lines
4. Titles
5. Travel and expenses
6. Timing of deadlines

None of these is a wholly unambiguous indicator of status or autonomy – there can scarcely be such an indicator in the prevailing circumstances of flexibility and uncertainty. There is inevitably an element of status disequilibrium – with particular specialists scoring high on one type of status, but low on another.

Firstly, then, *salary*. Table 4.9* shows salary to differ broadly in line with strength of non-revenue goal. Salaries of £3,000 and over are paid to 64 per cent of Foreign correspondents and to 67 per cent of Lobby men. But this level of salary goes to only 31 and 39 per cent of audience goal and advertising goal specialists. The highest and lowest proportions of salaries of £3,000 are distributed by fields as follows:

Highest:	Washington
	Political Lobby
	New York
	Fashion
	Aviation
	Football
	Bonn and Rome
	Labour
	Education
	Motoring
Lowest:	Crime

Clearly, salary levels not only indicate status, but also reflect special circumstances in particular fields – the youth of Education corres-

---

* Data on salary by age are in Table 3.12 above and data on salaries by seniority within specialist teams are in Table 4.10 below.

pondents, and the strong demand for Fashion journalists outside general national news organizations (e.g. on magazines).

Secondly, *volume and prominence of coverage*. The total number of words or of seconds (in broadcasting) is another indicator of status. But in some cases autonomy would involve writing less, not more; some Football specialists complain that they are expected to write the lead story on the sports page regardless of whether there is anything to justify such prominence – they see this as compulsion to overwrite or to exaggerate the importance of stories. Some Motoring correspondents would prefer to write shorter pieces about new car models, and longer pieces about the politics of transport. Some Lobby correspondents would prefer not to write political features of a certain kind.

Thirdly, the '*by-line*' is usually a less ambiguous indicator of status. Appending the name of their senior Political, Labour or Washington man, is seen by news executives as giving added 'weight' to the story. But for a more junior specialist by-lines are not automatic; by-lines are seen by him as a major aspect of control. One junior specialist recalled a disagreement with a senior news processor which ended with the chilling line from the latter: 'Right, Bloggs, just see how many by-lines you get now.' He got none at all for several months – as far as the readers, or Bloggs' news sources, could tell from reading the paper he might no longer be working for it.

Regular by-lines ensure that a specialist becomes recognized by news sources to some extent as a 'name' separate from the news organization. When a correspondent receives regular by-lines he is usually permitted to be somewhat more discursive. Presented and billed by the news organization as its resident 'name' expert, it seems logical that the expert should be allowed to offer some expert comments beyond the bare bones of the immediate news 'event'.

Fourthly, *titles*. Here there is a long-run process of inflation, with the number of titles containing the word 'Editor' increasing steadily. 'Our Labour Correspondent' becomes 'Our Labour Editor' and may eventually become 'Associate Editor (Labour)'. As elsewhere such inflation of titles is not purely a matter of fantasy and ego gratification or client (or news source) gratification. Title inflation is related to the structure of the organization – and reflects the increasing trend to a broad lateral span with shallow and imprecise vertical hierarchy – a trend in which the increasing numbers of specialists play an important part. In London the *Sunday Times*, with its several sections and inevitably broad lateral span, was the leader in title inflation.*

---

* The *Sunday Times* was listed in the standard directory with 22 'Editors' in 1964 and 24 in 1967. World's Press News *Directory of Newspaper and Magazine Personnel and Data*, 1964 and 1967.

Although such title inflation may reduce the market value of a title, it does not make all titles worthless. In a field where everyone else is being made an 'Editor' the man who is still only a 'Correspondent' may lose status and autonomy.

Fifthly, *travel* is another issue in which status and autonomy are involved. An Aviation correspondent may want to go to Toulouse, or a Football man may want to accompany a British team to Brazil, or a Washington correspondent may want to go with the President to Hawaii, or a Political correspondent may want to go with the Prime Minister to Washington. Audience goal specialists report having the highest expenses (Table 4.9); London-based Football correspondents travel frequently both outside London and abroad. However, the expenses figures of Football and Crime are both inflated by payments to news sources for information. Expenses are another ambiguous indicator of status – since within journalism payments to news sources are widely disapproved. But some news executives, while officially 'disapproving' of such practices, nevertheless, approve expense claims which include such payments. Such official turning of blind eyes concedes the Football and Crime specialists an element of autonomy.

Sixthly, another status indicator is the *timing of deadlines*. News processors are so burdened with work near this time that they can only handle what they regard as the most important material. Some specialists are asked to 'get your copy in early'; unless they do so their material is likely to be rejected by the processors. Consequently, working close to deadlines becomes a status indicator. Specialists were asked the time of their peak activity of the day. The centre point of this time band was then taken and the median centre points of peak activity were:

Earliest:	Fashion	13.30
	Motoring	17.00
	Education	17.00
	Football	17.30
	Bonn & Rome	17.30 (London time)
	Aviation	17.45
	New York	17.45 (London time)
	Crime	18.00
	Labour	18.00
	Political Lobby	18.15
Latest:	Washington	18.15 (London time)

Among these figures (which exclude Sunday and evening newspapers) there is one exceptional field, Fashion, which often appears on feature pages; these pages typically have earlier deadlines. But these times are useful general indicators of status. The other advertising goal field, Motoring, is also early – as is Education. Bonn and Rome coverage has an early time which partly indicates its lower status than the US postings. Of the two US centres, the Washington correspondents are later. The lateness of political Lobby and Labour coverage is not surprising. Crime looks out of place, however, for its generally low status – but this reflects partly the late working hours of criminals and the prominence given to some crime news for audience goal reasons in late edition changes.

The difference between 5 pm and 6.15 pm may appear small. But with final first edition deadlines around 9 pm, 75 minutes is a major distinction on this dimension of status. For a political Lobby correspondent to be only half-way through his peak work effort with the deadline under three hours away indicates little time or opportunity for processors to operate any detailed control. Normally all of the low status news (such as Motoring or Education) will be already processed and assigned positions in the content before the major political stories have reached the chief processors.

b. Status and autonomy within and between specialist teams

The majority of the specialists belonged to teams of two or more specialists working for a news organization in the same field. The number one man is normally unambiguously regarded both inside and outside the news organization as the boss. Members of a typical three-man team were paid, in 1968, as follows:

Number one	£3,700
Number two	£3,000
Number three	£2,400

The overall salary picture is shown in Table 4.10. Salaries of £3,000 and over were paid to 79 per cent of number ones, 30 per cent of numbers two and three, and 44 per cent of one-man teams.

A good deal of overlap is noticeable – and although most of this reflects different pay levels between different specialist fields (see Table 4.9) there were several examples of number twos being paid more than their number ones. Some correspondents described themselves as 'a very senior number two', and some number ones were openly anxious about the prominence of their subordinates. In other cases the number one man's control of his number two was limited by the latter having carved out for himself an important sub-specialism within the overall specialist field. Some new executives admit encouraging such situations in order to 'keep the number one man on his toes' – which could be interpreted as a deliberate attempt to keep him on his knees and to reduce the autonomy of both number one and two.

But such examples of disequilibrium are unusual. A number one specialist usually stands in an unambiguously superior position towards his number two. A crucial aspect of the number one man's

TABLE 4.10

SALARIES BY SENIORITY WITHIN SPECIALIST TEAMS

Annual salary	Number one specialist	Numbers two, three, four	One-man team	All specialists
	%	%	%	%
Less than £2,500	13	48	32	32
£2,500–£2,999	9	23	23	19
£3,000–£3,999	33	25	30	29
£4,000 and over	46	5	14	19
N	46	61	69	176

superior position lies in his choice of stories – a superiority which he can enforce day by day. By selecting for himself the number one story each day, the number one man will normally establish a superior range of personal contacts with news sources – thus reinforcing his relative status and autonomy. On very important stories the whole team may all cover the one story, but here again, the number one man is usually able to deploy his own team – if necessary using his number two to collect material for incorporation in the number one man's story.

To present a picture of specialist teams only in terms of internal conflict would be misleading. The reverse appears to be much more usual. Number one and number two have usually chosen to work together. They have much to gain from working in harmony as a team; if all three Lobby correspondents or all three Labour correspondents are united on a particular point they will be difficult to overrule. Any attempt to replace all three might be a severe blow to the news organization within a major news source area. Moreover, the collective personal contacts of a team – both within news sources and with competitor-colleagues – provides them with a formidable array of experience, weapons, and allies with which to resist news organization pressure.

Pressure from within the news organization comes not only from news executives, but also from specialist teams covering neighbouring news source areas. During the middle and late 1960's with the great increase in the British government's activities in the area of economic planning, there was competition between Lobby, Labour and Financial journalists as to which should get the lion's share of the new territory. News executives would often prefer the two contending specialists to work on a jointly written story – for instance the Lobby and Aviation man on a political aviation story, or the Labour and Aviation man on a story about aviation trade unions. However, specialists tend to see such arrangements as a bid by news executives to extend their control – since in such cases the executive is likely to define the shape of co-operation. There are also status problems; the Aviation man might well resent being asked to work with the number two Lobby man and even more with the number two Labour man.

There is usually only one Aviation correspondent per news organization. The status in any type of organization of those middle level personnel who lack subordinates is predictably unclear. Table 4.10 shows the salary pattern of one-man teams matching very closely with the salaries of all the selected specialists. Some one-man teams are, in effect, number one men without subordinates, while other one-man teams are really number three specialists without superiors. The problem is more complex, however, because the one-man teams are concentrated in certain fields – Bonn and Rome, Education, Aviation and Motoring. In these fields, specialists earning under £2,000 work in competition with opposite numbers – also one-man teams – who earn £4,000 or more. New specialists in such fields are likely to say they are 'less senior' than their immediate predecessors – recognition that such small fields lack internal career ladders, while status is tied closely to the individual.

c. Interaction within news organization

Table 4.11 shows the average (mean) frequency with which specialists in different fields said they interacted with executives and desks. This Table again reflects differences in status as well as the ambiguity and limitations of one more possible indicator of status; for example since both Editor and backbench are crucially important in terms of status, autonomy and control, specialists who interact most frequently with them appear to have the highest status and perhaps the most autonomy. Political Lobby correspondents have the highest average frequency of interaction with both Editor (1·5) and with backbench (1·4). In both cases mixed goal, audience, and advertising goal specialists have fairly similar scores. But in both cases the Foreign correspondents have a low frequency of contact – including very low contact (0·3) with the backbench. However, Foreign correspondents have very frequent (2·3, or just over 'several times a week') contact with the foreign desk – which is presided over by the Foreign editor.

TABLE 4.11

SPECIALISTS' FREQUENCY OF COMMUNICATION
WITHIN NEWS ORGANIZATION

Communication with	Communication by these specialists					
	Foreign	Political	Mixed	Audience	Advertising	All
Editor	0·7	1·5	0·9	0·6	0·7	0·87
Foreign desk	2·3	0·8	0·7	0·2	0·7	1·10
News desk	1·0	2·8	2·6	1·6	1·8	1·94
City (finance) desk	0·4	0·6	0·7	0·2	0·6	0·51
Features desk	0·8	0·9	0·9	0·5	1·6	0·90
Picture desk	0·5	0·4	1·0	1·2	1·7	0·88
Sub-editors	0·4	1·6	1·8	2·1	1·7	1·44
Backbench	0·3	1·4	0·9	0·8	1·0	0·85
N*	49	38	47	35	26	195

* Many specialists left one or two boxes blank. On internal evidence the majority of these appear intended to mean 'irregularly or never' and were counted as such. This is based on the following scoring: Daily=3; several times a week=2; between weekly and monthly=1; irregularly or never=0.

The special factor of expensive international telephone, or other, communication destroys the general validity of this particular indicator of status.

Nevertheless, for the London-based fields frequency of contact with the Editor remains a useful indicator of status. Here it is by individual fields:

Political Lobby	1·5
Aviation	1·2
Labour	0·9
Education	0·8
Crime	0·8
Motoring	0·7
Fashion	0·6
Football	0·5

Even here other factors are present. Aviation may score high because this field is covered mainly by one correspondent working alone; in Labour, however, there are teams of two or three correspondents for the main daily news organization and with the number one Labour man handling most contact with the Editor, the average frequency for all Labour specialists is reduced. In Football another special circumstance arises – Football correspondents communicate mainly with the *sports* desk which was not included in the question.

Table 4.11 reflects overall status imperfectly, precisely because it is also measuring internally specialized patterns of communication and control. A major distinction is between some specialists whose contact focuses primarily on a single desk or executive and other specialists who have several masters. The Foreign correspondents focus heavily on the foreign desk (2·3) and less on the news-desk (1·0) – the latter mainly in those news organizations which have no foreign desk. But the political Lobby correspondents have *four* foci of interaction – the news-desk (2·8), sub-editors (1·6), the Editor (1·5) and the backbench (1·4). The advertising goal specialists have no less than *five* points of at least 'between weekly and monthly' contact – the news-desk (1·8), picture-desk (1·7), sub-editors (1·7), the features desk (1·6) and also the backbench (1·0).

It is hardly surprising that the advertising goal specialists have a high frequency of interaction with the picture-desk – pictures are to be expected in any field which has a revenue goal. Frequency of interaction with picture-desk for specific fields was as follows:

Crime	2·0 (several times a week)
Fashion	1·6
Motoring	1·6
Aviation	1·5
Education	1·3
New York	1·0 (between weekly and monthly)
Football	0·7
Labour	0·6
Political Lobby	0·4
Bonn & Rome	0·4
Washington	0 (irregularly or never)

Here the revenue goal fields come out as having strong picture interest; Aviation again is closest, of the mixed fields, to those with an advertising goal. Washington is the least picture involved; New York is again the most audience orientated of the foreign postings.

Senior specialists can usually regard themselves as senior to most assistant desk personnel, and senior to at least some of the executives in charge of desks. The implications of all the possible sorts of constellations of interaction for autonomy and control depend on particular stories, particular personalities, and current status. On some stories a specialist may have great autonomy, but on others he will be firmly under the control of an executive who has a salient concern with that type of story. Certain personalities will make more of a specific balance of autonomy and control. A specialist's autonomy will depend on his current status – for instance if he has had a recent run of prominent stories, this may increase his short run autonomy. On any particular day, for instance when the Editor is off duty, the constellation may differ.

In some cases a specialist's interaction is focused on one senior executive – a senior Lobby man may talk to the Editor every day or a senior Foreign correspondent may talk to the Foreign editor every day. This relationship may imply autonomy in relation to most other possible sources of control – but nevertheless such daily contact also involves close surveillance by the one senior executive. The contrasting case is the advertising goal specialist who may appear to have many masters exerting control within the news organization. But a resourceful specialist may so manage these contacts – and play them off against external controls – as to expand his autonomy.

5

Specialist correspondent
as newsgatherer

Since the journalists in this study are defined as being 'specialist news-gatherers' it may seem confusing to describe their 'newsgathering role' as only one of three major work roles. Everett C. Hughes' term 'core activity' may be useful here. The core activity of specialist newsgathering journalists is gathering news – but it is not their only activity.

The term '*newsgathering*' specialist was used partly to distinguish these specialists from the critic, or gallery, or 'armchair' type of specialist in journalism. Apart from writing stories (the core activity in journalism at large), *gathering* stories – at press conferences, in personal interviews, or over the telephone – is their dominant activity (Table 5.1).

The position of the newsgatherers in relation to their news sources may differ according to the news organization goal which prevails in different fields of news; this possibility has not been considered in previous studies. The primary focus of Dan Nimmo's *Newsgathering in Washington* (1964) was upon newsgatherer/source interaction. Nimmo developed the following typology:

Newsgatherer Patterns	Source Patterns
Recorder	Informer
Expositor	Educator
Prescriber	Promoter

Here both journalists and sources are classified in terms of their propensity to adopt a 'neutral facts' or a 'biased opinion' stance. Nimmo's newsgathering *recorder* tends to be a 'neutral' news agency reporter; his *expositor* tends to be a specialist correspondent; his *prescriber* tends to be a columnist. Thus his classification implies different news organizational goals. But the distinction is blurred because most Washington news is of a 'mixed goal' kind.

A Foreign correspondent may be relatively immune from his news source's displeasure – a Foreign correspondent can comment on the local media to his distant and relatively uninvolved audience. In contrast, an audience goal specialist is dependent on his news sources and addresses a directly involved audience; the position of an advertising goal specialist also appears different because the news organization looks vulnerable to the relevant sanctions.

To rephrase this argument in terms of autonomy and control, the hypothesis reads as follows: *The greater the element of non-revenue goal, the more autonomy will the newsgatherer have in relation to his news sources; and the greater the element of revenue goal, the more will the newsgatherer be under the control of his news sources.*

1. NEWSGATHERING TECHNOLOGY

a. Individual news sources and the spoken word

In their work journalists encounter many 'exceptional cases' – to use Charles Perrow's term; prevailing definitions of news ensure that the 'search process' cannot be logical, systematic or analytical. Instead of rational procedures, emphasis is placed on 'experience and intuition'.

Occupational values stress that 'people make news'. 67 per cent (N = 203) thought that as news sources 'individuals are more important than organizations', while only 6 per cent thought organizations more important; 28 per cent thought they were equally important. The highest proportions stressing individuals were in the Political Lobby (81 per cent); lowest were Foreign correspondents (52 per cent). When specialists are asked about time spent on particular activities, those activities which involve gathering news from people are predominant. In Table 5.1 a non-gathering activity, 'writing and sending stories', came out top on the proportions of specialists spending both at least ten and five hours. But the next biggest proportions were as follows:

2. Telephoning sources – 39 (72)%
3. Dealing with documents – 33 (75)%
4. Face-to-face interviews with sources – 25 (58)%
5. Talking to other journalists – 15 (38)%

Dealing with documents is fairly impersonal, but all the other three activities involve talking to people. Political journalists emphasize impersonal documents and talking to both news sources and other journalists, but they spend little time telephoning sources; the audience goal Crime and Football specialists strongly emphasize telephoning sources and give weak emphasis to documents.

But the generally large amounts of time spent talking to individual sources – over the telephone or face to face – and to journalists, is the main finding in Table 5.1. This is as true of television as of press journalists, although the TV journalist has to interview on to film or tape, as well as into a notebook. The broadcast specialists collectively placed 'Writing and sending stories' as the most time-consuming single activity; dealing with documents was second, face-to-face interviews fourth, telephoning sources fifth, and communal meetings

TABLE 5.1

TIME SPENT ON NEWSGATHERING ACTIVITIES

(*Percentage of specialists spending 10 hours or more in an average week on specific activity, with percentage spending 5 hours or more a week in brackets.*)

	Foreign	Political	Mixed	Audience	Advertising	All
(a) Face-to-face interviews with sources	6 (39)	59 (87)	20 (59)	39 (64)	13 (48)	25 (58)
(b) Telephoning sources	32 (68)	19 (41)	52 (86)	61 (91)	30 (70)	39 (72)
(c) Communal meetings with sources (e.g. press conferences)	4 (28)	9 (44)	7 (43)	3 (12)	4 (48)	5 (34)
(d) Talking to other journalists	7 (28)	50 (81)	9 (34)	6 (30)	4 (22)	15 (38)
(e) Dealing with documents	39 (76)	34 (94)	43 (82)	12 (42)	26 (78)	33 (75)
(f) Dealing with letters	4 (13)	0 (3)	5 (11)	0 (0)	4 (35)	3 (11)
(g) Writing and sending stories	91 (98)	75 (97)	52 (86)	58 (85)	61 (87)	69 (91)
(h) Other	13 (20)	9 (9)	5 (14)	12 (21)	4 (13)	9 (16)
N	54	32	44	33	23	186

with sources sixth. The only major difference was that 'other' came third – mainly activities peculiar to broadcasting. Whether the TV specialist appears on the screen 'talking straight to camera' or whether he is interviewing a news source on the screen, the techniques of TV newsgathering differ from the press primarily by putting an even greater emphasis on individual personalities in the news source area.

The interview became a central technique in American journalism during and after the Civil War. It arrived somewhat later in London. Here is an account by an early Lobby correspondent of interviewing politicians at Westminster in the 1890's:

'Forty years ago when it was less common, a good and timely interview was a more notable achievement. Politicians, especially, were less approachable than they are now, and would-be interviewers had to put up with many a rebuff. . . . My plan was to engage the interviewee in conversation and to draw the necessary information out of him in a narrative form without raising his suspicions. Then, at the finish, I would ask his permission to publish the information. Sometimes I would be told that the identity of my informant should not be divulged; in others that I might attribute the statement to him discreetly.'[1]

The news interview remains a very personal encounter, including elements of trust, suspicion and ambiguity. It is still common practice for a journalist to conduct his 'interview' as a conversation. One specialist ticked '10 hours a week or more' for face-to-face interviews with sources, but added: 'Not quite the word. Drinking in pubs is more accurate.' However, notebooks are now more acceptable to news sources. 64 per cent of the specialists answered 'Yes' to using shorthand:

Foreign Correspondents	45% use shorthand
Political Lobby	74%
Mixed fields	79%
Audience fields	68%
Advertising fields	59%
All selected specialists (N = 196)	64%

All Crime correspondents used shorthand; the Lobby men were also very shorthand conscious. The Foreign correspondents included the lowest proportion of shorthand users:

'I believe shorthand is vital, but many people seem to get by very well without it – or by pestering people who do write it for vital quotes after press briefings.'

'I could do 120 w.p.m. but found it of no particular use. A journalist seldom wants more than a few lines of direct quote.'

'No. And it's a disadvantage – but I do manage all right. It just means you don't "direct quote" so often.'

'Yes. I consider ability to take a verbatim note invaluable and after these years in the US, I am still shocked at the dependence of American reporters upon transcripts and handouts.'

Shorthand places emphasis on the spoken word. This 'neutral' technique consequently carries a substantial freight of occupational ideology. Specialists are often to be seen sitting at their desks engaged in rambling telephone conversations and taking a shorthand note. Asked how many phone calls they made and received per day, some specialists gave answers such as:

'15–20 made; 10 received. This is wild guessing. Sometimes there are so many calls that the left ear becomes positively painful. On other days the phone hardly rings.'

Specialists have between 15 and 45 telephone conversations a day and they make more than they receive (Table 5.2).

TABLE 5.2

NUMBER OF NEWS SOURCE TELEPHONE CALLS PER DAY

(*Q.* '*About how many calls do you* make *to news sources per day?*')

	Calls made (mean)	Calls received (mean)	Total calls per day
Washington	10	5	15
New York	17	12	29
Bonn and Rome	17	6	23
Political Lobby	12	6	18
Aviation	20	14	34
Education	12	6	18
Labour	18	8	26
Crime	33	12	45
Football	18	5	23
Fashion	15	27	42
Motoring	14	9	23
			(N = 183)

Fashion, Crime and Aviation correspondents are especially heavy users of the telephone. Lobby correspondents, who work physically close to their sources at Westminster, use the telephone less. Fashion (where public relations is heavily developed) is the only field where more calls are received than made. In Football, where PR is weakly developed, there is an especially low ratio of calls received to calls made.

Specialists spend a large proportion of work time in talking to people – in single face-to-face meetings, in communal meetings, and on the telephone. The telephone and the 'neutral' technique of shorthand both reinforce the orientation of specialists towards *individual* news sources.

b. Search: travel to the scene

Another type of newsgathering activity is direct observation of events. Although these specialists are not of the 'gallery' type, Football specialists do spend a few hours a week watching Football

TABLE 5.3

TRAVEL: OUTSIDE LONDON AND ABROAD

	Mean number of days in year 1967–68		
	Within Britain but outside London	Abroad	Total combined
Political Lobby	17	8	25
Aviation	29	34	63
Education	57	10	67
Labour	34	10	44
Crime	33	9	42
Football	75	26	101
Fashion	15	36	51
Motoring	52	42	94

matches, Lobby correspondents usually observe direct at least the Prime Minister's Questions at Westminster, and Foreign correspondents may, for instance, watch a riot or a political demonstration. But the activity which most enables the specialist to 'see for himself' is travel. Away from central London, he can visit factories, schools, or 'the scene of the crime'; overseas travel allows a specialist to see 'with his own eyes' in other countries. The average number of days specialists said they spent out of London varied from 25 days in the Lobby correspondent's year to 101 days of the Football specialist's year (Table 5.3).

Outside London the technology of newsgathering remains the same – notebook and telephone; nights spent on such trips are usually in good hotels, because of the telephone facilities and the ready access to individual news sources, impromptu press briefings, other journalists. The main purpose of travel often is to get personal access to a 'name'. But being out of the capital city may make the specialist more dependent on one particular news source. Visits out of London, and even more visits abroad, can normally only be 'justified' if some substantial coverage results. One of the most acceptable explanations (to news executives) for such a visit is that a big 'name' is involved. This may be a London name who is himself travelling – such as a Minister visiting a factory in the British provinces or abroad.

On some occasions the news source also pays some or all of the travel expenses; this partly explains why the two advertising goal fields (Fashion or Motoring) do the most foreign travel. But the advertising revenue also makes news organizations willing to finance travel. *Motoring* specialists spent more days abroad than did those in any other field – 42 days in the year. This foreign travel took three main forms: visits to Grand Prix races and car rallies in Europe, car-testing trips abroad, and trips to foreign motor shows. The Motoring men also spent 52 days a year in the British provinces – visiting factories and races or in testing cars. The *Fashion* correspondents spend the second highest number of days abroad – mainly in Paris and other European fashion centres.

Football correspondents are the biggest travellers in the British provinces. Their 75 days a year includes visits to matches, but also visits to teams for news stories of the injury/transfer type. The Football correspondents averaged 26 days accompanying British teams abroad. The travel in this audience goal field is paid for by the news organization. Some Football journalists have been to thirty or more foreign countries and perhaps on twenty separate occasions to Madrid or Milan.

Crime in contrast involves little foreign travel and Crime men also travel out of London much less than Football specialists. The Crime correspondents concentrate on London crime and police sources, leaving all but exceptional crimes outside London to local agencies and stringers, who know their local police better.

Aviation differs from the other mixed fields, in having a high foreign travel element – 34 days. These trips are partly paid for by the news organization but an American aircraft company may invite British journalists on a free trip to the US at the time of an interesting space flight – which will enable Aviation specialists to justify the trip to news executives. This substantial element of free plane flights underlines the advertising goal element.

Education specialists, however, with an average of only 10 days abroad, regard a short trip to Sweden or France as an unusual opportunity. But they travel much more within Britain; these correspondents frequently visit comprehensive schools in Yorkshire, teachers' conferences at the seaside, or technological universities in the Midlands.

Labour correspondents resemble the Education men in the lack of foreign travel. But the Labour specialists seldom go to look at the factory where a strike is taking place; they cover the national negotiations which – with British national bargaining – take place in London. Trips to the provinces by Labour correspondents are primarily to annual conferences of major trade unions.

Political Lobby correspondents are an extreme case of lack of travel. The Lobby correspondents' visits to the provinces consist mainly of attending the annual autumn conferences of the national political parties. Nor do Lobby correspondents have any regular pattern of foreign travel. But some of the senior Lobby men accompany the Prime Minister on his foreign visits; on these trips a major purpose of the Lobby men is to maintain or establish personal contact with the Prime Minister and his senior advisers.

Foreign correspondents do the most travelling abroad – outside the country in which they are based. Correspondents based in Washington and New York had been on trips to Canada, the West Indies, and Latin America. Those based in Bonn had often been on trips to Eastern Europe and in 1968 a number had been for extended periods in Czechoslovakia both before and after the Russian invasion; correspondents based on Rome had covered other Mediterranean countries such as Greece. Several specialists based in America had spent 50 to 100 days in the US hinterland – by the end of May 1968, even before the completion of the primary stage of the Presidential election. One correspondent had travelled 60,000 miles within the USA during the last year.

That Latin America is visited more by Football specialists, France more by Fashion and Aviation correspondents, and North Africa more by Motoring than by any other kind of specialist could be seen as indicating the commercialism and provincialism of the British national news media – especially since the political men travel so little. But some political Lobby men are ex-Foreign correspondents; moreover foreign politics are covered by roving as well as foreign-based correspondents. There are also solid arguments for covering Latin America from New York rather than from London – or from Buenos Aires.

The least debatable conclusion is that – despite the importance of travel in the image and self-image of journalists – specialists (both domestic and foreign) stay tethered primarily to the capital. These specialist journalists are constrained not by their laziness or by excessive loyalty to the capital, but by definitions of news values which stress élite individuals – more of whom are in the capital. Travel cuts the specialist off from 'hot' news events in London – where unpredictable newsworthy happenings happen more frequently. As a 'search procedure' travel often adds little to the notebook and the telephone.

c. Search: scanning the media output

The output of his own news organization gives the correspondent the latest bulletin on organizational status and rank; but much of the output will also be *news* to him. Most specialists take several newspapers at home and see others at the office. In newspaper offices newspapers litter the desks and often the floors. All specialists tend to read – apart from their own field – the political, foreign and diplomatic news; after this come the mixed fields (Table 5.4). The least reading is done of revenue fields.

Journalists' personal preferences, occupational socialization and specialist concerns are not easily divisible:

'Like most former general reporters I remain interested in newspapers as a whole.'

'Most experienced journalists not only believe it necessary to follow other major events but want to and like it.'

'I read the others more out of personal than professional interest in the subjects.'

The biggest radio following is of the breakfast-time news and news magazine programmes; the next biggest is the 1 pm radio news programme; then the 6 pm news (which some hear from transistors on their desks). The most quoted type of TV programme was of course 'news', followed by the late evening news comment programmes. From weekly TV the most quoted were all 'factual' programmes.

Most specialists listen to about an hour of morning and/or lunchtime radio, read up to half a dozen morning newspapers, plus two evening papers, and then watch TV news in the evening. All specialists also read relevant specialized magazines. Apart from the other meanings that such output has for him, this extensive exposure serves the correspondent as a preliminary search procedure. Aviation correspondents, for instance, say they read most heavily Foreign, Diplomatic, Lobby, Financial, and Labour news. Yesterday's developments in Foreign and Diplomatic news may have implications for the highly international Aviation industry; Lobby news is important, as one specialist said, because 'Politics and Aviation are indivisible'. Finance is potentially important because many Aviation stories are

TABLE 5.4

READING NEWS FROM OTHER SPECIALIST FIELDS

(Q. 'When reading newspapers do you pay much attention to these areas of news other than your own?')

Specialists from these fields	Read these fields the most				Read these fields the least	
	1	2	3	4	8	9
US WASHINGTON	Diplomatic	Lobby	Finance	Labour	Football	Motoring
US NEW YORK	Diplomatic	Lobby	Education	Aviation / Labour	Motoring	Football
BONN/ROME	Diplomatic	Lobby	Finance	Education	Motoring	Football
POLITICAL LOBBY	Diplomatic	Foreign	Labour	Finance	Football	Motoring
LABOUR	Lobby	Foreign	Finance	Diplomatic	Football	Motoring
EDUCATION	Lobby	Foreign	Diplomatic	Labour	Crime	Motoring
AVIATION	Foreign	Diplomatic	Lobby	Finance	Motoring	Crime
CRIME	Lobby	Diplomatic	Foreign	Finance	Aviation	Football
FOOTBALL	Foreign	Lobby	Diplomatic	Crime	Aviation	Finance
MOTORING	Foreign	Finance	Lobby	Labour / Diplomatic	Education	Football
FASHION	Foreign	Diplomatic	Education	Lobby	Aviation	Football

Notes (1) This is based on the following scoring: 'None' = 0; 'A little' = 1; 'A fair amount' = 2; 'Much' = 3. The order is of the mean score for all the specialists in each field. (2) Specialists were not asked about their reading of Fashion news.

concerned with the financing of projects. This scanning of the output of other journalists reflects the lack of any more systematic search procedures.

d. Weak search technology: personality and 'experience'

Despite much talk about the future use of computerized information retrieval systems, Fleet Street specialists had very little search apparatus available. Research assistance was almost non-existent, secretarial assistance minimal, even newspaper cuttings rather unsystematically deployed, and the personal 'contact book' of news source telephone numbers was still a major search tool.

The great majority of specialists worked either from an open plan office (like general reporters) or from a closed but shared office – perhaps six specialists sharing one secretary. Audience specialists were the most likely to work from an open office, and Foreign correspondents the most likely to have an unshared private office. Among the London-based specialists the advertising goal specialists (Fashion and Motoring) have the most secretarial support – 32 hours each on average. The Lobby men have the least secretarial support; only a few news organizations have at Westminster even one secretary regularly in attendance. The most usual situation is of a specialist with a few of hours secretarial time a week:

'3–5 hours a week. Mostly for answering letters, making hotel bookings etc. – NOT for any activity directly concerned with reporting.'

'We share with about a dozen other specialists. Our one secretary opens mail, takes phone messages and types odd letters.'

A substantial minority of specialists complained that they had to type all their own letters. Some specialists said they spent as much as 5–9 hours a week dealing with letters, although 1–4 hours was more typical. The other major complaint related to 'cuttings'.

A specialist is repeatedly confronted with subjects on which, to say the least, he feels a need to refresh his memory. This he usually does by looking at cuttings of previous stories from several newspapers. Two-thirds of specialists used the office cuttings library 'a fair amount', or 'much'. But most specialists complain about the inefficiency of their office cuttings library; 87 per cent of specialists have their own personal filing system and 68 per cent carry files with them at least sometimes (Table 5.5). Aviation correspondents were representative – keeping up their files took them two hours a week.

The Lobby correspondents spent the least time on cutting and filing, and they were also the least likely to have any personal files; the low level of secretarial service in the Lobby is one obvious explanation, but the very scale of the task of filing possibly relevant political material may seem to make the task hopeless – especially since there are *some* relevant reference books. Lobby men, like other specialists, rely heavily on searching other men's minds – rather than searching through files. The continuous physical presence of other specialists in the Lobby offices at Westminster makes searching the minds of competitor-colleagues especially easy. Public relations officers in Whitehall, or in other large non-government organizations, are often,

TABLE 5.5

CARRYING A PERSONAL FILE OF CUTTINGS

	Foreign	Political	Mixed	Audience	Advertising	All (N = 201)
	%	%	%	%	%	%
Have no personal files	5	38	9	13	4	13
Never carry files	16	9	19	18	41	19
Sometimes or nearly always carry personal files	79	53	72	68	55	68

in effect, used by a journalist as temporary research assistants – for instance to get the details and dates of previous Ministerial statements. A third type of personal and oral search is into the mind of some authority or leading 'name' in the subject area; here the specialist only requires a telephone and a contact book listing home as well as office numbers.

BBC news specialists have slightly more elaborate search apparatus than press journalists, including better office facilities and secretarial help. Unlike a Fleet Street specialist who can phone back regularly to his news desk, a BBC specialist may be called with requests for material by producers of half-a-dozen different news and current affairs programmes. But the BBC arrangements for making search support available to news specialists are closer to Fleet Street than to current affairs programming. In the latter case the role of 'research assistant' is well defined – for instance, in preliminary reading of press material, and for screening of potential interviewees. The vastly greater financial resources available for a single current affairs TV programme as against a single press story, and the more compressed character of TV, are other factors. All current affairs programmes are relatively unspecialized; and despite brave talk about lack of dependence upon specialist sources, current affairs TV is dependent upon the advice of a few outside expert advisers who may be paid a 'consultant' fee. One of the main categories of such 'experts' are none other than the specialist correspondents. Current affairs programmes are also very dependent upon the stories of press specialists – in the original choice of topic as well as in the treatment, including the definition of what the main partisan views are and hence where the non-partisan 'neutral' ground lies.

Both news values and newsgathering techniques stress the primacy of individuals. An effective specialist is largely defined as a person who is on personal terms with important persons in the relevant field. The weakness of technology and the stress upon oral search behaviour derives partly from the definition of news as being exceptional – and the consequent tendency to place a lower value upon widely available printed material ('Bumph', 'Handouts'). This approach depends heavily on last week's stories (in the form of a bundle of press cuttings), and reliance upon the spoken words of 'names' often also involves relying upon people in positions of power.

Such investigation as does take place is frequently into someone's memory. This memory may belong to an 'experienced' competitor-colleague; or the specialist may search his own memory and rely upon his own 'experience'. Thus 'experience' also is defined in a highly personal manner. The individual specialist's experience is most briefly codified in his telephone contact book; some specialists show considerable pride in displaying their encyclopaedic collection of home phone numbers of prominent people they 'know'. This contact book is the personal property of the specialist – unlike the office files of the 'rational' administrator. The specialist not only carries it around on his person, but when he leaves the news organization he can take away with him the contact book and its codified experience.

2. SPECIALISTS AND THE NEWS SOURCE AREA

a. The news source area: structure and publicity stance

In Table 5.6 a summary of characteristics salient in relations with specialist journalists is placed under four main headings:

1. Special historical or other factors
2. Monopoly of the field by a single source organization

3. Monopoly of one important part of the field by a single source
4. The prevalent publicity stance of major sources

Another relevant variable is the general goal of the field as seen by the news organizations; this goal shapes the kind of news the organization wants from the field and shapes the specialist's view of the source – as well, perhaps, as the source's view of the specialist.

In the *Advertising goal fields*, Fashion and Motoring, major news source organizations see news stories as one means to sales success. The strength of commercial organizations which are also major news sources is shown by the control which both fashion organizations and car manufacturers exert in the marketing of new designs; embargoes of length and inflexibility which would not be tolerated in most specialist fields were firmly enforced. Motoring journalists and Fashion journalists were given embargoed details of new cars and new fashions often some weeks in advance and were then forced to maintain silence until the embargo ended.

Fashion journalists are mostly women with magazine, not newspaper, backgrounds – which reduces their career opportunities within their present news organization. Motoring correspondents are unusually involved in situations (international racing, rallies) where there are audience pressures towards patriotism. Fashion journalists say that fashion is basically frivolous and commercial anyway. Motoring correspondents say it might be wrong harshly to criticize new cars; they only have the cars a few days; the manufacturer has invested large sums in the model; criticism might damage an industry which earns foreign currency for Britain.

Major manufacturers and retailers (especially in Fashion) are uninhibitedly promotional in their publicity stance. However, in Fashion small firms (which do little advertising) are often strongly criticized; in Motoring the Ministry of Transport seems to serve as a scapegoat and is seen by specialists as 'bureaucratic' in the popular pejorative sense.

Audience goal: In Crime and Football there is very little in the way of either comfort or public relations activity. Here news organizations are providing coverage for which there is a known vigorous public demand. In both audience goal fields there is one very strong type of source. Scotland Yard has a monopoly of much crime information; Football clubs similarly are hierarchically organized with managers in possession of much of the key information – since they pick teams and negotiate transfers. In the police and in major football clubs regulations forbid talking to journalists; policemen or football players who talk to journalists can be disciplined. In Britain there are severe legal restraints in Crime reporting and control of the

TABLE 5.6

SOURCE STRUCTURE AND PUBLICITY STANCE BY FIELD

	Special historical or other factors	Monopoly of field	Monopoly of part of field	Prevalent source publicity stance
Advertising goal				
Fashion	women journalists	none	fashion houses	promotional
Motoring	foreign competition	none	manufacturers' new models	promotional
Audience goal				
Football	northern origins	none	top managers	negative
Crime	legal restraints	police	Scotland Yard	negative
Mixed goal				
Education	recent origin	none	none	cautious and promotional
Aviation	foreign competition, defence	none	none	cautious and promotional
Labour	strike negotiations	none	none	negative and promotional
Political goal				
Lobby	British constitution fictions	none	prime minister	cautious and promotional
Non-revenue goal				
USA	diplomatic centre, us domestic news	none	none	uninterested and promotional
Bonn	East Germany	none	none	cautious and promotional
Rome	papacy, humour	none	papacy	negative, cautious and promotional

police is (compared with some other countries) concentrated at the centre. Football began in the North of England and has (like the world of criminals and policemen) a strongly working-class flavour. Directors of football clubs have, according to Football specialists, a 'millowner' mentality.

Mixed goal: In Education, Aviation and Labour journalism the mixture of goals is matched by a mixture of news sources and a mixture also of publicity stances in the source area; in contrast to advertising and audience goal fields, there was some difference of opinion among specialists as to which were the three leading news sources. Education correspondents agreed that the biggest single source was the Department of Education but agreed less about numbers two and three; the teachers' unions, the Association of Local Education Authorities, the National Union of Students, and head-teachers' organizations were all quoted. The educational system was seen as decentralized – with much power in the hands of teachers. Publicity stances were seen as exceedingly cautious in certain areas (the professional image of schoolteachers) and highly promotional in others (teachers' pay, students).

Aviation specialists also saw their field as lacking a single dominant source. Anglo-French projects, sales of British aircraft to foreign airlines and the purchase of military and civil aircraft from the United States all increased the number of news sources possessing important information about British Aviation. The Ministry of Defence was seen as in sharp internal conflict. The biggest single source was 'Government', but different correspondents placed the three relevant Ministries in different orders of importance. The Aviation world was seen as basically a three-sided affair of manufacturers, customers, and governments. This tripartite pattern (in both military and civil aviation) is seen as making the source area fairly open. The large financial implications of some single decisions lead to vigorous public relations activity and advertising. The promotional approach accompanies caution (Defence); the advertising is mainly by airlines, whereas manufacturers are more important news sources – so there is little source-advertiser overlap.

Labour correspondence concentrates on negotiations where national strikes are possible or under way. There is no single dominant source. The Ministry was the biggest single source, but other government (especially economic planning) bodies were important. Major sources included the Confederation of British Industries, the Trades Union Congress, and the big unions. The source area was again seen in a tripartite shape – with the unions putting up demands to management and government bodies trying to umpire the disputes – which makes for another open situation. Publicity stances vary from the promotional (the ministry and some big unions leaders) to the negative (some employers, some unofficial strikers).

Political Lobby has the unusual factor as a specialist field of operating not only within Parliamentary restraints (such as privilege) but also within the same building as the MPS. The Prime Minister is the dominant source of information as to what he, the Prime Minister, is going to do next; but he is often not the dominant source of information as to what the Cabinet will do next – since other Cabinet Ministers talk to journalists. This field also has a strongly tripartite element; on major decisions the relevant Cabinet Minister must consult the major interests involved (e.g. industry, unions, pressure groups, foreign governments), the relevant civil servants, and some of the government's own MPS in Westminster. These preliminary soundings and negotiations make the field fairly open – with the exception of decisions which the Prime Minister makes without consulting the whole Cabinet. The presence of an Opposition party at Westminster makes for a promotional attempt 'to win the publicity battle'. But the secrecy of the system of political communication (resulting from 'Cabinet collective responsibility', 'Civil Service anonymity', 'Parliament supremacy') also induces elements of caution.

Non-revenue: For British Foreign correspondents reporting from the United States, West Germany and Italy, the news source area is fairly open. Quasi-legal restraints are few, since countries of this sort cannot in practice expel journalists from other 'friendly' nations. The supply of information available in the local media in a democratic country is very considerable – at least in relation to the demands of news organizations in London. Foreign correspondents are especially interested in the foreign policy of the country they cover; some information is also supplied to them by the news organization in London which may have special knowledge of the London end of, for instance, London-Washington negotiations. For British correspondents in the USA there are two main types of news interest: (1) US domestic news in general; with the availability of the great American news agency and broadcast networks this is a very open area. (2) Diplomatic news broadly defined – especially concerned with 'world peace' and US relations with Europe in general and Britain in particular. New York has the United Nations, and Washington has the World Bank, the Organization of American States, and the number one foreign Embassies of many nations – in addition to the US Federal government. Access for (at least some) British correspondents is fairly good to various sources of US foreign policy news – White House assistants, State Department area specialists, members of Foreign Relations Committees of the Senate and House and their staffs; in addition to the British and other Embassies there are Defense, Commerce, FTC and other agencies relevant to certain areas. Whether or not access is open for American journalists *relative to the amount of information potentially available and actively in demand by them,* access for most British journalists is excellent relative to the much smaller amount of information in which they are interested.

Bonn, according to experienced British Foreign correspondents, is, after Washington, the most open capital to cover. Government press relations practices in Bonn follow the Washington model – with, it is said, middle level civil servants more accessible (and better informed) than in Paris. Another factor in 1968 in Bonn was the coalition between the two major parties; political control of Ministries was divided between the parties, leading to inter-departmental rivalries and increased openness. A factor different from Washington, however, was less easy personal access for British correspondents to the top politicians themselves. In addition to the officially free and open access approach in Bonn, there is also an element of considerable caution partly reflecting a lingering suspicion of certain elements of the British press, and perhaps also the delicate diplomatic position of the Bonn government.

In Bonn caution was common, but not indifference. In America there was a wider range varying from a promotional flavour ('I was a Rhodes scholar myself', and in New York the transatlantic promotion of entertainment stars), to at the other extreme outright indifference ('The *Daily Express* carries no votes in Illinois').

The Italian government and industry are of limited interest to most (but not all) London news organizations. There are three main interests in Rome: The Papacy (mainly in 1968 'The Pope and the Pill'); secondly the film industry, Hollywood-in-Europe, and La Dolce Vita; thirdly the exotic human interest story, 'Sicilian peasant chains daughter to kitchen table'); much of the latter material comes from news agencies including the local ANSA, but the Italian newspapers (and TV especially) are not highly regarded by British correspondents. The Rome film industry has a Hollywood promotional approach; Italian politicians are cautious (perhaps in view of their own highly partisan media) and not generous with interviews. In contrast to Washington and Bonn, Rome political sources are difficult to contact especially during the afternoon and on the telephone. The publicity stance of the Papacy is even more negative than that of British Football clubs or Scotland Yard. The Ecumenical Council in its very nature was more open, but the Papacy itself is hierarchical and secretive – 'They keep discussing communication but know nothing about it'. The journalists on the Vatican newspaper *Osservatore*

Romano are also believed to be ill informed, and much speculation in the Italian press generally (for instance on Papal visits abroad) is believed to be inaccurate.

With the exceptions of the Papacy in Rome and the Prime Minister in London, however, the broad structure of the source area correlates strongly with the goal of the specialist field. At the non-revenue end of the spectrum there is little in the way of source monopoly, and publicity stances are varied. Mixed goal fields are basically similar. Audience fields contain some source monopoly and have a negative publicity stance. Advertising fields contain some source monopoly and have a promotional publicity stance (protected by advertising and news source conjunction).

b. News sources: goals and payments

Specialists were asked whether there were any news sources 'especially *favourably* disposed to your editorial organization?' Among Foreign correspondents 72 per cent of quality newspaper men claim especially favourably disposed sources against only 52 per cent of popular newspaper specialists. Among correspondents in mixed goal fields (including the political Lobby) 75 per cent of quality newspaper men make this claim against 42 per cent of popular newspaper specialists. But among the revenue goal (both audience and advertising) correspondents a higher proportion of popular newspaper specialists (66 per cent) report favourable news sources than among quality newspaper correspondents (only 50 per cent); here the news sources favour the newspapers with the big battalions of readers. The preference for popular newspapers is especially strong in the audience goal fields of Crime and Football.

Do payments by news sources to journalists play any part in these preferences? The answer is a fairly definite No. Such payments would be seen as 'bribes'. For news sources these payments would carry more potential danger than possible benefit. Sources by the late 1960's attempted to exert control over specialists by other safer means – especially in revenue fields.

Some direct payments do, however, pass in the other direction. Most Foreign and Lobby correspondents think there is none in their fields; among mixed specialists somewhat more think payments are made, and among revenue specialists more still. It is in the audience goal fields that cash payments to sources are said to be most common; in Crime and Football journalism there is a close connection between the negative publicity stance of major sources and the prevalence of payment to source individuals. Some journalists claim that payments are necessary because the sources are so negative; the

TABLE 5.7

PAYMENTS TO NEWS SOURCES

Amount of such payments	Claimed to prevail in their own fields by these specialists					
	Foreign	Political	Mixed	Audience	Advertising	All (N=192)
'None'	% 63	% 82	% 28	% 8	% 58	% 47
'A little'	31	18	61	33	42	38
'Fair amount' or 'much'	6	0	11	58	0	15

sources on the other hand may see the prevalence of such payments as one reason for negative attitudes to journalists. 58 per cent of Crime and Football specialists said there was either a 'fair amount' or 'much' of such payments.

'£3 to £25 for a good news tip.' (Crime)

'Much payment, but not to Police.' (Crime)

'We often pay club employees and "friends" of players for tip-off information.' (Football)

'In relation to soccer I am strongly against this. It is also strongly condemned by my newspaper. But it happens.' (Football)

Most payments are made by a few popular newspapers – although other popular newspapers do not provide funds for paying sources. Most such payments are made to members of the public (e.g. who happen to witness a crime) or people on the fringes of the source area (e.g. small-time criminals, or people on the fringes of professional football). Payments to policemen and to football players occur less frequently than in the past; in both cases the disciplinary threats on the source side are severe.

In the mixed fields 61 per cent of specialists say there is 'a little' payment to sources:

'A little. It would be wrong to say "none", but the proportion is minute.' (Labour)

'Obviously payment is often indirect in form of lunches and drinks, but I pay students directly.' (Education)

'A little. Usually tips about crashes etc.' (Aviation)

Certain popular newspapers are widely known to pay for reliable tips. On certain occasions an unofficial strike leader may have important information; or an employee on an airport involved in servicing aircraft may have information about a politically important special flight abroad. Such provision of information overlaps into a local part-time 'correspondent' – such as the Editor of a student newspaper paid a small regular fee as the local 'University correspondent'.

There have in the past been scandals connected with payments to Members of Parliament;[2] penalties to both journalist and MP for doing this – it is a breach of Parliamentary Privilege – probably ensure that it now rarely or never occurs:

'None. Paid-for information is always highly suspect. Lobby journalists do not need this incentive.'

'None. Apart from paid articles.'

Nevertheless a few Lobby correspondents say there is 'a little' payment to sources; this is payment not to MPs, but to irregular sources – such as a member of a local party providing information on the constituency problems of a prominent politician.

Most British Foreign correspondents in the US say there is no payment to sources. The minority who answered that there were some payments were either thinking of the practices of American journalists (especially in New York) or of small payments to irregular sources:

'A little. Mostly to people like policemen and gatekeepers for physical whereabouts info.'

'Only in exceptional cases. A poverty-stricken mother with a large family in Alabama. And only afterwards, for inconvenience caused.'

c. News sources and sanctions

Two-thirds of specialists regard news sources in general as being positively helpful and/or cordial. The tougher sorts of sanctions in most specialist fields are completely unknown. Once again the audience goal specialists are less likely than the others to see sources as positive. Only a minority of both Football and Crime specialists see their sources as positive. In contrast Motoring has the highest proportion of specialists saying that sources are positive. Among the other fields about two-thirds say sources are positive:

'Mainly helpful. Only rarely otherwise.' (Aviation)

'Very few people are unhelpful.' (Education)

'It's only the minor ones who are hostile – that's why they're minor.' (Labour)

'Cordial and helpful – but the relationship is bound to be largely personal.' (Lobby)

'Helpful. Except in a crisis.' (Washington)

The general picture of most sources being basically cordial is supported by Table 5.8. The proportions reporting sanctions being used is lowest among Foreign correspondents – and highest among audience and advertising revenue goal specialists. The type of sanction most widely experienced by specialists is the 'Letter of correction/complaint sent to Editor by source' and only 56 per cent have experienced this mild sanction even once. 'Insistence that correction appear in print' was reported by 46 per cent. A complaint or *threat* of a complaint to the Press Council was reported by only 14 per cent of specialists. Moreover of all the sanctions in Table 5.8 about half the specialists were reporting its having been used against them *once* only.

TABLE 5.8

USE OF SANCTIONS BY NEWS SOURCES AGAINST SPECIALISTS

	Percentage of specialists saying they have personally encountered sanction at least once					
	Foreign	Political	Mixed	Audience	Advertising	All (N=199)
	%	%	%	%	%	%
(a) 'Insistence that correction appear in print'	31	32	57	58	62	46
(b) 'Request by source for apology from you privately'	10	13	19	33	35	20
(c) 'Complaint, or threat of complaint, to Press Council'	2	8	21	28	12	14
(d) 'Letter of correction/complaint sent to *Editor* by source'	38	58	68	67	77	56

What about tougher sorts of sanctions? The specialists were asked about four tougher sorts of sanctions, but negligible proportions had experienced these even once:

(1) 'Elimination from mailing list.'

(2) 'Prohibition from attending briefings.'

(3) 'Prohibition from attending conferences.'

(4) 'Supplied with false or unreliable information from source in order that this will involve you in trouble with Editor, news-desk etc.'

Examples of all these sanctions had been reported in the preliminary interviews – but the questionnaire responses indicated that the use of such sanctions was very unusual indeed.

Why are the tougher possible sanctions very rarely used and even the milder sanctions used only infrequently? Some of the specialists' comments may be helpful:

'Insistence that a correction *must* appear is the best way of ensuring that it isn't printed.' (Aviation)

'Usually complaints are based on third hand knowledge. During my years in Fleet Street I have – after replying to the complaint – never received any further response.'

'Corrections usually result from misunderstandings or human error.'

'Sources tend to regard us as part of the same world, and accept that they have to live with us – and may one day need our sympathy.' (Labour)

'False information is invariably due to people trying to appear informed when they are not. If you are trying to get information honestly and have taken the trouble to do your homework, most people of any stature are helpful. The less important the more pompous.' (Lobby)

'Elimination from mailing list. Never. Dammit.' (New York)

'None of these in the US. I've had complaining letters when based elsewhere.' (Washington)

Source attempts to stop a particular specialist from getting information are usually ineffective – because his competitor-colleagues are likely to help him, and because some other news sources may become more friendly. On such occasions competitor-colleagues emphasize the *colleague* side of their relationship and define the attempts as victimization. Consequently even if news source individuals become estranged from a specialist this does not usually take the form of harrying him with excessive complaints or withdrawing the standard flow of information.

d. Specialist attitudes

Education and Labour correspondents were pro-Labour in 1968; and Motoring, Fashion and Crime were pro-Conservative (Table 4.2). In the divided world of national politics the Lobby correspondents were divided between Conservative and Labour. In this, as in other fields, there appears to be a connection between the political views of specialists and those of the majority of their news sources. Labour correspondents, for instance, have the same anti-Conservative views as their trade union news sources. A broad similarity between the views of major sources and specialists seems likely to develop in at least three ways: Firstly there is some pre-selection on the basis of previous interest. If a man dislikes foreigners, trade unionists or schoolteachers he may be less likely to become (or to remain) a Foreign, Labour or Education correspondent. Secondly, the specialist merely by being in the field of coverage acquires *some* interests in common with major sources. Thirdly, continued exposure to the field may well increase his sympathy for the problems of major sources.

The specialists were asked: 'On what public policies or programmes in your field would you like:

a. to see more public money spent?
b. to see less public money spent?'

The most frequently quoted answers were as follows:

	Spend more on	Spend less on
Washington and New York	Education, Poverty, American Cities	us Defence
Political Lobby	Welfare, Education	Whitehall Administration, Defence
Labour	Industrial Training and Welfare, Education	New Whitehall Ministries
Education	Nursery, Primary and Slum Schools, Teachers	Universities
Aviation	Air Safety, Large subsonic jets	Prestige and 'Political' (e.g. Anglo-French) projects

	Spend more on	Spend less on
Crime	Prisons and Modernization of Police	—
Football	Coaching and Grounds	—
Fashion	Training and supporting young designers	Badly planned export promotions (e.g. British Weeks)
Motoring	Roads and Motorways	'Restrictive' (e.g. speed) legislation

There is a strong preference among most specialists for spending of a 'liberal' kind. Education was especially popular as a field for more expenditure and defence for less. Even among Crime correspondents the wish for more expenditure on the police (new technology, regional crime squads) was bracketed with the wish for modernization of prison buildings. There was a strong general preference for the less dramatic, less prestige, and more modest-looking sorts of expenditure. Even if big dramatic projects (and especially their failures or drawbacks) fit with new values, they do not fit so well with the private opinions of specialist journalists. Among preferences for spending less public money, specialists' favourite choices include 'Whitehall', and 'Bureaucracy'. Economic planning and government assistance to industry are particularly unpopular.

e. Autonomy and control in the news source area

Although the specialist fields are partly defined in terms of major news sources, these sources usually lack any monopoly control. Moreover, despite apparently possessing strong sanctions against correspondents, the sources use such sanctions very little. Nor do the personal demeanours which correspondents find it necessary to adopt with news sources present a simple picture. The predominant responses were as follows:

'Caution, Discretion'   – necessary fairly often or always.
'Toughness, Aggression' – necessary sometimes.
'Deference'   – necessary sometimes or never.

The majority of specialists claim to use all three demeanours at least 'sometimes' (Table 5.9).

At this stage two possible ways of explaining the apparent inconsistencies are worth noting. Firstly, to view the relationship as one of news correspondents against news sources may be mistaken. For

TABLE 5.9

DEMEANOUR WITH NEWS SOURCES

(*Q. Which of these demeanours is necessary with major news sources?*')

Demeanour	Percentage saying demeanour necessary at least 'sometimes'					
	Foreign	Political	Mixed	Audience	Advertising	All (N = 190)
	%	%	%	%	%	%
'Deference'	65	33	56	65	59	56
'Caution, Discretion'	100	100	100	100	93	99
'Toughness, Aggression'	75	78	69	91	70	76

instance, the data consistently suggest that the revenue goal correspondents (both audience and advertising) are the most under control, whereas the non-revenue Foreign correspondents have the most
autonomy. In both cases this appears to result from a broad compat-
ibility between the goals of news organizations and news sources in
the relevant areas. Secondly, there are similar indications that
specialist correspondents feel themselves controlled by (and autonomous within the limits of) broadly held 'news values'. Moreover not
only the specialists and news organization executives share these
values – news values are also broadly accepted by news sources.

These points will be further discussed below. The confusing
variety of demeanours which specialists claim to be sometimes necessary (Table 5.9) reflect the great variety of news sources. Obviously
also there is huge variety in the character of individual sources.
Whereas the 'biggest' news sources tend to be large (often government) organizations, most of the 'best' news sources – as seen by
specialists – are individuals.

3. GOVERNMENT AND ORGANIZATIONS AS SOURCES

a. Government control?

Government in one shape or another plays a leading part in the news
source area. Even the Football correspondents have their 'Minister
of Sport'; for the Motoring correspondents the Ministry of Transport is one of the most important single sources. For the Crime correspondents the police are overwhelmingly the major source, while

the second source is the Home Office. Labour, Aviation and Education correspondents all have one or more Ministries as a major source. The central concern of the political Lobby correspondents is the political running of the government by the Cabinet. For Foreign correspondents the government of the country they cover is central.

Common to several London-based fields is a government Ministry seen as the single biggest source. But this Ministry is not monolithic. People at the top – including both the political 'masters' and the 'non-political' civil servants – may be willing to talk. One or more other Ministries may also be in the same source area, as well as trade associations, companies, and pressure organizations. There may be knowledgeable occupational groups (e.g. pilots in Aviation, teachers in Education) backed by strong 'professional' trade unions. There may also be at Westminster some politicians well informed on the relevant area. This pattern of a Ministry which, although the major source,* is neither internally monolithic nor externally monopolistic, makes it difficult for specialists to answer whether there is a news source organization which could make the specialist's job impossible 'if the word went down the line that no members of the organization were to talk to you':

'If policemen spread stories (and my personal behaviour supported this) that I was not to be trusted my job would be almost impossible. But it's unlikely to happen to someone of my experience and reputation.' (Crime)

'Yes. Several organizations – Board of Trade, Ministry of Defence, Min. Tech. In practice such an instruction would never be obeyed universally. It has been tried against at least one correspondent and failed. In fact it recoiled because people sympathized with him.' (Aviation)

'Yes. The Ministry perhaps, but most of the news could be got in other ways and they could not refuse straight "hard news".' (Education)

'No. A thousand times No. There is no solidarity in politics. To be blackballed by one will merely encourage others to confide.' (Political Lobby)

'No. It would be difficult if the White House or State Department blacklisted me. But one's colleagues would always fill one in.' (Washington)

* The presence of a major government source organization is a key factor in the setting up of a new specialist field. Editors want to be sure that there will be 'enough' news to keep a specialist busy. More than one Editor said he regarded an active government organization as one such indication.

22 per cent of all specialists (N = 200) said there was an organization which could, by denying information, make their job impossible. The highest proportion were for the mixed fields (26 per cent), the political Lobby (33 per cent) and the audience goal field (28 per cent). Only 15 per cent of Foreign and 11 per cent of advertising goal correspondents thought such veto powers existed. These were mostly government organizations of some kind.

b. *Source organizations, public relations and specialists*

The history of public relations in Whitehall is to a large extent the history of public relations in Britain. Although the Ministry of Information was disbanded at the end of the 1914–18 war, several Departments retained public relations activities. During the second war there was a huge increase and by 1945 the Ministry of Information had a total staff of 6,550 in Britain and abroad.[3] After the war many of these people initiated public relations activities in commercial organizations.

Chief Information Officers meet regularly under the chairmanship of the Chief 10 Downing Street PRO to co-ordinate government publicity activities in advance and to prevent clashes on particular days. Similar attempts are made in the Motor industry, for instance, by the Society of Motor Manufacturers and Traders – in the form of a diary of forthcoming events – but this is limited by commercial competition.

While a car company cannot deny that its main objective is selling cars at a profit, the claims of Whitehall Ministries to be serving the public sound more believable to journalists. Whereas a car manufacturer satisfies criteria of news value when it has a strike, builds a new factory, launches a new model or sets some kind of record, a government Ministry touches its particular world in ways which satisfy news values more frequently. Most Ministries have either mediating and crisis settling goals or service goals which bring them into contact with individuals in 'human interest' situations; Ministries gather information (accident, employment, output, export); Ministries bring together prominent personalities in situations of conflict and decision. Daily journalists can regard Ministries as operating on the same daily frequency. Whereas *daily* production figures from a car company would not be regarded as news, *daily* road death figures from the Ministry of Transport were regarded as news, especially (as on public holidays) when 'there isn't much news'.

The form of public relations least favoured by journalists is that conducted by public relations departments and subsidiaries of advertising agencies; here one PR executive may be responsible for a bizarrely assorted collection of products and services from several different companies.[4] In the middle range of acceptability are PR activities as conducted direct by large commercial undertakings. Towards the acceptable end are major government organizations. The most acceptable type to journalists would probably be the public relations activity of organizations which are both non-commercial and non-governmental. The difficulty from a PR point of view is that independence from the government tends to have an inverse correlation with news values – such as volume (especially of money), conflict, and suitable frequency of activity.

Despite their criticism of public relations in general, in specific cases journalists usually prefer to deal with organizations which have an active public relations wing. In three fields where public relations is little developed specialists covering what they regard as unhelpful and arrogant organizations told stories which showed the organization as bumbling and incompetent in the very area where it believes its own expertise to exist – the Police with security, leading Football clubs playing international matches, and the Papacy with the life and death of the Pope:

A *Police* story is that the modern scientifically equipped police stations increasingly common in London have large plate-glass windows which enable criminals to watch detectives at work. Criminals can thus see which detectives are on duty, and by timing their crime accordingly can in part choose which detective gets the case to solve.

A *Football* story is that foreign journalists – especially from Latin countries – are accustomed to much fuller access to players before and after a match than is allowed in Britain. A common aspect of visits by foreign club teams is that the accompanying foreign journalists insist on visiting 'their' players' dressing rooms. Sturdy British officials block the way insisting that none shall pass, and – journalists say – bitter exchanges of both words and punches sometimes ensue.

A *Papal* story is that, in view of the excessive secrecy of the institution, journalists cannot rely upon the news to be immediately announced when a Pope dies. During the final illness of Pope John XXIII a journalist from the Rome paper *Il Tempo* made an arrangement with a servant in the Papal chambers who undertook to open a particular window as a signal that the Pope had just died. *Il Tempo* was thus able to splash exclusive news of the Pope's death. But the window had been opened because the afternoon was warm. The Pope was still alive.

Whatever the truth of such anecdotes, in the late 1960's Scotland Yard began introducing new PR measures, including the employment of PROS with journalism experience. A few Football clubs were following the lead of Coventry in the same manner; there were some signs that the World Cup which brought many foreign Football journalists to London in 1966 had slightly strengthened this trend. Similarly the Ecumenical Council in Rome saw extraordinary – and temporary – changes in press relations introduced; but by 1968 there was a permanent Vatican press room and a Monsignor PRO to whom questions could be put once a week (even if most questions did not receive immediate answers). Nevertheless, despite such faltering first steps, there is a widespread belief among journalists that the establishment or major enlargement of a PR department is usually followed by greatly improved access for journalists. The decision to employ more PROS and especially ex-journalists is often the outward and visible sign of a decision taken at the top of an organization to adopt a more 'positive' public relations policy.

The specialists were asked: 'On an average weekday how many separate PR letters have you got (*including* invitations, tickets, handouts, circulars, texts of speeches and "publications" of a PR type, but excluding material on general sale)?' The mean answer for each field was the following number of PR letters per weekday:

	PR letters per day
Washington	21
New York	19
Bonn and Rome	22
Political Lobby	7
Labour	20
Education	15
Aviation	20
Crime	4
Football	6
Motoring	27
Fashion	25

Advertising goal correspondents get the most PR letters; the Crime and Football men predictably get the least. The political Lobby figure of only 7 PR letters per day is hardly in keeping with their reputation among some other journalists of being 'handout hussars'. But Lobby men receive more literature of a general sale type – namely government publications.

Government publications are issued through PR or 'Press and

Information' divisions. The basic rule is that such documents are
issued to Lobby correspondents only; the Lobby men receive these
documents usually a day or two *before* Members of Parliament. This
is traditional practice but is in conflict with the other tradition of the
supremacy of Parliament as the forum in which new government
policies must be first announced. This conflict between traditional
'tradition' and traditional practice is one of several which occurs in
the Lobby system of political journalism. Whitehall trusts the Lobby
to protect this 'constitutional' embargo (and coverage by the Lobby
men is often a passport to front page treatment). If he thinks the
document of little political interest, the Lobby man will channel the
document back to his news organization, where it will usually be
handed to another specialist. There is little danger of anyone in the
news organization breaking the embargo – partly because embargoes
are usually honoured anyhow, and if the story has potential political
excitement the Lobby men will in any case keep it for themselves.

The basic Whitehall rule that all government (HMSO) documents go
only to Lobby correspondents is – like most other 'rules' and 'traditions' concerning the Lobby – much honoured in the breach. For
instance, both the Lobby and the Labour correspondents would receive embargoed copies of a White Paper about trade union legislation or a Departmental Committee report on regional planning. But
in other cases the Ministry does not trust the specialists in question
and the documents go only to the Lobby. Sometimes a specialist who
has not received a document is allowed to have one if he comes to
the Ministry and collects it personally – this identifies the individual
entrusted with the document beyond any doubt, and underlines the
importance of an embargo on a government document.

Although government documents are of great importance for
Lobby correspondents they are less important for other specialists.
Labour correspondents receive many publications produced by trade
unions; Education correspondents receive a great variety of publications, small surveys, speeches and reports from teachers', parents'
and students' organizations. Aviation correspondents are deluged
with the house magazine type of publication – international airlines
are especially prolific here. Such publications occasionally contain
important statements or articles; even job advertisements can indicate the start of new projects.

But public relations departments are important to specialist
journalists in other ways than through literature and handouts.
Specialists were asked: 'When contacting a source organization that
has a PR staff, in what proportion of cases do you go (at least in the
first instance) to a PR man?' The median percentages were as
follows:

	%
Washington	70
New York	70
Bonn/Rome	65
Political Lobby	55
Labour	60
Education	65
Aviation	70
Crime	40
Football	20
Motoring	80
Fashion	50

With the predictable exception of Football and Crime all other fields had an average of 50 per cent or more. Many specialists emphasized 'in the first instance' enquiries to PR departments are often about times of press conferences, small matters of past history, or routine checking:

'50%. Wherever possible I avoid PR personnel. Most, but not all, PR staff are mainly advertisers – particularly in private industry. Government department PR staff, however, are often good.' (Labour)

'60%. This procedure of initially contacting PR staff is virtually necessary when dealing with major US Government Departments – such as White House, State Department or Defense.' (Washington)

'In 70%. But this includes a high proportion of routine enquiries.' (Aviation)

When an interview is arranged by the PRO he usually also sits in on the interview. This standard practice may 'protect' the source individual from the specialist; but the PRO may 'help' the specialist to ask more fruitful questions – sometimes 'protecting' him from his ignorance. Both sides agree, however, that further meetings often take place subsequently without a PRO present.

Specialists in general acknowledge that Whitehall PROs are honest, if cautious. PROs, like journalists, are also aware of the need to protect confidences. If a single specialist phones up with a 'hot' set of questions – this will not be told to other specialists who phone that day; but if half a dozen specialists all telephone with the same line of questions, they will be told that other journalists are 'on to the story'.

Any picture of a smouldering state of conflict between specialists and PROs would be quite misleading.

The specialists who find the relevant PROs least helpful are the Crime correspondents. There was a 'press room' at Scotland Yard but a locked door between this room and the rest of the building symbolized the structural situation. The Crime correspondents' main complaints about the PROs at Scotland Yard in 1968 were that they didn't understand journalism and were not themselves in possession of adequate information. By contrast in Motoring, where the sanction of advertising withdrawal is present, some PROs think that the ease with which they get their publicity material used makes PR activity itself look too easy.

In another field where many stories are of crises and conflict, relations between the Ministry and the Labour correspondents seemed especially harmonious. Why in the midst of so many stories of strikes and threatened strikes does this Department have such a good reputation among journalists? To paraphrase a previous argument, Ministries in general are more like news organizations than industrial companies are; Ministries pursue information-gathering, and arbitrating, activities. But a Ministry in the Labour field (in a country with *national* bargaining) is even more like a news organization than are most other Ministries. The Ministry acts as an umpire in national negotiations, sees itself as trying to break down failures in communication and consequently as needing to adopt a vigorous information policy. The Ministry is a clearing house for local Labour information. The Ministry also operates in national negotiations on the same daily *frequency* as most news organizations; a very frequent press release service is supplemented by much telephoning to Labour correspondents. The Ministry appears to provide a fuller and faster service of bad news than is available elsewhere. The Ministry is seen by specialists as having relatively little bias in situations of threatened strikes – its vested interest is seen as merely wanting to be involved in getting a settlement. Labour specialists might not expect the Ministry PROs to be quite so forthcoming with news which did reflect badly on the Ministry itself, for instance a case of racial discrimination by a local employment exchange, but Labour correspondents regard this kind of local story as rather marginal to their national interests. The Labour field merely shows in a somewhat extreme form what public relations has to offer specialists. Specialists in a competitive position want two main kinds of information:

(1) All the basic information which is widely available to competitors.

(2) Other information which is not available to competitors.

On most days and most stories there is more of the first kind of information; and in supplying this first type of information public relations departments play an important part.

Specialists describe most public relations material as junk. But they may also admit that of fifteen or twenty PR letters they receive each day, one or two may well be used as the basis for a story. By helping specialists to cover 'all' the news, to work at speed, to meet deadlines, and to present lively material briefly, public relations has much success. However, with this very success there goes an element of failure. Although specialists use much public relations material, they tend to see anything that emerges in this form as devalued; more-over the speed and efficiency of public relations activity allows specialists time to continue looking for other stories.

c. Press conferences and briefings

Some press conferences are seen by the public on television, and consequently are somewhat looked down on – 'virtually a public meeting', 'nothing interesting gets said in big press conferences'. Some of these remarks reflect (mild) jealousy by some press journalists of television. But two major criticisms of such conferences have substance: firstly, if general reporters are present, the very wide range of requirements of those present may lead to some irrelevant questioning and to some restraint on the part of the news source. Secondly, anything said at such occasions is so widely available that it is somewhat devalued within journalism.

But even if these big press conferences are like public meetings, they are often like rather important public meetings. Firstly a journalist sees how a particular performer performs. Secondly something may be gleaned from other journalists present. Thirdly it may be possible to ask the leading performer more private questions after the press conference. Fourthly such a press conference may provide 'leads' for subsequent telephone searching.

The preference of both sources and specialists to confine at least some, and probably most, meetings to specialist correspondents only is given shape in most established specialist fields in London journalism through a specialist 'group'; one purpose of such groups is to exclude general reporters and to restrict certain conferences to 'full-time specialists only'. But there are fewer press conferences and briefings than some people imagine; the overall figure is only two or three per week (Table 5.10). There are big seasonal differences; Motoring specialists are deluged with such meetings at the time of the London motor show, and United Nations correspondents during the months when the UN General Assembly is in session.

Specialist correspondent as newsgatherer

TABLE 5.10

FREQUENCY OF PRESS CONFERENCES AND BRIEFINGS

(*Q.* '*How many times in 30 days do you go to a formal press conference or briefing—where all or most of the people in the field are invited, for a pre-arranged time and place?*')

Type of conference or briefing	Average (mean) number per 30 days					
	Foreign	Political	Mixed	Audience	Advertising	All
(a) 'Not for use or writing'	0·6	0·8	0·5	nil	1·2	0·6
(b) 'Not for attribution'	1·2	20·7	2·2	0·1	0·5	4·5
(c) 'Entirely on the record'	5·9	2·5	5·8	0·5	7·4	4·4
(d) 'Mixture of on and off'	2·1	1·4	2·3	0·9	3·3	1·9
Total number of conferences and briefings in 30 days*	10·4	27·7	10·0	1·6	11·1	11·7†

* There are discrepancies in all the totals. These totals are averages of the specialists' own estimates.
† N=190.

The *not for use or writing* type of briefing is rare in all fields – including Foreign correspondence in Washington; many such meetings are for individuals or small groups of specialists and hence do not come within the definition in the question of 'all or most of the people in the field' being invited. The *not for attribution* type of briefing is more frequent but not common, except in the political Lobby – these, averaging 21 a month, are the famous 'Lobby briefings'. They are given twice a day by the Prime Minister's chief PRO – in the mornings (for evening newspaper Lobby men primarily) at 10 Downing Street, and in the late afternoon in the 'Lobby room' at Westminster. These briefings are sometimes given by the Prime Minister himself. Other regular weekly briefings of a 'not for attribution' sort are given by the Leader of the House or the Leader of the Opposition. Irregular *ad hoc* briefings are given by other Ministers – usually to explain some kind of new policy.

Not for attribution briefings are much less frequent in other fields, partly because individual departmental Ministers are less newsworthy than the Prime Minister (the daily delphic utterances of whose PRO attract a steady audience), and such Ministers with much smaller responsibilities will have less frequent statements to make of the kind which could be regarded by back-bench MPs as major government policy. In mixed fields such as Aviation, Education and Labour, not for attribution briefings by the senior Minister occur at roughly monthly frequency. Labour correspondents on average receive more such briefings (2·9 per 30 days) than do Education specialists (1·0) partly because more Ministers want to talk to the Labour men. But not all 'not for attribution' briefings are given by Ministers – for example Labour correspondents get them from people like the General Secretary of the Trades Union Congress. Such briefings occur because prominent individual news sources want sometimes to talk in a preliminary way about ideas and plans to which they will not be firmly and explicitly committed in public in the form of an 'on-the-record' statement.

The *entirely on the record* press conference is the most common type in most fields. The press conference which is a *mixture of on and off* the record is self-explanatory. At some 'not for attribution' conferences the source gives one substantial on the record quote. The reverse may happen at an 'on the record conference'.

British Foreign correspondents go to fewer press conferences than one might expect. Foreign correspondents both in the United States and Europe prefer to use the reports on these conferences carried by the local national news agencies. The general pattern, however, is similar to mixed goal fields in London. The mixed goal correspondents attend about 10 conferences or briefings a month, the majority being on the record. Some of these press conferences deal with published documents or are preceded by some kind of public relations handout. In the case of a government document of major importance the relevant Minister might give separate briefings to the Lobby, to one or more other groups of British specialists, and to one or more groups of foreign journalists, plus making television and radio appearances.

The Motoring and Fashion correspondents are similar, in the number and pattern of press conferences, to the mixed fields. It is the audience goal fields which are again deviant; both Crime and Football specialists average under two press conferences or briefings a month. Specialists in both fields regard this as one more indication of the negative attitudes of news sources. Football press conferences take place at annual occasions such as those of the Football League or the Football Association; press conferences are also given by managers on trips to games in foreign countries. But back in Britain the general lack of press conferences continues. The Crime correspondents would like regular background briefings such as are given by Ministers in the mixed fields; and they would welcome frequent *ad hoc* conferences or briefings given by police officers in charge of unsolved crimes. Such press conferences are given, say the Crime specialists, only when the Police want to use the press and television to trace a missing person or suspect.

d. Source organizations and specialist exchange

Asked who helps whom more, 40 per cent of specialists say (Table 5.11) that sources help the journalists more:

> 'They benefit from our information and the publicity we give them, but very few depend on this alone.' (Labour)

> 'The chance for reciprocation in favours is small.' (Football)

> 'Foreign journalists have little to trade.' (Washington)

A much smaller proportion – only 9 per cent of all the specialists – think that 'the journalists help the sources more'.

> 'News items are even more valuable than advertising to the motor industry.' (Motoring)

> 'Soccer gets more free publicity than any other sport but in most cases we have to go out and fight for stories.' (Football)

> 'By the desired focus of attention internationally.' (New York)

The answer receiving the largest percentage of support, however, (51 per cent) was 'It's about equal.'

> 'Successful contact keeping relies on an exchange of information.' (Aviation)

> 'I think we are one big community.' (Motoring)

> 'It's a reciprocal world.' (Football)

> 'There's a lot one can tell most Embassies.' (Washington)

The only fields where the majority think the sources help more are Washington, Bonn/Rome, Labour and Education; all these are fields in which government source organizations play an important part. On the other hand the single field with the highest proportion saying 'it's equal' is Aviation, where government sources are again important. The difference may be that Aviation had three Ministries

TABLE 5.11

SOURCES AND JOURNALISTS: WHO HELPS WHOM MORE?

	Foreign	Political	Mixed	Audience	Advertising	All (N=196)
	%	%	%	%	%	%
(a) 'The sources help the journalists more'	51	46	44	24	27	40
(b) 'It's about equal'	43	51	47	59	62	51
(c) 'The journalists help the sources more'	6	3	9	16	12	9

(Defence, Trade and Technology) plus two major nationalized airlines (BEA, BOAC) to deal with – in addition to foreign governments and airlines. The other most notable point is that all the revenue fields – audience and advertising – collectively see the balance as being fairly equal. This may follow from the commercial benefits which specialists in a revenue field think they are bestowing on sources.

But can these activities be regarded as an exchange? The question confuses the specialists themselves; they know that the marginal utility of publicity or information can never be tested. Two standard criticisms of much sociological exchange theory may be relevant:

(1) All social interaction can be viewed as exchange.

(2) Exchange theory is weak at the middle level – above the small group level of exchange between individuals and below the political-economic level of exchange between organizations or governments.

It is precisely at this middle level that the present 'exchange' situation is located. At the organizational level a number of source organizations, which compete and co-operate with each other, confront a number of news organizations, which also compete and co-operate. Individual news sources or news organizations could be seen as constrained by their competing (and co-operating) organizations and by their overlapping customers and audience. But this level of analysis would be too remote to explain most of what happens in source-specialist interaction.

The routinized provision of information – such as public relations and press conferences – is clearly not a simple exchange between an individual source and an individual specialist. There is a strong *collective* element here – the transactions are between *groups* of specialists and press relations *divisions* within news source organizations. The interaction situation contains contractual and quasi-legal elements. The 'release' time written on a press handout is usually ignored only with dire consequences for the journalist. Similarly if a specialist repeatedly produces prominent stories, which a source organization can convince the Editor contain major and culpable factual mistakes, the Editor may feel that he has no alternative but to move the specialist from the field in question – on the grounds that the specialist will no longer be trusted by the sources.

Another contractual element is that neither side can easily withdraw. Public Relations officers in a government Department cannot deny a stream of basic information and handouts to a specialist; a news organization could get friendly MPs to ask questions in Parliament, which would be a serious setback for the PR division concerned. With government PROs in a situation of quasi-legal obligation to provide at least some information, other source organizations will be at a disadvantage unless they also provide information. Nor can source organizations withdraw facilities from one correspondent, unless he lacks the minimal support of his competitor-colleagues. Most specialists are predisposed to pursue the objective of improved access to news sources for all specialists in the field.

Nor can specialists completely deny publicity to prominent source organizations. Specialists are allowed considerable tactical autonomy and, as experienced and occupationally socialized journalists, their view of news values will be broadly similar to that of relevant news executives. But if a specialist is ill, or for some reason fails to send a story, the news organization can still use an agency version, or assign a general reporter, or use the PR handouts.

Thus in the case of a major news source and a major news organization neither individual sources nor individual specialists can more than partially withdraw from the information-publicity 'exchange'. There is no open market and no directly alternative suppliers or consumers of the service in question. (The only possible alternatives are general reporters instead of specialists, and on the other side some other news source.)

Individual specialists frequently bypass the public relations personnel. But the whole group of specialists in a field cannot always bypass the PR personnel. If the Minister, for instance, is going to talk to a specialist group collectively, this meeting will be arranged, and attended, by a PR man. From time to time there are conflicts, disputes and complaints about particular stories or particular incidents.

In the audience goal fields the usual source response is a complaint that the specialist has been inaccurate; sources such as Scotland Yard and the Vatican may merely state that there has been an inaccuracy – without supplying an alternative 'accurate' version.

In other fields where the sources are seen as less negative a common practice is for the source to provide the specialist with the 'accurate' version – and possibly some further detail. When the specialist next produces a story on the same subject whether within days or weeks – he will use the 'accurate' material in the new story.

e. *Organizational sources: the critical news dilemma*

On the question of critical news coverage there are at least two pieces of conventional wisdom:

(1) Journalists – dependent on major news sources and hence uncritical of them – are natural supporters of the *status quo*.

(2) Journalists – dependent upon producing negative news and thus obsessed with conflict, failure and violence – are natural anarchists.

A 'critical dilemma' certainly exists for specialist journalists; but the dilemma exists also for the news sources. News values emphasize conflict – which often implies conflicting sources of information. The source dilemma is how to provide information which includes conflict and yet is not too damaging to the source organization.

Specialists are under news organization pressure to produce stories of a bad news type. Norms of criticism are partly set by general reporters, feature writers, columnists, leader writers, TV current affairs journalists, and specialist newsgatherers working on the border of the field. Sunday newspaper specialists tend to look out for slightly 'offbeat' or 'post-mortem' stories; weeklies with their more 'comment' kind of approach also push the norms in a critical direction. Sometimes a specialist publication exerts a similar influence.

Major national source organizations, such as Whitehall Departments, are so large and segmented that it is unclear where the 'organization' ends and its customers, suppliers, or its political 'masters' begin. Moreover the men at the top – such as political bosses struggling with a new Ministry, trade union leaders handling unofficial strikers, or leaders of umbrella associations trying to lead member organizations – are often engaged in a struggle for power with their nominal subordinates or supporters. Such a 'boss' may use critical publicity in an attempt to beat some of his 'subordinates' into line.

Organizations sometimes seek 'bad news' coverage of their own activities. The cancellation of a major aircraft project is a serious loss for the main manufacturers and subsidiary suppliers involved, who may supply detailed information about the decision – for instance blaming Treasury incompetence.

'Tame Seal' is one of several derogatory terms used by journalists about a specialist whom they regard as completely uncritical of a major news source. Such terms, however, also illustrate the limitations of source control over specialists. The more successful the source organization is at turning a specialist into a Tame Seal, the lower will be the specialist's reputation within his news organization and among other journalists. With the exception of advertising goal fields, Tame Seal stories tend to get low prominence in the output.

Public relations activity becomes tied to the *daily* frequency of most specialists. The specialists want a flow of news every day and at great speed. Major source organizations can help to meet this need, but they are less successful at getting information into the specialist output about their own lower frequency or less dramatic activities. The public relations supply of news pushes back the starting line of what specialists regard as 'real' news.

4. INDIVIDUALS AS NEWS SOURCES

a. Organizational and individual sources

For the national specialist the junior PRO has relatively little to offer. The prominent 'name', by contrast, knows many things the specialist would like to hear and he has the power to give 'exclusive' information. Many specialists describe their own relations with sources in terms of exchange and power; some Lobby correspondents see themselves as dependent on certain Cabinet Ministers while having little time to waste in talking to many Members of Parliament. Education correspondents admit to regarding their relations with the head of a major educational institution quite differently from their relations with an ordinary teacher met casually at a conference.

But among media Performers there is a very rapid turnover; many of the names in the headlines or faces on the TV screen will not be there in five years' time. The insecurity-at-the-top theme plays a part in specialists' perceptions of the balance of exchange and power. A Cabinet Minister may have been having publicity which he regards as wholly bad. Or another Minister, despite being in the Cabinet, may be getting very little publicity at all. In either case the Minister in question may be extremely anxious to get some 'neutral' publicity. Paradoxically an unknown Civil Servant within the same Ministry may be in a stronger position on some issues of potential news value. He may be on important committees and willing to hand on information in a discreet manner to a trusted journalist. With little risk to himself and the ability to provide this service for perhaps a decade or more, such a relatively 'minor'-seeming source may be in a strong exchange and power position.

Another type of individual source who is difficult to classify is the top individual in a large organization somewhat on the fringes of the specialist area. The head of an American domestic airline would not come within the list of day-to-day major sources for a British Aviation correspondent. But if the head of such an airline is considering buying options on British-built aircraft he may suddenly become a major source. Moreover although he may have important information for a British Aviation correspondent, he himself may be able to learn a good deal from the correspondent.

b. Performers as individual sources

Specialists were asked: 'Some specialists say that in their field there is a small number of key individuals and that over half the work consists of finding out what these people are up to. Is this so of your field?' 59 per cent said Yes with variations by goal as follows:

	%
Foreign	40
Political Lobby	84
Mixed fields	60
Audience fields	51
Advertising fields	73
All selected specialists	59 (N = 200)

The field with the highest proportion saying Yes was Fashion (designers especially). The next highest were the Lobby correspondents who identified the key people as being in opposition to each other, for instance not only the Prime Minister and other top Ministers, but leaders of factions in the government party and the official opposition. Other specialists identified their 'key individuals':

'Yes. Top management/politicians.' (Aviation)

'Yes. The leading figures of the teachers' Unions, local authorities, Ministry and top educationists.' (Education)

'Yes. Ministers, Union leaders, industrialists and "Civil Servants" in politics and both sides of industry. The important people are either innovators or so placed that their actions affect large groups.' (Labour)

'Yes. Middle and senior rank CID officers.' (Crime)

'Yes. Administrators and officials and players connected with the game's top dozen clubs.' (Football)

'Yes. In each political party, ministry or other organization there is some key man who either runs the show or knows all about it.' (Bonn)

'Yes. Basically the policy makers – Cabinet officials, government Department and private business heads, Chairmen of Congressional Committees.' (Washington)

'Yes. In the UN – the Leaders pro-tem of ideological or area groups of states.' (New York)

News criteria such as personalization and conflict tend to define 'important decisions' and 'key individuals' each in terms of the other. There are two main ways of 'finding out what these people are up to'. One is to talk to the assistants, intimates, allies (and perhaps opponents) of the key individuals in question. The other is to find out from the key individual direct, which is usually the most desirable. Access to a big name satisfies news values with a minimum expenditure of the specialist's scarce time. The big name can give a story more importance even if the connection is only a comment; a specialist with an item of fresh news phones a big name for his comment (enabling the story to appear: 'Minister denies charge . . .'). The top names have more information not only about their own but also about other organizations. Cabinet Ministers through Cabinet committees and Cabinet meetings know about important decisions in other Ministries. A 'name' who is unwilling to talk about his own organization will often talk about another organization of which he has knowledge. Such umbrella information may concern a subject strong in news value – for instance a clash between two large organizations or several big names. Big name individuals also are aware about *who* is taking a decision elsewhere and *when* the decision will be taken. Finally, regular access to personal conversations with top names in the news source area may become cumulative and help to open doors elsewhere.

But the meeting with one individual journalist is, for the name source, uneconomical in time – journalists are most keen for personal interviews when source individuals are most busy. Such personal interviews also may antagonize competing specialists. One resulting compromise is the short private interview after a press conference. Another is the small 'secret' briefing for a few correspondents. In Washington there is a tradition of 'backgrounders' – meetings between a senior political figure and a small number of correspondents, often over dinner. The source gets, on an off-the-record basis, publicity through *several* news organizations; the journalists get relatively lengthy and relaxed access to the 'name'. British correspondents in the us have long adopted this American custom. In the 1960's there were at least two such backgrounder groups to which some British Washington correspondents belonged. One was an all-British group, and the other a more exclusive European group. An example in the late summer of 1965 of an *ad hoc* small group meeting was a briefing given by President Lyndon Johnson shortly before he went to San Francisco to address the special anniversary meeting of the United Nations. The briefing, for a dozen correspondents of various European media, took place at the house of Max Freedman (a former *Guardian* correspondent and friend of L.B.J.) in Washington. One British journalist present reported President Johnson as making three main points:

(1) That a story by James Reston in the *New York Times* to the effect that the us would help the un out of its debt situation had originated from the State Department. President Johnson would make no such statement at San Francisco.

(2) 'He gave us a pep talk about our importance in "explaining" us policy abroad. (Which I do not regard as my function.)'

(3) President Johnson said that at the end of 1965 he would concentrate less on getting his legislation through Congress and would turn his attention more to foreign affairs.

In London the late hours and 10 pm voting habits of Parliament, plus the size of the city, made for a tradition of political *lunching*. A few specialists – who perhaps work for the same multi-media organization, or who co-operate in other ways – may take a prominent performer out to lunch.

Another compromise form of personal contact between a name source and individual specialist is the evening or week-end telephone call. One Lobby man said he knew four Cabinet Ministers sufficiently well to leave a message asking them to ring him back. The week-end is an especially popular time for phoning sources. Evening and weekends, of course, are the time when name sources are free of their advisers, staffs, or Civil Servants.

c. Civil Servants and other non-performers as individual news sources

The 'tradition' of an anonymous and politically neutral Civil Service appears to leave the matter of explaining the policy of a government Department in the hands of the temporary political 'masters' and the public relations department. Silence on the part of the Civil Servants and close co-ordination between the politician-Ministers and PROS would thus ensure that the Ministry spoke with a single voice. This 'tradition' obtains, if to a lesser degree, in most large organizations; but, needless to say, the tradition is honoured a fair amount in the breach: Firstly, the name performers in political or directorial control may themselves be internally split. Examples include the common political practice of 'balancing' a right-wing and a left-wing Minister, or the directors of previously competing companies on a merged board. Secondly, a Foreign Ministry spokesman may be wooden and unhelpful at press conferences, but his personal contacts with Foreign correspondents may be quite different. London-based specialists say that a top PRO may be willing to say: 'This is the on-the-record line. But my own off-the-record assessment is this.' Lobby correspondents reported that during Mr Harold Wilson's first four years as Prime Minister there were internal disagreements within his Downing Street PR staff, as well as lack of communication between PROS and the political boss.

Thirdly some of the neutral and anonymous Civil Servants do talk to journalists. Specialists were asked: 'What proportion of all your dealings with the news sources are with Civil Servants?' The highest figure, 50 per cent, was for the federal capital of Washington and for Crime (policemen being Civil Servants); the lowest proportions are for Football and Motoring – where coverage is of the industry rather than the Ministry of Transport. Perhaps the most interesting figures are for the mixed fields – 15 to 25 per cent – and the Political Lobby, where it is 30 per cent. Some caution should be exercised in looking at these figures, since PROS in Ministries are Civil Servants.

However, answers to an open question (about what 'grade or type of Civil Servant' they talk to most frequently) establish that specialists do have frequent dealings with Civil Servants other than PROS:

'Under Secretary and above.' (Aviation)

'Middle ranking Civil Servants in the Department of Education and Chief Education officers of Local Education Authorities.' (Education)

'Senior police officers.' (Crime)

'From senior press officers to Permanent Secretaries.' (Labour)

'Permanent Secretary, Assistant secretary, Minister's Private secretary.' (Lobby)

'It is easier and much more profitable, to develop a personal relationship with the Assistant to the Assistant to the Secretary of State, than with Dean Rusk himself. Further, Americans don't generally become self-conscious until their late forties. And the below middle age generation tends to be profoundly sceptical.' (Washington)

A minority of specialists, however, said that they rarely dealt with Civil Servants apart from PROS or those in lower positions (such as 'executive' grades). In some teams of two or three specialists one man (not necessarily the number one) may have most of the dealings with Civil Servants.

Specialists were asked: 'In your own field how often do you think the *major* decisions are made mainly by Civil Servants?' The very wide differences between fields included big differences within goal types in the proportion of specialists saying that in their field Civil Servants make major decisions 'fairly often' or 'always':

60% or more of specialists:	Aviation
	Motoring
40%–50% of specialists:	Education
	Labour
	Crime
	Washington
	New York
33% or less of specialists:	Political Lobby
	Bonn & Rome
None of the specialists:	Fashion
	Football

Aviation was the specific field where the highest proportion of correspondents believed Civil Servants to be making the major decisions always or fairly often. The political Lobby on the other hand had one of the lowest proportions saying this; for Lobby correspondents news is defined as what politicians do and in particular what the British Cabinet does. But in Aviation the major decisions are seen by correspondents as primarily concerning big projects – and government decisions in research, finance, and airline policy are widely agreed to be basic.

The long incubation period of aircraft projects is a further distinctive feature of the Aviation field; another feature is its great technological complexity – which seems likely to make Civil Servants (including scientific Civil Servants) relatively more important than short-stay political Ministers. Moreover the long-term planning of aircraft projects, quite apart from personalization or élite performers, fits such news value criteria as 'volume' ('X hundred million pound project'). Advanced aircraft projects are suitable for stories about new technology, wrapped up in a single identifiable package.

Nevertheless even in Aviation, the specialists say that only 25 per cent of their source dealings are with Civil Servants, and politicians are regarded as major sources. In the present state of political science we are unable to say how important politicians are relative to Civil Servants in governing Britain. But many, even quite senior, Civil Servants probably have little information which would be of interest to journalists. The kinds of decisions primarily taken by politicians are more likely to fit journalists' conceptions of news values than are the kind of decisions primarily taken by Civil Servants.

'The more senior the more freely they talk.' The highest reaches of the Civil Service are the most 'political' – in the sense of having the most widespread contact with politicians and involvement in political decisions. The giving of information to journalists is one means of supporting, or of opposing, a political 'master'.

Other individual sources, although not media performers or public names themselves, are at the level of 'advising' or reporting directly to such names. An obvious example in politics are second rank members of the government; at least some amongst them – including some determined to become 'names' themselves – may be even more talkative than the more talkative Cabinet Ministers. Despite a particularly strict rule that policemen must not talk to Crime journalists, it is accepted in the upper reaches of the police force that this rule must be broken. Again in Football, the other audience specialism in which there is a firm rule against talking to journalists, this rule is inevitably broken. One Football journalist talked about how the *Daily Express* got the exclusive story late in 1967 that Dave Sexton would be the new Chelsea manager:

'The decision is made one day and perhaps half a dozen people know that day. By the next day a dozen people know, the next day two dozen – the information moves out in ripples. Probably the *Express* got the story from some local contact – a player or some other employee of the club, or maybe a freelance or local journalist. There are many backdoors in Football.'

'Backdoors' are perhaps especially numerous in national politics – where anything which has been discussed in the Cabinet may ripple out to at least some journalist within hours or days. Prime Ministers and other leading performers cannot, as a general rule, make major decisions without consultation. The increasing complexity of decisions tends to involve increasing access for journalists (although the access may not increase as fast as the complexity).

Even in the military field the centrality of technological considerations involves – in the case of Britain – the rippling out of information to other countries, such as the United States, Germany and France. Technical specialists who oppose organizational policies often give information to journalists. The very breadth and scale of technology – the numbers of experts and sub-contractors – is an important aspect leading to journalists' access. The scope and extent of government activity in industry, planning, and elsewhere leads to protracted negotiations – and a standard tactic in such negotiations is leaking information to journalists. These developments also bring professional politicians – including MPs with constituency interests – into the area of decision. Members of Parliament may not be very effective at gathering information, but they are obvious allies for many commercial and other interests – and many MPs in turn are often not averse to publicizing such information as they have. Moreover the increasing complexity of decisions has led to many developments in pre-testing reaction, from the trying out of drafts on interested parties to market research studies of general public response. Senior people inside and outside large organizations receive a variety of such pre-testing documents – and some of these documents reach journalist acquaintances.

d. Élite specialists, 'experience' and the personal approach

In any field of journalism one or two specialist correspondents may develop superior access to sources, and become to some extent performers in their own right. One example was the Paris correspondent of *The Times*, De Blowitz, and his coverage of the Berlin Congress of 1878.[5] Apparently in order to influence British opinion, Bismarck broke his custom and gave De Blowitz 'a memorable interview of five hours' duration' over dinner. De Blowitz's final coup was to obtain the full text of the treaty which *The Times* published in London at the same moment as the document was being signed in Berlin. De Blowitz never revealed who gave him the treaty, but *The Times* historian thinks it was probably the French Foreign Minister. The basic tactic of De Blowitz – to move from one top name to another until all the other names also want to talk – is still used. It is easy to see how this procession becomes cumulative; but it is less easy, for most specialists, to get the process in motion.

There were one or two such élite correspondents within several of the specialist fields covered by the present study. Such correspondents were usually working for one of the 'quality' newspapers.

Television journalists in general are less suitable for special revelations – and the less detailed coverage of TV often means that these journalists possess less detailed knowledge of the field generally. But in Foreign correspondence BBC men – and Reuters correspondents – perhaps because of their large international audience, appear more likely to have élite contacts.

Sometimes 'experience' is deliberately planned and cultivated in advance; for instance the youngest Football specialist may be assigned to cover the England Under 23 team – in the expectation that some of these players will later be in the full England team. Some Political Lobby correspondents in early 1968 – over two years before the 1970 General Election – were already saying that they must pay more attention to likely members of the next Conservative Cabinet. Ambitious source individuals will also be cultivating publicity and 'experience' in dealing with journalists.

Prominent news source individuals will often have a record of rapid movement both hierarchically and geographically. A young Football journalist in Manchester may get to know a leading player, who ten years later shows up as manager of a team in the London area. Policemen similarly move from place to place on their promotion ladder. The Lobby correspondent of a provincial paper may get to know a local MP who later becomes a Minister; or a Lobby man may have contact with a young Civil Servant in a Minister's private office – who ten or fifteen years later may have become a much more senior Civil Servant. But Foreign correspondents are perhaps the most subject of all to the experience of finding old sources popping up in new places:

'Any correspondent who has served in several overseas posts is liable to find diplomat friends occupying senior posts in, say, the US State Department. By virtue of oldish acquaintance he'll use them as contacts, however senior they may have become.' (Washington)

Another aspect of 'experience' is ability to draw conclusions from what to a novice might seem rather flimsy clues. Senior Football specialists say they acquire an ability to narrow down the possibilities:

'If the Second Division league leaders are worried about their goalkeeper they will be prepared to buy a better replacement, in order to ensure their promotion to the First Division. If you know enough about the game you can list six possible goalkeepers they might be after. Then if you spot their manager watching a match involving one of these six goalkeepers, you're on to a big transfer story.'

This practice of 'putting yourself into the source's position' is common also in other fields. When the likely issue in a decision has been narrowed down, a small verbal slip at a press conference may suddenly acquire significance. Of course this practice of 'seeing it from his point of view', and using 'instinct and experience' can also be regarded as 'pure speculation'.

Two very senior Fleet Street News executives gave the following accounts of the personal approach to news sources:

(1) A political journalist got to know the secretary of a Conservative shadow Minister. In bed with the secretary at a seaside hotel the night before the annual Conservative Party Conference, the journalist discovered that her boss was going to make an unusually important speech next morning. He immediately got out of bed, and phoned the theme of the speech to his Fleet Street office in time for that night's late editions.

(2) The problem in covering the United Nations is to get hold of advance texts of resolutions which the third world nations are bringing forward. There are two ways of getting these texts. One is to have a white secretary who sleeps around with men in the African and Asian delegations. The second way is to station permanently at the bar in the delegates' lounge a journalist who looks like one of the potted palm trees and drinks like a fish.

Although many journalists have tales of this sort to tell – with the moral that the personal approach often pays off – such approaches are said to be more often of a food and drink, rather than a sexual, nature.

A few specialists said they tried to lunch with a source every day and a few said they tried to avoid all source lunching. Two fields where lunching is especially prevalent – Aviation and Motoring – are also fields in which there is much public relations activity. The two heaviest drinking fields appear to be Crime and Labour. There is a 'local' pub for each police station in central London – although it is never the pub nearest to the police station; Crime correspondents frequent these pubs as a means of breaking down the distance between themselves and policemen. For Labour correspondents, drinking is important in establishing personal relations with trade union leaders. Labour specialists say there is a noticeable difference in this respect between union and management negotiators; after a meeting, while the management men get into their chauffeur-driven cars and disappear, the trade union leaders are much more likely to take a pint of beer with the Labour correspondents.

The propensity of Labour correspondents to drink informally with union men, but not with management, arises partly from differences in status, salary, and way of life between the two potential source groups. But a good deal of drinking and lunching results from sources and journalists being in the same place at the same time – rather than from pre-arranged meetings; these places include the traditional Pall Mall gentlemen's clubs – but more important are pubs near to Ministries or other source organizations, restaurants in Soho and elsewhere, and other clubs of a specialized interest sort. Many specialists say it is largely a matter of 'hitting it off' and genuinely liking the man. Most are also agreed that there is a strong age-grading phenomenon – of ambitious young specialists having ambitious young sources, and older specialists older sources. Specialists talk about 'my generation' of policemen, MPs or footballers.

Both an individual source and a specialist may develop a common interest in building up the source's name – the source wanting to become a 'name', the journalist wanting to build up his asset ('I knew him before he became famous'). In some source-specialist situations this element of working together is more explicit. The source may write a signed article for the newspaper, which the specialist may help to commission or sub-edit; in television interviews there is an element of the reporter and the source putting on a dual performance and establishing a shared experience. Another situation where exchange becomes more explicit is when a journalist 'ghost' writes a book for the source – something especially common in Football journalism.

Although most of the information supplying comes from the source side, there are also several kinds of feedback of information from the journalist to the source individual:

(1) The simplest kind is the supply of 'stop-press' news from the journalist to a source. 'We tell them a lot of things which they would hear within an hour or two.'

(2) Sources are interested in gossip about their own field of activity. Since journalists are in the gossip and information gathering business full-time, they will usually have plenty of fresh gossip.

(3) Specialist journalists may act as unofficial 'go-betweens' or 'conciliators' on a word of mouth basis; an obvious example is the industrial dispute.

(4) Specialists may perform a somewhat similar role between groups or individuals within a single organization. Cabinet Ministers may consult specialists as to the wishes of their own backbenchers, or backbenchers may want to know about the intentions of their own Ministers.

Such provision of 'information' by specialists to news sources shades off into the supply of advice and 'suggestions'. Professional footballers ask Football correspondents for advice on career problems. Lobby correspondents 'suggest' to MPs that they put down a particular Parliamentary Question.

In exchange for information about a particular decision or conflict, a specialist can offer individual sources who opposed the course taken an opportunity to 'get back at' the perpetrators of the decision. There is the prominent politician who was over-ruled by the Cabinet, or was sacked – yet still has much interesting information in his possession; there is the highly placed man in the Aviation industry – such as a designer, test pilot, or export salesman – who thinks the blame for some failure should be placed elsewhere; there is the detective who was moved off a particular crime; or there is the prominent footballer who was dropped from the first team by the new manager. All information supplied by an individual source has some motive behind it – which the specialist must evaluate. One source may seem to be trying to get back into the first team; another source may seem to be heading for the third world war:

'On April 2, 1954, I sat in Mr John Foster Dulles's ante-room at the State Department, waiting to see him. . . . After a long pause, he spoke, emphasizing every word: "I can tell you that American aircraft carriers are at this moment steaming into the Gulf of Tonkin, ready to strike. . . ."

'He went on to explain that the US Government was convinced that it could not afford to let Indo-China go Communist. He favoured intervention, but President Eisenhower had made such action dependent on Britain's deciding to go in and Prime Minister Anthony Eden was stubbornly opposed to the idea.

'I knew, as Mr Dulles must have known, that the British Cabinet was to meet in two days' time, on Sunday, to make its decision for or against support. A lot depended on that Cabinet meeting, and I was certain as I sat down to write my weekly despatch to the *Sunday Times* (in which I could not quote from the interview) that in indicating such sensational developments Mr Dulles was hoping to use one more avenue to influence the decision in London.'[6]

In the standard situation of a press conference, or with a mailed handout, there are certain agreed conditions – in particular a set time at which the material may be used. But this quasi-contractual element does not exist in dealings between an individual journalist and an individual source. Sometimes the source will say that his remarks are off-the-record or not for use, but where source and journalist know each other, this may be left understood rather than explicitly stated. Despite the special circumstances of some such meetings and the extreme 'frankness' with which the source may talk, usually no explicit bargaining over the exchange takes place. Henry Brandon says '... I was certain ... that in indicating such sensational developments Mr Dulles was hoping ...'. Even when the story could influence a decision to make war, there is no explicit bargaining of an 'If I tell you this, you must undertake to say that' character.

The same lack of explicit undertakings occurred in Lobby journalism of the 1890's.[7] Specialists say they are rarely approached on an explicit bargaining basis – and if so apprached tend to become sharply hostile toward the bargaining source. Thus the exchange of publicity for information takes on certain elements of 'pure' exchange of the small group or friendship type. The very 'purity' of the exchange, however, leads to a certain interpersonal distance. The specialist does not ask the source's motives, and the source does not ask the specialist how he will word his story.

e. Individual sources: the critical news dilemma

Specialists admit to treating major regular sources differently from minor irregular ones. Here is an account of a British Foreign correspondent handling a minor irregular United Nations military source in 1962 during the Katanga secession from the Congo:

> 'One enterprising *Daily Express* reporter had asked a high-ranking Swedish Officer about his medals; some of them, he learned, had been bestowed by the Germans in World War II, for successfully helping them to cross the country, once on their way in, once on their way out. Since the *Express* was both violently anti-UN and violently anti-German ... this made a fine story.'[8]

But even though a *major* news source individual would be unlikely to receive this kind of treatment from a specialist there are certain techniques which can be used for managing the critical dilemma:

(1) Criticize the organization rather than the man. One City editor said that because of his friendly personal relations with the current Chancellor of the Exchequer, he directed his regular criticisms mainly at the Treasury rather than its political boss.

(2) The 'moral division of labour' approach. Here the man is criticized, but the story is written by a general reporter.

(3) Division of labour within a team of specialists. Among Lobby correspondents some teams operate in such a way that in practice

one man writes stories critical of Labour and another man writes stories critical of the Conservatives.

(4) Criticism does not always lead to source withdrawal. Some sources persevere and try to persuade the correspondent of the error of his ways.

(5) Specialists with a number of élite sources may find it easy to drop one source and establish relations with another. Criticism is said by some journalists to produce a new friend for each old friend it loses.

(6) Some specialists are less dependent on any individual source, because they choose to compete in originality of comment and criticism rather than in original newsgathering. This is especially possible for a very well-known specialist.

Leo Rosten reports one Washington correspondent in the 1930's as saying: 'Almost every correspondent has special news-sources whose displeasure he consciously or unconsciously fears';[9] but Rosten's study included regional newspaper correspondents. For a national specialist individual sources may be people whom he is very unlikely to want to criticize – for instance the assistant of a 'name' source, elder statesmen, or others who are sources but not performers. There is also a big turnover rate in all fields among leading performers. Division One Football club managers seem to come and go nearly as fast as Cabinet Ministers. Moreover in situations when a specialist experiences pressure to be critical of a source, this is often because the competition also is being critical. He will not then be the only specialist producing critical coverage; with careful wording of the story, or minor qualifications, a particular source may find the story more 'acceptable' than the headline on the story would suggest.

Different specialists have different individual sources; stories which are bad news from a particular source's point of view will be used without much inhibition by at least some specialists. If the story is 'big' enough, the other specialists must also cover the story. Competition, then, is a prime spur to carrying critical stories despite possible source displeasure; and competition, given prevalent definitions of news, is usually competition to be critical or to produce stories which certain sources will see as 'critical'.

5. THE NEWSGATHERING ROLE

Do source–journalist relations involve an exchange of information for publicity? A simple exchange model, especially in the context of national journalism, appears to omit too many variables – such as the audience, critical or 'bad' news values, the strength of non-revenue or 'non-rational' goals, and the importance of the competitor-colleague group of journalists with its own norms of behaviour. Most exchange models suggest structured interaction, balance, careful calculation of interest, the gradual development of norms of exchange behaviour. Such exchange models ignore the instability of news, the loosely structured (or chaotic) character of the social interaction, and especially the lack of time for care, gradualness or full communication about the dispositions of different parties relevant to the rapidly changing 'current' story.

Exchange notions *of a kind* are present in the minds of most newsgathering specialists. But is this saying more than: 'In general, newsgathering journalists in pursuit of information on the whole act in what they believe to be their own self-interest, and they perceive their news sources as similarly motivated in their pursuit of publicity'?

A basic difficulty is that not only organizations but also individuals are involved on both sides. In dealing with news source organizations, journalists (and their employing news organizations) are in some situations involved in a quasi-contractual relationship – for instance in the case of 'embargoed' documents. In contrast the relationship between an individual journalist and an individual news source conforms more closely to friendship or the 'personal' relationship type of exchange. The first, organizational, level is 'above' the level at which the Blau and Homans kind of sociological exchange analysis is most effective; the second, individual, level is 'below' this small group level.*

Did the newsgathering role differ consistently with the goal prevailing in the field? More particularly were non-revenue specialists the most autonomous and the revenue goal specialist the most under control? The major difficulty arises here from the ambiguity of such terms as 'autonomy' and 'control'. This can be illustrated by the sharp differences between the two types of revenue goal. The advertising goal specialists face a source area whose publicity stance is mainly promotional; there is little friction between journalists and sources. In contrast audience goal specialists face sources which have a negative publicity stance – and friction between journalists and sources is highly prevalent. *Advertising* goal specialists (Fashion, Motoring) are the only ones to receive more telephone calls than they make, there is little payment to news sources; public relations material is voluminous; dependence on PR personnel is heavy; press

* An exchange perspective can be applied to almost any interpersonal relationship, but this perspective appears less suitable for analysing differences between one 'exchange' relationship and another.

conferences are fairly frequent. But *audience* goal specialists (Crime, Football) receive an extremely low ratio of calls from sources; payments to news sources are common; public relations material is almost non-existent; these specialists contact PR personnel relatively rarely; press conferences are infrequent. Yet despite these major differences, these two categories of specialists are the two least likely to say that the 'sources help the journalists' more than *vice versa*. The common factor here is presumably the commercial character of news sources in both fields – and the low salience of political and governmental sources.

The non-revenue, the political Lobby, and the other mixed goal specialists – all fields where political and governmental sources are central – are fairly similar in relation to the newsgathering role. In all three cases the news source area is neither heavily negative nor heavily promotional, but rather varied; the ratio of phone calls received to those made is at an intermediate level in all three cases. Payment to news sources is at a low level in all three. The use of sanctions by news sources is – compared with both audience and advertising goal fields – low in all three cases. Public relations activity in both non-revenue Foreign correspondence and the mixed fields appears similar – a medium volume of handouts, medium frequency of press conference, high tendency to go to PR personnel in the first instance. In all three fields the majority see the sources helping the journalists more than *vice versa*. This reflects these journalists' perceptions of their sources' motives as being other than straightforwardly commercial.

Such evidence suggests that rather than an autonomy and control dichotomy we should perhaps be thinking in terms of: What *kinds* of control? Commercial or political? But this also seems too simple a dichotomy. Another complicating point in relation to 'control' (or autonomy) is the difference between organizational and individual news sources. Here there are some major contrasts between goal types; key individual news sources appeared much less salient for Foreign correspondents than for political Lobby correspondents.

A more helpful way of looking comparatively at autonomy and control might be to regard some fields as ones in which autonomy and control is a contested issue in relation to the newsgathering role – but in other fields this issue is not contested. An example of the latter are the advertising goal fields. Here autonomy and control is not a strongly contested issue – because the news sources exercise control in other ways (via the news organization and its definition of the advertising goal itself). By contrast, in the audience goal fields autonomy and control is a salient issue – partly because the major control lies elsewhere, in the strong interest of the audience.

Clearly, there are severe limitations on the autonomy of any journalist in his newsgathering role. Moreover, while at least some sources – like the employing news organization – will be able to exercise some negative control, the autonomy of the specialist is also limited by several factors other than the attitude of his news sources and his employers. One obvious example is the present state of newsgathering technology – which places such stress on telephone, pencil and notebook. This is not an argument for technological determinism; different social systems manage to produce different kinds of journalism – despite similar technology. But the newsgathering technology – within certain broad social values and certain occupational 'news values' – does strongly shape what is *impossible*.

6

Specialist correspondent as competitor-colleague

1. COMPETITOR-COLLEAGUES: COMPETITION

a. Exclusive news: Bismarck and The Times *correspondent*

On February 6th 1852, *The Times* carried a leader referring to 'the earliest and most correct intelligence'. 'Early' referred primarily to publishing information before politicians chose to reveal it. But after the appearance in 1855 of a number of tax free competitors, journalists came to devote equal energy to obtaining intelligence 'early' in the sense of before the competition. Indeed the arguments for the abolition of 'taxes on knowledge' were to a great extent arguments, not merely against the government, but against the artificial semi-monopoly of *The Times*. The debates on this issue, and most subsequent debates on the issue of 'press freedom' in multi-party countries, centred on the issue of *competition*.

Competition between newspapers, of course, existed long before 1855; and even *The Times* at the height of its prestige stressed competition. De Blowitz, in his exclusive at the Berlin Congress of 1878, exhibited a number of aspects of journalistic competition:

(1) *Competition for access* to news sources. De Blowitz successfully outdid his rivals by getting superior access to Bismarck and other prominent figures.

(2) *Competition in speed.* De Blowitz obtained the gist of the preamble to the Treaty at noon on Friday (12th July, 1878). Since *The Times* did not appear on Sunday he had to get it into the Saturday edition. Having anticipated that no German post office would be willing to cable such a document he had prepared a transmission route through Brussels – where he dispatched his assistant (with the Treaty sewn into the lining of his coat).

(3) *News organization's emphasis on exclusive news. The Times* printed a special late Saturday morning edition containing a French text of the Treaty and an English translation.

(4) *Interpersonal competition between journalist 'colleagues'.* 'One

of my fellow-correspondents, the most talkative of them all, asked the reason for my sudden departure. I confided to him that I was enraged – that Prince Bismarck, in spite of the service rendered by me, as he himself had described it, to peace, had just refused to give me the Treaty. . . . My colleague departed to repeat my words, and all my brethren, sharing my indignation, came to condole with me.'[1]

(5) *Emphasis on the exceptional dramatic 'scoop'*. His coverage of the day-to-day background of the Congress was probably more valuable to the readers of *The Times*; but De Blowitz himself in his autobiography stresses the drama, intrigue (and somewhat less the luck) of the Treaty scoop.[2]

These five aspects of competition in journalism have changed only in detail since 1878.

b. Competition, news organization, and audience

The argument against giving so much competitive emphasis to exclusive and late news was made in the 1966 Economist Intelligence Unit report:

'There is a great desire to be exclusive in most editorial departments and many Editors are prepared to go to very considerable lengths to attempt to be exclusive. . . . It is assumed by many editorial executives that late news is vital to the circulation and health of their publication. . . . Even some journalists admit that many of the changes made in the last edition are of a technical nature directed towards their competitors rather than to their own readership. It might be revealing to examine how many newspaper readers know what edition they receive, and what effect, if any, this has on their buying pattern.'[3]

The EIU report noted that the *Evening Standard* in 1966 was printing eight separate editions during a period of nine hours.

But other equally impressionistic evidence can be quoted to support the contention that concentration on late and exclusive news does benefit a news organization. The EIU report fails to grasp the fundamental point that late or exclusive news policy is only one part of the broad multi-goal strategy. In most cases this strategy includes the presentation of some particular kind of image or 'personality' to a certain type of audience, which in turn makes any rules as to the effectiveness of certain kinds of competition unlikely to be of general applicability.

Competition within journalism must be seen in the context of competition between news organization and between media, or multi-media, organizations. It must also be seen in the context not only of competition between news organizations *within* one multi-media organization,* but competition between the news department and other departments leading to a coalition audience goal which all major departments can support.

To ask whether newspaper readers know what edition they receive may be posing the wrong question. The readers may not know what edition it is, but readers in certain outlying regions do tend to prefer editions specially aimed at their region. Scottish readers may well not know which nationals are printed in Scotland; but the *Scottish Daily Express* and the *Daily Record* – both printed in Glasgow and both packed with Scottish news – did dominate the morning paper field in Scotland in the 1960's.

For a social scientist in search of some objective measure of 'competition' it is tempting to use the advertising industry's National Readership Survey (JICNARS) figures for readership duplication. But duplication is only one aspect of competition. For eight out of nine national dailies in 1968 the biggest overlapping readership came from one of three papers – the two biggest 'populars', *Daily Mirror* and *Daily Express*, and the biggest selling 'prestige', *The Daily Telegraph*. But these were not necessarily the newspapers which executives (both editorial and non-editorial) would quote as their leading competitors. Some readers may read a paper at home or work but not regard it as their 'own' paper; moreover in the eyes of media executives not all readers are equal. There is the general preference for young educated affluent readers – for both revenue and non-revenue reasons.

c. Competition as seen by specialists

Specialists on the 'populars' regarded other populars, especially the *Daily Mail*, *Daily Express* and *Daily Mirror*, as the biggest competition. By specialists on the 'quality' news organizations, other 'quality' organizations were regarded as the main competition. But the popular specialists tend to regard the 'quality' specialists as serious competition, whereas the quality specialists are unlikely to regard the popular specialists as serious competition.

The most competitive news organizations, as seen by the selected national specialists overall, were *The Times*, *The Daily Telegraph*,

---

* The weak performance of *The Sun* during the 1960's was partly due to its being discouraged from competing vigorously with the *Daily Mirror*, another IPC owned paper. For instance, in 1968, no less than 48 per cent of *The Sun*'s readers also read the *Daily Mirror* (JICNARS).

Daily Mail and *Daily Express*. In terms of socio-economic status of the readers this centre of competition is somewhat above the middle point. On the other hand if one looks at the *numbers* of specialist journalists themselves this up-market bias largely disappears since quality newspapers have several times more specialists, in relation to their circulation, than do the large circulation newspapers. If the specialists are taken overall *The Times*, *The Daily Telegraph*, *Daily Mail* and *Daily Express* do indeed occupy the middle ground and are thus a 'rational' choice as the major foci for competition.

Other noticeable aspects of competitiveness as seen by specialists include the following:

(1) The audience goal fields (Crime and Football) are seen as competitively dominated by the popular newspapers.

(2) In the advertising goal fields the quality newspapers are again dominant – with the Sunday qualities making an unusually strong showing.

(3) Of the agencies, Reuters makes a strong showing in Foreign correspondence; but despite its dominance here in terms of men and resources it is not regarded as the most competitive organization – many Foreign correspondents regarding it as more help than competition. The domestic Press Association, aimed as it is primarily at the British provincial newspapers, is not regarded as strong competition.

(4) Broadcast news is not regarded, by these mainly newspaper correspondents, as very serious competition; the main exception here is in the Political Lobby – the only specialist field where the numbers of broadcast correspondents are comparable with those of the large newspapers. In all fields the BBC news (with its larger number of specialists and much greater – including radio – number of bulletins) is regarded as stronger competition than ITN.

(5) The London evening newspapers were regarded overall as about equal in competitive seriousness to the broadcast news organizations.

(6) Among the Sunday newspapers the qualities are regarded as much more serious competition than the populars in all but the audience goal fields.

(7) The only news organization regarded almost uniformly as no competition at all is the Communist *Morning Star*. This newspaper has few specialist correspondents. Its best competitive performance is in Labour correspondence; here it is regarded by other

specialists as well-informed on certain kinds of story – such as unofficial strikes.

But the main finding on competitiveness as seen by other specialists is the strength of the quality daily newspapers. This is underlined – in Foreign, Lobby, and the mixed fields – by the strength of the two least central quality dailies, *The Guardian* (seen as seventh, second equal, and second) and *The Financial Times* (seen as third, seventh equal, and seventh).

d. Competition and 'exclusive' stories

Competition is so deeply embedded in the ideology and occupational language of (British) journalism that 'news' comes to be seen as (a) What the competition is saying, and (b) What the competition is not saying, but would if it could. Not only news is defined in terms of competition; specialization also is seen as a means by which a news organization may compete more effectively in a given area. *Autonomy* is granted to a specialist in the interests of competition; and the more effectively a specialist is seen to compete, the more independent he becomes of organizational controls. But *control* of specialists also operates through the mechanism of competition; a specialist can be 'programmed' to compete against a certain news organization; his material is processed in the light of what the competition is saying in its early editions.

The status of a specialist, within his own news organization and in the occupation generally, depends largely upon how other journalists regard his competitive effectiveness. Just as an 'event' once it becomes 'news' is more likely to remain news for some time, so a specialist who has produced what his news organization regards as a major 'exclusive' will be given extra prominence for some while afterwards. Most journalists say that the exclusive story has become a rarity. Leo Rosten said in the 1930's that 'real "scoops" in Washington are uncommon'.[4] It would be surprising if he had said anything else, in view of the definition of 'exclusive' news as being uncommon.

Whereas journalists discuss the unusual occasions when some major (and reliable) story is carried exclusively by one news organization, what they spend much more time and energy on each day is *covering* the main news – which their competitors are likely to have in similar form. Trying to get news that other specialists do not, or will not, have is a largely optional extra. There are usually more opportunities for originality in details than in dramatic unique whole stories. These opportunities include: (a) *'Angles'* or 'lines': this is an original theme with which to link together several pieces of information

TABLE 6.1

COMPETITIVENESS OF NEWS ORGANIZATIONS AS SEEN BY OTHER SPECIALISTS IN SAME FIELD

Mean Score	(Bonn, Rome, Washington, New York) Foreign	(Lobby) Political	(Aviation, Education, Labour) Mixed	(Crime, Football) Audience	(Fashion, Motoring) Advertising	
2·0						FAIRLY SERIOUS COMPETITION
1·9			Times	{ D. Mail, D. Express		
1·8						
1·7		Times	Guardian			
1·6						
1·5		{ Guardian, D. Mail	{ Sun, D. Express	Ev. News	{ Times, Sun. Times	
1·4	Times	D. Telegraph	{ D. Telegraph, D. Mail	{ Sun, D. Mirror		
1·3	D. Telegraph	{ BBC News, D. Express		{ People, News of the World		
1·2	Fin. Times	{ Sun, Fin. Times	Fin. Times	{ Ev. Standard, D. Telegraph	{ D. Telegraph, D. Mail	
1·1	{ Reuters, Sun. Times	ITN News	Sun. Times	Sun. Express	Observer	
1·0	D. Express	Sun. Times	{ Sun. Telegraph, Observer		{ D. Mirror, D. Express	A LITTLE COMPETITION

	Guardian	Ev. Standard	Fin. Times
0·9			
0·8	{ Ev. Standard, D. Mirror }; { Observer, D. Mail, BBC News }	BBC News; { Sun. Mirror, Times, ITN News }	{ D. Sketch, BBC News }; { Sun. Express, Guardian }
0·7	D. Mirror; { Sun. Mirror, Observer }	{ D. Mirror, ITN News }	{ Sun. Mirror, Ev. Standard }
0·6	Sun. Telegraph; { D. Sketch, Sun. Telegraph }	{ Observer, Sun. Times }	{ Sun, D. Sketch }
0·5	{ Ev. Standard, ITN News }; Press Association	{ Ev. News, D. Sketch }; Sun. Telegraph	Ev. News
0·4	Sun. Express; People	{ Morning Star, Sun. Express }; { Guardian, Press Assoc. }	BBC News
0·3	{ Sun, D. Sketch, Ev. News }	{ News of the World, Morning Star }	ITN News
0·2	{ People, Sun. Mirror }	{ Sun. Mirror, Press Assoc. }	News of the World
0·1	News of the World	{ News of the World, People }	Fin. Times; { Press Assoc., Morning Star, People }
0	Morning Star	Morning Star	

NO COMPETITION AT ALL

Note: This table is based on the average of all the other specialists in each individual field using this scoring system: Scoring of Competition: Very serious = 3; Fairly serious = 2; A little = 1; No competition = 0.

each one of which may be available to competitors. (b) *Details:* often one specialist will produce a story which contains one quote, one name, one fact which the competition do not have. (c) *Interpretation:* it is generally agreed in British national journalism that merely reporting bald 'facts' is impossible and/or undesirable. (d) *Speed:* this includes speed in writing the story, or speed in dictating it – perhaps with a shorthand note of the opening few sentences. Speed also includes speed in getting and dispatching one story, so as to be ready for another. Speed can mean getting the story into one edition earlier than the competition. (e) *Breadth of coverage:* in some busy fields, where a news organization may have more than one specialist, there can be a dozen or more possible national stories in a day – of which most organizations will not carry more than, say, three. But *The Daily Telegraph* and news agencies in most fields, and some national newspapers in certain fields, prefer to carry more than the average number of stories. (f) *Chasing up:* another type of competition occurs when a specialist is telephoned at home, after the first editions are available, with the information that a rival is running an 'exclusive' story: 'X is shooting down another aircraft project tonight.' Competition here can include declining to follow the story; one competitive technique is to telephone sources and then dictate a story which denies some points in the competing story: 'Contrary to rumours circulating last night . . .'

In order to obtain specific examples of what they thought of as 'exclusive' stories the specialists were asked a bald question: 'What has been the biggest exclusive story in your field in the last twelve months?'

> *Washington:* The most quoted exclusive was: '*The Financial Times* story that McNamara was leaving the Defense Dept. for the World Bank.'*

> *New York:* There was a wide range – in keeping with the shape of this field – varying from human interest and personalities to financial stories.

> *Bonn and Rome:* Easily the leading subject was the Russian invasion of Czechoslovakia; a variety of different Czech stories were quoted, such as: 'Possibly *Express* time beat on Prague invasion, by having staff reporter present.'

> *Political Lobby:* There were two leading subjects here for exclusive

---

* According to the US journalism trade press *The Financial Times* carried this story 'speculatively' on Monday 27th November, 1967 – before any major American news organization. *Editor and Publisher*, 9th December, 1967.

stories, firstly the devaluation of Sterling in 1967, and secondly the subsequent Cabinet re-shuffle: 'Possibly the *Daily Mail* story the day before devaluation.' 'Perhaps Callaghan's resignation from Chancellorship, but dividing line between speculation and fact on this was rather thin.'

Labour: One story here was widely quoted: 'News that Mrs Barbara Castle, then Transport Minister, intended to replace Sir Stanley Raymond as Chairman of British Rail.'

Education: Here there were two most quoted stories: '*Sunday Times* leak on the Public Schools Commission final report.' 'Forecast of postponement in raising school leaving age to 16.'

Aviation: No single exclusive story was chosen as the major one of the year; individual specialists quoted a wide range of stories mostly concerned with cancellation of aircraft projects, or purchase (e.g. of the American F111 swing-wing plane) or delays (e.g. in Concorde's first flight).

Crime: There was no single widely quoted choice but the leader seemed to be: 'Arrests of the Kray brothers gang.'

Football: The leading exclusive was: 'Dave Sexton taking over as new manager of Chelsea which *Daily Express* predicted.'

Motoring and Fashion: Most correspondents agreed that exclusives were either virtually unknown or rather trivial. One Motoring correspondent replied: 'On the Continent there are many "exclusive" stories written due to embargo-breaking. On the whole here we do not break an embargo.'

Many specialists denied the concept of 'exclusive' stories:

'Most of them are wrong anyway. And printed in the knowledge that they are wrong. I could argue you a thesis that the wronger the journalist, the safer his job: "Our scoop – right or wrong!" '

'In political journalism there is plenty of exclusive surmise, but exclusive hard news stories are rare.'

'Exclusive to me is a dirty word. It means absolutely nothing to the reader whether you have the story on your own or share it with 10 others. The trouble with Fleet Street is that you are too often judged on what your rivals have done and not on what you have done yourself. Exclusive stories are always 90% luck.'

These remarks cannot all be dismissed as sour grapes, since some specialists quoted by their competitor-colleagues as having produced recent exclusives nevertheless make such derogatory comments. Another ambivalent aspect is that those quoted as having produced exclusives invariably themselves also quote their own specific story, whereas others make such remarks as:

> 'I can't remember these things unless they involve me! I don't think they did this year.'

Most quoted cases were big news events in the relevant fields – the departure of the American Secretary of Defense, devaluation, a change of Chancellor, the sacking of the chief executive of British Rail. The last was the story which received the strongest vote as major exclusive story in any single field. Such a story is sudden, obviously 'big', relatively unambiguous, culturally proximate (many newspapers are read on British Rail trains), somewhat unexpected, but meaningful; such a sacking is highly negative and stresses personality and conflict ('Barbara Castle sacks Raymond').

Some stories have been hinted at previously; it has been said that a 'decision will be announced soon', and hence there is dispute as to when the story did first appear – and consequently which story, if any, was 'exclusive' news rather than 'surmise'. Hence the exclusivity of a 'genuine exclusive' resides partly in the way the story is presented:

(a) Frequency. The announcement is sudden.

(b) Lack of ambiguity. The *sacking* aspect is emphasized, whereas if the story had emerged more slowly, other complexities and ambiguities might have emerged also.

(c) Unexpectedness is deliberately heightened.

The news organization or the specialists, or both, may manipulate these aspects. Some morning newspapers deliberately hold back exclusive stories from the first one or two editions – which makes it more difficult for the competition to check the story for inclusion in their later editions. The news organization also tends to give much bigger emphasis to stories it expects to be exclusive.

Such projection of an 'exclusive' story by the news organization has obvious implications for the status of the individual specialist. Several men who had produced exclusives which were still being talked about in the field months or even years afterwards, said that this particular 'famous' exclusive had been much easier to obtain than other less-remembered stories. But they are still aware that in the largely oral memory of the occupation, the occasional 'major' exclusive stands out.

In some teams the senior specialist concentrates on trying to get such major exclusives, while the rest of the team cover the rest of the news. Such concentration upon exclusive stories carries further status implications; the senior specialist is defined as superior to ordinary stories, and may work for several days without producing anything usable. When such a trusted specialist does produce an exclusive the news organization will tend to give the story prominent coverage.

A specialist who predicts in a splash story that some prominent individual will shortly be sacked is sticking his neck out in front of a very large audience. Successful risk-taking underlines for all to see that the correspondent in question really is well informed. But the risk is likely to increase with the exclusivity. To be exclusive the story must be 'early' – before other journalists announce the event, and before the news sources announce it. 'Early intelligence' also carries the traditional implication that the public is to some extent let in on decisions as they are being taken; this is flattering to the public and may indeed lead to 'public opinion' of some kind or other having some influence. But 'early' intelligence may be so early that the decision does not go in the predicted direction; or the 'public opinion impact' may be taken into account. The exclusive prediction that X is going to be sacked by Y may turn out to be false – if Y changes his mind.

A journalist may sit at his typewriter weighing the trustworthiness of a source, trying to decide whether to take the risk of producing an exclusive story. Often there is a period of waiting – of hours or days – after the story has appeared and before the predicted event has yet had a chance to happen. Occupational mythology records the case of a Foreign correspondent who gets a cable from his Foreign desk: 'Your exclusive still exclusive.' A specialist who has produced an 'exclusive' story about which he is somewhat anxious may 'give' it to his competitor-colleagues after the first edition deadlines – in the hope that they will use it also, and leave him in a less exposed position.

There is wide recognition within the occupation that to produce an important exclusive requires not merely luck and successful access to sources, but also judgement and courage. The personal experiences of individual journalists, the ideology of the occupation, and its tendency to see the world in terms of individuals, all help to focus attention upon those few correspondents who have a reputation for producing exclusive stories.

e. Competition and uncertainty

Some pieces of information could either make the splash story or rate one paragraph on page 17. Suppose an Aviation specialist is told by a 'usually reliable source' that political pressure is developing to cancel a particular aircraft project; this could be a 'big story' – strong in news value, money wasted, blame, political repercussions, unemployment. But there may already have been a number of stories in the press about possible cancellation. What one specialist may regard as one more rumour along the same lines as the previous rumours, another specialist may regard as a major exclusive.

Who decides whether a story is big or little, and whether an exclusive is really an exclusive? Some political Lobby correspondents discuss with the chief processor or the Editor what 'weight' should be attached to a story. If it is agreed that a political story is 'big' it will normally be made the lead story; but in some of the lower status fields this will depend on the supply of stories on the day from other fields. In such fields the processors themselves must decide what weight to give a story. How do they tell whether an exclusive-looking story in Education is important or not? The obvious place to look for guidance is in the output of the competition. If the competitors have some of the story but not so much as 'our Education correspondent' then he may seem entitled to prominent display for a story which appears partly exclusive and fairly important. But what if the competition does not have the story at all? The processors must decide whether the Education correspondent has an important completely exclusive story or something that is relatively worthless.

The circular definition of 'news' – news is what the competition says is news – means, according to some specialists, that it is possible to have a story which is so exclusive that processors play it down and the competition do not follow it up; but the same story may be repeated a week later by another correspondent and be eagerly followed up by the competition. The original correspondent now experiences pressure from his own processors to follow up a competing 'exclusive', which he is quite certain he produced a week earlier and which the processors ignored. There will usually be room for differences of opinion as to which story was really 'exclusive', which was 'speculative', which 'hard', and so on.

But it is widely agreed that the hallmark of a really indisputable 'exclusive' is being followed up by the competition. Competition for exclusives thus becomes competition to get something the competitors will acknowledge as an exclusive through following it up. Some specialists deliberately hold back 'exclusive' information and only use it when they think the competition will feel compelled to follow.

One specialist said that when he was a novice in the field with no reputation, if he had produced an exclusive story that the Minister in the relevant field was about to resign, his news organization would have been very cautious about using it at all. Now, however, that the specialist had an established status the reaction would be quite different: 'Oh good, we'll keep the splash for you.' If the correspondent has a high status in his field it will also be more difficult for his competitors not to follow his story, at least in part; their processors will alert them to the exclusive-looking story by the usually reliable correspondent on the *Daily X*, and some of these competing specialists may at least run stories which say 'Rumours to the effect that . . . were denied last night. . . .' A spate of these stories may lead to the Minister in question making a statement, and even if the resignation does not occur it may still look – for instance to competing processors – that there 'was something' in the original 'exclusive' story.

According to some specialists there is an element of poker playing involved; such specialists are reluctant to follow up other correspondents' stories: 'You must retain the psychological initiative.' Other specialists – less confident of their status – if they find themselves alone on a story with no competing specialists in sight, immediately assume that there must be some more important story happening elsewhere and that they themselves 'are on the wrong story'. Both reactions to being alone on a story, although very different in terms of status implications and self confidence, involve two common assumptions about news values and competition, namely:

(1) Uncertainty is always present.

(2) News values are defined, in part, by the interpersonal behaviour of competitor-colleagues who are competing with each other on a day-to-day basis.

Given these two factors it is not hard to predict that competition will be modified by co-operative activities. It is difficult to think of any sociological study of an occupation, profession, or industry which does not reveal ways in which members of an occupation seek to manage uncertainty, and to reduce what they may regard as 'unreasonable' levels of competition; employees typically seek to wrest some measure of control over occupational uncertainties away from ultimate employers or customers and into the hands of co-workers who are involved together in frequent social interaction within a particular line of work activity.

2. COMPETITOR-COLLEAGUES: GROUP EXCHANGE

a. *Exchange and competitor-colleagues*

Warren Breed was of the opinion that on a complex 'beat' with numerous sources there would be 'pooling' of information between competing journalists:

> 'Reporters are freed from many overlapping contacts by foot, phone and in person; they are protected against scoops by rivals; and the concomitant anxiety of punishment; and they get more raw news-material. Sources are subject to less interviewing. Such is the justification of the pool.'[5]

Two accounts of political journalism in the late Victorian period illustrate two very different sorts of co-operation. The first account is of the standard practice for taking a shorthand note of a big political speech in the country:

> 'About eight reporters are, as a rule, "in the ring"; and working in alphabetical order, hand over hand, note-taking for two minutes, and, transcribing on flimsy, they manage to keep written up to the speaker.... If you do not take a good note, and falter in transcription; if you fail to take up your next turn at the moment the chief, watch in hand, gives you the hint, the note-taking arrangement is thrown out of gear, and all around the ring there is either muttered thunder or icy reticence. But with skilful reporters – and the men allowed "in the ring" are generally known to be thoroughly up to their work – the task of reporting a great political meeting is a comparatively light one.'[6]

In this example eight reporters from competing papers co-operate in a manner somewhat similar to a team of Debate reporters at Westminster all working for one organization.

A quite different sort of co-operation was a partnership between two competing Lobby correspondents in the 1890's; this operated not on an *ad hoc*, but on a more regular, basis:

> 'One field of enterprise that was exploited successfully in my time by a few was the obtaining of early information of the proceedings and the reports of Select Committees and Royal Commissions, which were numerous at this period. W. E. Pitt, of *The Times*, an old Press Association colleague of mine, made a great speciality of such things, and I frequently worked with him in securing early information of the reports of these bodies before they were issued officially. In addition to the claims of my own paper, I was a

regular contributor in my spare time to several other journals of such news, and where my interests and those of *The Times* did not clash, Pitt and I exchanged the results of our efforts. As my interests, apart from the *Pall Mall Gazette*, were distributed among provincial newspapers, Pitt's achievements stood out more prominently. . . .'[7]

Co-operative activities of both a collective *ad hoc* kind, and a regular partnership character, were found by Rosten in Washington:

'Contact between correspondents is continuous, professional morale is high, co-operation is widespread. Information is shared, advice is given freely, the fruits of individual labor pooled. The National Press Club serves primarily as a clearing house for the exchange of facts, tips, leads and gossip. After a press conference, for instance, correspondents compare notes, consult colleagues on the "angle" to be followed in interpretation, and seek the opinion of reporters more expert in certain fields of news.

'The advantages of co-operation are obvious. (1) Through a division of labour with friends, one correspondent is "covered" on events which he could not possibly report in person. . . . (2) Co-operation entails a sharing of expert knowledge. . . . (3) In the same way, familiarity with regional situations is put to co-operative uses.

'Co-operation reaches its most explicit form in the "Blacksheet". The Blacksheet is a carbon copy of a news-dispatch, which one newspaperman gives to another. The correspondent receiving a Blacksheet from a colleague is free to use it as he sees fit. . . . The stories on Herbert Hoover's acceptance of the Republican Presidential nomination, which appeared in the Baltimore *Evening Sun* and the New York *Herald Tribune* in August 1932, were practically identical and betrayed the undiscriminating use of the Blacksheet.'[8]

In these quotations about late Victorian Britain and 1930's Washington there are indications of several occupational norms:

(1) On a fairly casual basis ('advice is freely given') or in a routine situation (such as taking down a speech or a press conference) most journalists will help most others.

(2) In more intimate forms of co-operation personal friendship ('an old Press Association colleague') and equality are stressed.

(3) This intimate or partnership co-operation is most respectable if it takes place between journalists who are not very direct com-

petitors. Higginbottom, working for the evening *Pall Mall Gazette*, was not in direct competition with *The Times*; Rosten quoted a New York *morning* and a Baltimore *evening* co-operating – and he calls 'undiscriminating' the identical use of a carbon, not the co-operation itself.

(4) Journalists think co-operation should be carried on in a fairly secretive manner – some disapproval by outsiders is to be expected.

In sociology, following the lead of several founding fathers – such as Simmel, Mauss, and Malinowski[9] – there has developed a substantial body of theoretical work, which uses 'Exchange' as a central concept. The relevance of the exchange perspective to newsgatherer/news source relations was discussed in the previous chapter. But it seemed likely that relations between journalists *within* specialist groups would be the area where, for instance, Peter Blau's *Exchange and Power in Social Life* would be most applicable.

However, theoretical formulations on exchange almost invariably make assumptions which are not valid for groups of competitor-colleague correspondents. Homans, for instance, assumes that the 'investment' of chronological age will have some kind of standardised value.[10] This assumption is not valid in journalism where lack of a career structure and occupational ideology ('it's a young man's trade') make age a rather ambiguous variable; this is especially so of specialist journalists – few of whom are below the age of 30.

Peter Blau's 'mutual consultation' type of exchange is relevant to the sort of situation Blau has himself analysed – officials working from an office of a government agency and applying codified regulations to specific 'cases' in the local economy.[11] Within such a government agency there is one body of relevant principles upon whose application the officials can consult with each other; there is also one official hierarchy and – in a fairly small office – one main pattern of status. Neither of these conditions obtains within a group of specialist journalists. There is no single body of knowledge even within one news organization, much less so between say *The Financial Times* and the *News of the World*; nor is there any recognised hierarchy within the group of competitor-colleagues.

Analyses of power and influence based on a marginal utility approach to exchange make assumptions which are not justified in the case of a group of specialist journalists. Terms such as 'power' and 'coercive' are not appropriate for the internal structure of a group of correspondents. Much or most of the power and 'coercive means' relevant to such groups are located outside them – in the hands of news sources, news organization executives, the occupation of journalism at large, and ultimately the audience. The assumption that a power-holder will dispose of 'commodities' which the 'other participants cannot do without' and which they 'cannot replace' by 'other commodities'[12] does not obtain. The crucial commodity is information – and another journalist is unlikely to have an extensive monopoly of information; moreover even when a journalist does possess 'exclusive' information its value varies according to the news organization which employs the specialist; if, for instance, his news organization does not value 'exclusive' information highly, or is satisfied with 'comment' type pieces, then its correspondent will quite easily be able 'to do without' any commodities that any other specialist may happen to possess.

Warren Hagstrom applies exchange notions to the case of academic scientists; these scientists 'give' their research findings to scientific journals in return for recognition from their scientific colleagues.[13] Here again the situation differs from that of specialist journalists. Journalists sell their contributions in return for money – which constitutes one among several sorts of highly regarded reward within journalism.

The economic concept of marginal utility has only limited applicability to the situation of specialist journalists. The assumption of perfect knowledge of the alternative choices is more than usually false because of such occupational norms as the confidentiality of news sources; rigidly fixed deadlines defeat any chance of careful weighing of the choices.

Laboratory groups of psychology students, members of a single department in a work organization, gangs, juries, committees – all such groups have clear boundaries. But among competitor-colleague groups of correspondents one of the contentious issues is where the boundaries of the group lie; there are usually marginal categories of members such as part-time specialists and those working for organizations other than *national* newspapers, radio/TV and agencies. Nevertheless these specialists spontaneously refer to specialists working for competing organizations as 'colleagues'; most specialists probably spend several hours a week in very close physical proximity to each other. Moreover the 'group behaviour' continues even when they are not physically together – they talk regularly on the phone for instance, and even when not so communicating are anticipating, and reacting to, each other's behaviour.

Leaving aside the question of how representative is the sharply boundaried group, one can list certain aspects of these groups which set them apart from many of the studies of groups and exchange. Firstly an individual only becomes a member of such a group by being a paid employee of a news organization which is in commercial competition with news organizations employing the other group members. Secondly there is some diffuse exchange of such intangibles as esteem and of minor acts of colleaguely help. But the most important type of exchange is a very specific exchange of certain sorts of highly perishable information related to particular events 'in the news today'. Thirdly from the point of view of power and leadership a competitor-colleague group is unstructured and segmented into internally competing sub-groups (e.g. daily, evening, Sunday newspapers). Consequently there is no single group structure or group leadership. Power and leadership within the group appear primarily within 'teams' – number one, two and three correspondents working for a single news organization. Another way of looking at such groups is that the characteristic 'bulge in the middle' of national news organizations is exaggerated further within specialist groups because neither the top dogs (executives) nor the bottom dogs (junior reporters or sub-editors) are represented.

b. *Group associations*

British specialist journalists, like those in other countries, form their own group associations. Probably the earliest of these was the Westminster Press Gallery which started in 1881. Their constitutions vary considerably in detail, but most correspondents' associations cover a roughly similar set of activities:

(a) A mailing list of members is sent to source organizations.

(b) Meetings of a 'social' nature in which prominent individual sources are invited for drinks or a meal and sometimes to speak.

(c) More serious meetings are also arranged with prominent sources – such as a monthly off-the-record session with a relevant Cabinet Minister.

(d) The making of collective representations on specific issues – which can vary from a complaint about correspondents being made to stand outside in the rain, to a long-standing grudge about the way a certain source organization releases documents.

(e) The handling of complaints from sources to the effect, for instance, that a specific correspondent has broken an embargo. In some such cases a correspondent is 'expelled' from the association.

In *Foreign Correspondence* in none of the four selected centres was there a British correspondents' association. A British group within the Overseas Press Club of New York broke up in 1944 over accusations of one correspondent reporting an off-the-record briefing given by Wendell Willkie.

The Political *Lobby* is in sharp contrast to all other specialist fields in that in practice membership of the association is compulsory. The Lobby association is a sub-division of the more inclusive Press Gallery. Apart from forcing him to be a member, the Lobby association does not have any other special powers over the individual correspondent. The Lobby Committee, however, is rather more powerful than other such committees in relation to sources; this Committee decides whether or not to issue invitations for *ad hoc* briefings from specific Ministers. The Lobby Committee also, of course, has consultations with the PROs of the Prime Minister and Leader of the Opposition on arrangements for regular off-the-record briefings. The Lobby includes the provincial Lobby correspondents and has just over 100 members.

The *Labour* correspondents make up one segment of the Labour and Industrial Correspondents Group (founded 1937). This is another large association, because some news organizations each have several members; it includes Labour and Industrial specialists who work for large provincial news organizations out of their London office. The *Education* Correspondents' Group (founded 1962) is one of several associations which have modelled themselves on the Labour and Industrial Group. The *Aviation* correspondents during the late 1960's had no such organization. A previous one had been disbanded. Some of the functions of a Secretary or Chairman were performed by the current 'doyen'.

The *Crime* Reporters Association (founded 1945) is another one with an internal division – between the Crime news correspondents and the men who report at the Law Courts. An unusual objective of this medium-sized association is to arrange a system of code numbers which a Crime correspondent must quote on the telephone when speaking to Police sources – to prevent impersonation by criminals. The *Football* Writers Association is large, about 200 specialists, including provincial Football correspondents. This association pre-dates an umbrella organization, the Sports Writers Association.

The Guild of *Motoring* Writers is large, including provincial and magazine journalists and some people who are not full-time journalists. One unusual aspect is that two years of 'experience' are required before a Motoring specialist is eligible for membership; another unusual aspect was that in 1968 only about half of the most prominent correspondents on the national news organizations were members.

Other journalists – for instance feature writers – are inclined to accuse specialists' associations of being restrictive and collusive; some specialists in the relevant fields similarly criticize the group associations. Words like 'brainwashing' and 'conspiracy' were heard. Yet these *tend* to be self-disproving prophecies. Unlike the Japanese clubs[14] most British specialist associations do not attempt to operate an exclusive association, nor to use sanctions against those correspondents who prefer not to join. In most fields there are some prominent correspondents who choose not to belong and claim that they do not suffer from this; when a correspondent resigns, or is asked to resign, from membership over an embargo-breaking dispute, care appears to be taken to avoid victimising the man. A few national Editors are vigorously opposed to specialist associations, and it is accepted that correspondents from these news organizations may feel unable to join. Again the occupational ideology which sees journalism as an 'open' occupation tends to support the norm that a specialist should not suffer from non-membership. Consequently the mailing list of current correspondents in the field which is sent to news sources includes in some cases the names of prominent non-members; the latter may also attend meetings with sources arranged by the association. It is perhaps because the Political Lobby is the one specialist field in which membership is compulsory that the activities of the Lobby are especially subject to criticism from other journalists. (The key factors here, however, relate to the rules of the British political system rather than to the rules of the Lobby correspondents' association.)

The correspondents' associations are also subject to much internal conflict. The *exclusive* arguments are that more intimate dealings with sources are possible if numbers are kept down and only full-time experienced specialists are present. But as fields expand, arguments for inclusive definitions strengthen; argument centres upon whether any single news organizations may have one, two, three or more members; there is the related question of full and 'associate' membership. In some associations there are anomalies and bendings of the rules – to allow conscientious office holders to remain for lengthy periods. The associations lack not only strong sanctions, but also the most rudimentary organizational resources; they typically have no office, few records, and no secretarial assistance.

The association's strategy often is to ally itself to the status-enhancing or empire-building intentions of a source individual or organization. For instance, the development of the Education Correspondents' Group was strongly encouraged by successive Ministers of Education (both Conservative and Labour) and a Ministry PRO. Similarly the Labour and Industrial Correspondents increased their status and empire by successfully laying claim to cover new post-1964 economic planning activities in Whitehall; they were assisted in this by prominent source individuals and PROs at, for instance, the Department of Economic Affairs and the Prices and Incomes Board.* Such alliances may lead to charges of conspiracy or collusion with news sources; but the familiar dilemma for both news sources and specialists remains that consolidation of a subject area by a specialist group requires plentiful supplies of *bad* news.

The leading characteristic of the correspondents' associations is their weakness. There is little evidence that the great majority of their 'activities' would not happen anyway. Although Aviation was a field lacking such an association more than one national Editor, when discussing his disquiet over collective activities, included Aviation in his list.

c. General information exchange

79 per cent of specialists agree with this statement: 'The proprietors co-operate in various ways as well as competing in other ways. It's inevitable that specialist journalists also both co-operate and compete' (Table 6.2). Mutual assistance between news organizations is common. It is usual in cases of difficult telephone communication from abroad for competing news organizations to co-operate. During the Russian occupation of Czechoslovakia in 1968 Foreign correspondents' stories went by various zig-zag telephone routes through Eastern and Central Europe and often ended up in the wrong Fleet Street office; the same thing happens in the telephoning of Football stories from, for instance, Spain; news organizations pass such stories straight back to their competitors. Television camera or sound men from competing organizations will also help each other – for instance if a piece of equipment breaks down.

On the issue of 'consultation' specialist opinion was more evenly divided between those who agreed and disagreed with this statement: 'Consultation between competing specialists is merely anticipating in part what happens anyway when the competing first editions become available.' The 45 per cent who agreed made some qualifications:

'The implication that co-operation is somehow *sinful* is one to which I cannot subscribe.' (Washington)

'I would co-operate on (say) an out of town murder, but I would never dream of phoning up an opposite number and comparing notes about any kind of story from the office.' (Crime)

* An earlier example of this phenomenon was the active support of Ernest Bevin, as Minister of Labour, 1940–45.

TABLE 6.2

ATTITUDES TO SPECIALIST CO-OPERATION

		Foreign	Political	Mixed	Audience	Advertising	All
		%	%	%	%	%	%
(a) 'The proprietors co-operate and compete. It's inevitable that specialist journalists also both co-operate and compete'*	AGREE	80	82	71	91	69	79
	DON'T KNOW	8	3	0	6	8	5
	DISAGREE	12	15	29	3	23	16
(b) 'Consultation between competing specialists merely anticipates what happens when the competing first editions are available'*	AGREE	40	46	46	55	42	45
	DON'T KNOW	16	0	5	0	17	8
	DISAGREE	44	54	49	45	42	47

N=(a) 191; (b) 172.

*Abbreviated. Full wording appears on previous page.

TABLE 6.3

GENERAL EXCHANGE BEHAVIOUR

		Foreign	Political	Mixed	Audience	Advertising	All
		%	%	%	%	%	%
(a) 'On most days I will tell any specialist who asks what story or stories I am working on'	YES	16	21	14	6	0	13
	DON'T KNOW IT DEPENDS	50	39	45	49	35	45
	NO	34	39	40	46	65	43
(b) 'I will hand on any piece of information which the other specialists are bound to get before the deadline anyway'	YES	26	59	49	47	27	42
	DON'T KNOW IT DEPENDS	40	16	31	24	38	30
	NO	34	24	20	29	35	28

N = (a) 191; (b) 192.

'This is true but not very significant. One does not co-operate for this reason and a first edition exclusive is still a good thing.' (Education)

'You can swop ideas without giving anything away.' (Labour)

General co-operation is usual when an important meeting breaks up and source individuals exit from several different doors; Labour correspondents, for instance, have a common interest in pooling the comments of several different trade union and management negotiators, rather than clinging exclusively to part of the story and missing the rest. The tendency for physical proximity to produce collective 'consultation' seems to be widely acknowledged. But, of course, people do not get physically into the same place on a purely random basis. Specialists also said that when in possession of interesting pieces of information they tried to avoid meeting their opposite numbers.

Table 6.3 shows that 43 per cent of all specialists will not tell any specialist what story they are working on; but only 28 per cent will definitely *not* hand on information which other specialists will get before the next deadline. The strongest evidence of widespread co-operative behaviour is that 42 per cent of specialists say 'Yes' to handing on information which others specialists will get before the next deadline:

(a) (On most days I will tell . . .) 'Only tell if we're both on same job. Someone might say – no story here – and I could agree or disagree.'

(b) (I will hand on any piece of information . . .) 'Only if I know we're both working on the same story. Would not go out of my way to pass on information.' (Motoring)

(a) No. (b) D.K., depends. 'On a big story I'd rather die first than pass it on. I might share something smaller if the other specialist is struggling and I like him.' (Football)

(a) D.K., depends. (b) Yes. 'Journalists only ask when they expect other journalists to be friendly. You don't help people you don't respect.' (Education)

(a) D.K., depends. (b) Yes. 'It depends on chance, i.e. if you happen to meet them or talk to them on the phone.' (Labour)

(a) D.K., depends. (b) Yes. 'The Lobby practice is: if a story is common knowledge everyone helps each other, but if you get a little exclusive you go off on your own and do it.' (Political Lobby)

(a) Yes. (b) Yes. 'Mutual assistance may fill possible gaps for me. I'd be a fool not to offer a cheap premium for a useful insurance.' (New York)

(a) and (b) D.K., depends. 'Very little day to day exchange of information. More on out of town assignments, especially when circumstances difficult (riots, revolts).' (Washington)

d. Group norms and structure

Despite some differences between fields, certain sorts of statements recur frequently. One can begin with the most general and move to the slightly more specific:

Norm One: A competitor-colleague is a 'colleague'. Specialists refer spontaneously to competitors as 'colleagues'.

Norm Two. Those who are unusually vulnerable should be helped. The most obvious example is the case of the newcomer to the field. There is a reluctance to see a competitor-colleague perform so badly that he is in danger of losing his job.

Norm Three: Routine information should be shared, but not potential exclusives. This is one of the most quoted norms and probably the one which allows of the widest range of interpretation.

Norm Four: There should be an element of reciprocity even in general exchange. In most groups probably *about half* of the national specialists engage in a good deal of general exchange activity – or present themselves to others as 'extrovert', 'friendly', 'not secretive', or generally willing to gossip about the day's current stories. Among the other half of the group there will be somewhat less general exchange and hence less reciprocity. The term 'lone-wolf' is used by some specialists about themselves.

Norm Five: All specialists of one frequency collectively help all specialists of another frequency. In some circumstances all Sunday journalists are prepared to give things to all non-Sunday specialists and *vice versa*; evenings to mornings and *vice versa*; similarly with agency journalists and all others, and radio/TV journalists and all others. In each case the specialists under the greatest time pressure can rely on small acts of assistance from those specialists whose frequency gives them more latitude.

Norm Six: First edition exclusives are 'given' to the competition for the second edition.

'You know whom you can trust, and if you can help a chap by telling him what's in your first edition, you may save him time and trouble – if only by giving him time to think up some reason for disparaging it to his own news-desk.'

The specialist who has an exclusive story or detail in his first edition makes a favourable impression with his news organization and impresses his competitor-colleagues (at least if they feel compelled to follow him). Having improved his status as an effective competitor, he is now able also to behave as a good colleague by warning his competitor-colleagues – so that they hear of the story before their own news-desk phones them:

'I want to beat my opposite number but not kill him off altogether.'

One specialist was said to behave 'apologetically' to competitors after achieving an exclusive story.

So much for the six norms. But what about the social structure of the competitor-colleague group? Specialists were asked: 'In your own field do you think there are one or two outstanding individual journalists or does it vary according to type of editorial organization and story?' A substantial number of journalists said there were certain outstanding individuals; but nearly as many said that being 'outstanding' depended upon what type of organization a man worked for – or that some were especially good on certain types of stories. Some of the 'outstanding' specialists were not in the field at all by the definition of this study. Individual specialists who become unusually senior, prominent, or highly paid may move into a half-in, half-out, position – as a columnist, as the number one man of a somewhat wider area – or they may be allowed to do an unusually large amount of freelancing; in some cases senior correspondents move into semi-retirement but re-emerge for important stories. This all makes for a relatively leaderless group of specialists. In this rather structureless group, any man who stays fully in the group is only equal to the others – promotion leads out and away.

These groups lack not only clearly defined leadership, they also usually lack clearly defined 'isolates'. The most respected members of the group are often the least gregarious – 'You won't see X for days on end, and then he pops up with a scoop.'

The most lengthy discussion between competitor-colleagues on a general exchange basis takes place when there is least to discuss – for instance morning paper journalists over a mid-day drink when they know the main 'event' of the day is several hours away. On a seemingly empty day a specialist who cannot think of anything else to do will phone up a number of competitor-colleagues, partly to check that they are in their offices (and hence his is not missing some news event elsewhere) and partly as a standard journalist's reaction – if in doubt, make some phone calls.

But specialists also exchange comments on the ' "angle" to be followed in interpretation' – in Leo Rosten's phrase about Washington correspondents. A press conference often jumps from one topic to another – leaving several possibilities for the story; specialists may say 'it's the £50 million', or 'it's the computer point', or 'nothing new there'. Some specialists may say that they are definitely doing a particular story. It is usually obvious from the questioning in a press conference which aspects some specialists believe the best line to be. If one specialist has a private conversation with a leading source, this is less likely to lead to information being exchanged. But in a situation weak in news value, the specialists have a greater collective interest in working together against the danger that this will be a day when they all fail to produce any stories at all.

The greatest significance of colleague exchange lies not in the information exchange on particular days, but in the on-going 'group culture' which develops over time through such exchanges. In an occupation which has weakly developed search procedures, one common type of search is search into the memories of competitor-colleagues. Although little reference is made to books, this does not necessarily mean that the specialists with the longest experience perform as walking encyclopaedias for all group members. The 'group memory' is probably most important over a time span somewhat longer than 'what happened at last year's meeting (conference, debate, negotiations)', as represented in 12 months' old press cuttings; the period might be perhaps two to five years into the past. This is a length of time covered by the specialist experience of many or most specialists.

3. Partnership exchange

a. Exchange 'partnerships'

'Younger correspondents are more likely to exchange Blacksheets with correspondents not much older. Correspondents working for arch-Republican or arch-Democratic papers, or themselves allied emotionally with either party, will tend to find in each other's Blacksheets a gratifying coincidence of attitude. Members of the Gridiron Club tend to exchange Blacksheets with others who sport the insignia of the order.'

Leo Rosten, *The Washington Correspondents* (1937)

In the present study one main hypothesis was laid down on the question of partnership co-operation: That *partnerships would involve directly competing specialists*. From this main hypothesis others followed:

(1) Co-operating specialists would work for news organizations of similar frequency. In particular popular morning paper specialists would co-operate with competing popular morning paper specialists.

(2) Number ones would co-operate with number ones, number twos with number twos, etc.

(3) Co-operation would be greatest where competition was thought to be greatest.

(4) The stronger the pressure from the news organization towards competition and 'scoops', the more likely would specialists be to react by safeguarding their autonomy and co-operating with the opposition.

Table 6 4 shows that 50 per cent of all specialists were aware of competing *against* such a partnership and 23 per cent said they belonged to such a partnership. Among Foreign and advertising goal specialists partnerships were less common; but among political, mixed and audience goal specialists 70 per cent were aware of competing against partnerships, and 30 per cent said they belonged to partnerships.

Among the non-partners those who were vigorously opposed to such partnerships were outnumbered roughly two to one by those who adopted a neutral or calculative attitude; this latter category, who claimed not to be co-operating partners but did not disapprove of such co-operation, expressed a variety of attitudes. Obviously these overlapped, but main types of attitude included:

(1) *Specialist engages in loose or* ad hoc *co-operation* with one or two specialists but claims this is not a regular 'partnership':

(a) (Compete against?) 'Tendency of foreign correspondents to team up, especially in national groups.'

(b) (Belong partnership) 'No. Not specifically. On occasions with a colleague from a non-competing newspaper or one in same organization.'

(b) 'No. But I sometimes work with another Lobby man (not always the same one) on a story.'

(b) 'No. I co-operate informally with one paper in particular, on run-of-the-mill stories, but will not commit myself to a firm partnership including exclusive stories.'

(a) 'Yes, there is nothing fixed – but we do tend these days to hunt in pairs.'

TABLE 6.4

SPECIALIST PARTNERSHIP: COMPETING AGAINST AND BELONGING TO

		Foreign	Political	Mixed	Audience	Advertising	All
		Bonn, Rome, New York, Washington	Lobby	Labour Education Aviation	Crime Football	Motoring Fashion	Selected correspondents (N = 192)
		%	%	%	%	%	%
(a) 'Are you aware of competing against two or more specialists who co-operate in a partnership?'	YES	14	74	67	71	27	50
(b) 'Do you belong to such a partnership?'	YES	14	39	22	29	12	23

(2) *Specialist doesn't belong to a partnership because his new organization is unsuitable.* This reply usually comes from a news agency or broadcast specialist who says he lacks direct competition and has deadlines so frequent that no press specialist would want to share stories with him:

(b) 'No. I find most newspaper correspondents unwilling to share significant information with agencies/radio/TV which would make it available to their competitors.'

(b) 'No. Because the BBC with hourly deadlines is too much of a competitor. It would be unfair of me to take this advantage.'

(b) 'TV hasn't really enough to give to make it worth while – although there are some permanent relationships.'

(b) 'No. The press seldom work in partnership with an agency man because agency stories are circulated on a nationwide basis.'

(b) 'No. On a Sunday paper you are not involved in stories where correspondents find themselves together or "hunting in packs".'

(3) *Other reasons for non-partnership which make the assumption of equality between partners.* Some specialists indicate that they have not established partnerships because a suitably equal opposite number is not available:

(b) 'No: working alone frees me from obligation to, in many cases, slower moving reporters.'

(b) 'In general I feel I would have more to give than to take and therefore it's not worth my while.'

(b) 'No. It is more to my advantage to work alone because my field of contacts is probably wider than that of any competitor.'

(4) *Specialist prefers to be an individualist.* This category differs only slightly from the previous one. Some specialists say that there is no point in co-operation because the advantages in information gained are outweighed by the disadvantages in information given away. Answers in this category often express hostility but with few 'professional' or ideological overtones:

(b) 'No: confidence in my own ability. Lone hunters do not have to share the trap lines.'

(b) 'No. I have done in the past. There is nothing wrong with them. But my own staff is strong enough to make it unnecessary.'

(a) 'Yes. Between them they're not much good.'

(b) 'No. I'm a loner and prefer to drop my own bricks and take in my own credit.'

(a) 'Yes. I no longer need to read both papers.'

(b) 'No. No one including myself will share a really good story.'

(5) *Specialist strongly disapproves of partnerships.* This disapproval is usually on grounds of 'professional' or 'ethical' misbehaviour, or of disloyalty to the correspondent's employer. Such strong disapproval is expressed by only a small minority of the non-partners:

(b) 'Exclusivity is the aim of every good reporter – not playing PRO.'

(b) 'Employers might as well rely solely on PA and Reuters.'

(b) 'It leads to people thinking that a false story is true "because X, Y and Z all say it".'

(b) 'Collaboration has grave dangers, i.e. presenting the public with facts which appear to be corroborated from independent sources, but really are one man's shared story.'

b. Partnership exchange: equality

The quarter of specialists who said they did belong to a partnership were asked three further specific questions:

(1) Do you phone or talk to each other almost every day?

(2) Do you sometimes divide up newsgathering activities and swop information later?

(3) Do you sometimes give each other blacks (carbons) of stories?

The first two of these activities were much more common than the third. Of 45 specialists who said they had partners, specific types of partnership activity were reported as follows:

(1) Talk to partner almost every day   39
(2) Sometimes divide up newsgathering   37
(3) Sometimes exchange carbons   15

9 of the 15 carbon exchangers were in the Political Lobby. Outside the Political Lobby the exchanging of carbons is rare, perhaps because specialists in other fields usually return to their offices to type out the story – where they are physically separated from their partner who will be sitting in his office. In the case of stories which are phoned in to the office most specialists will not have a carbon – more often they will merely have a shorthand or longhand note. But since Lobby men share communal offices at Westminster, carbons can be handed across from one desk to another. Sometimes this is a story which summarises a government document; in other cases a carbon may be useful mainly in showing a correspondent what 'line' his partner has taken or what 'weight' and 'strength' he has attached to some recent political moves.

Partnerships in the Lobby differ also in the *size* of partnerships. Taking just the two most common partnership activities – talking every day and sharing newsgathering – a co-operating Lobby correspondent typically has two partners, while specialists in other fields have only one.

Co-operators do not differ dramatically from other specialists in terms of education; 30 per cent of partners were educated beyond age 20 – as against 34 per cent of non-partners. The co-operators are a little younger; 58 per cent of partners are under age 40 – as against 42 per cent of partners. There is some difference in seniority in the news organization. Compared with specialists in general, co-operators are less likely to be one-man teams and more likely to be number two or three specialists. It is the *number two* position which is most common; there are 17 number twos to 12 number ones.

Equality is the basic norm in exchange partnerships. Two (or three) specialists exchange information and other kinds of help in such a way that the partners think they are benefiting fairly equally. When a team of say three specialists, A1, A2 and A3, co-operate with another team, B1, B2 and B3, A1 will normally co-operate mainly with B1. On some stories A1 may find himself 'working with' B2 or B3; but number one specialists work on number one stories which usually makes opportunities for co-operation between A1 and B1 much more frequent. In line with the way specialists tend to perceive such situations, the relationship of A1, A2 and A3 with B1, B2 and B3 is regarded here as only three (not the maximum of nine) – and these three partnerships tend toward equality.

Partnership co-operation is firstly on a regular day-to-day basis, and secondly is usually restricted to one or two partners. Partnership co-operation is more regular and positively structured. In partnership exchange the telephone call to a partner will usually be every day (or nearly every day) and at a probably busy time – when both partners are approaching the first edition early evening deadline. (Sunday paper specialists ring each other on Saturday.) Such calls take place in conditions of time scarcity and specialists are keen that the co-operation should save time and be mutually rewarding:

> 'The key here is that one must match oneself with a partner of equal talent and assiduity if the liaison is to work. A lazy partner is useless.'

The same specialist expounded on this point in the interview:

> 'X says this co-operation between them is pretty well known in the field, but not to his own news-desk. His partner, Y, rings up during the interview and they tell each other what they are doing. X says at one time he used to exchange stories with the predecessor to the present man on the *Daily Z* – but this lapsed. The Z man was less useful because he was not such a good journalist as Y.'

Another benefit of partnership co-operation is the chance to talk over difficult stories with a competitor-colleague:

> 'A co-operates with B. He's never made any secret of this and it's known to both their offices. He likes having one person with whom he can discuss things and on whom he can try out his judgement of a difficult story. And although both are on quality dailies, they are not the most direct competitors.'

One of the commonest sorts of partnership co-operation is the dividing of newsgathering, and balancing of individual strengths. For instance one Labour correspondent might have especially strong individual contacts in a particular trade union, whereas his partner would have such contacts in another union:

> 'The co-operation is on "known" stories where information is re-quired from several sources some of which will be more accessible to one partner or another.'

Specialists say that such co-operation saves news sources trouble.

The more specific and detailed partnership form of co-operation involves also a stronger contractual element in the exchange. In a partnership of two or three specialists, the limited size – and the time saved by the partnership – leaves room for some post-mortem discussions (and argument) on yesterday's behaviour. A fairly detailed partnership agreement evolves – as to what will be exchanged, what the main 'exclusive' exceptions will be, and how far in advance of edition times (and other competitor-colleagues) the partner will be warned of exclusive items.

Many stories do not have an equal news value as between the two news organizations; even directly competing news organizations have differences in the length, number, subject-matter, regional and political appeal, of stories which interest them. Thus a correspondent on *The Guardian* might be able to use a story with a North of England angle which his *Financial Times* partner did not want, while the opposite would be true of some financial stories. A *Daily Express* specialist might be able to use a story for which his *Daily Mirror* partner had no use – simply because one paper uses a greater total number of stories than the other. In the Political Lobby especially it is said to be possible for partner A's story to occupy one paragraph in his own paper, while the same story is made the splash front page of his partner B, to whom he gave it.

A news source may ask the correspondent not to 'hand on' information. And the most 'exclusive' stories, also, will not be exchanged; but the definition of 'exclusive' in the context of partnership co-operation is much more limited than in the case of collective co-operation. The attitude was widespread that co-operation up to a certain point was legitimate, while beyond a certain point co-operation was unacceptable:

(a) (Compete against?) 'Yes: Two number ones on rival papers are notorious for "sharing the load".'

(b) (Belong partnership?) 'Yes, but not to the extremes that the above mentioned take it.'

In some cases a number two specialist feels obliged to co-operate with a particular competing number two, because his own number one co-operates with the same competing organization's number one. But number ones and twos do not always co-operate with specialists from the same competing organization. In a largish field like the Political Lobby or Football the size of specialist teams makes for a fairly complex pattern, such as:

$$A_1 \qquad B_1 \qquad C_1\!\!-\!\!-\!\!-\!\!-D_1\!\!-\!\!-\!\!-\!\!-Q$$
$$A_2\!\!-\!\!-\!\!-\!\!-B_2\!\!-\!\!-\!\!-\!\!-C_2\!\!-\!\!-\!\!-\!\!-D_2$$
$$B_3\!\!-\!\!-\!\!-\!\!-C_3$$

One complexity is teams of different sizes between different news organizations. In this pattern A, B, C, D would all be *daily* newspapers and Q might be a Sunday paper. B_2 and C_2 are each shown as having two partners, but A_2 and D_2 as having only one partner.

A simpler pattern is found in the smaller, mainly one-man team, fields – such as Aviation, Education, or some smaller Foreign correspondence centres:

A——B   C——D   P——Q

The definition of 'partnership' obviously implies that the numbers of partners must be small. But why are most partnerships only of two correspondents, while Lobby partnerships of three (or four) are common? The major saving of time may be lost if the partnership becomes bigger; a correspondent with two partners must make twice the number of warning telephone calls and may feel that the extra gain is outweighed by the extra costs in time. The Lobby might be different here, with all correspondents working out of the same set of offices at Westminster. Another obvious difference in the Lobby is the availability of a category of specialists who are highly know-ledgeable, work on the same frequencies and deadlines, and are not directly competing – these are the *provincial* Lobby correspondents.

A number of national Lobby correspondents had, when previously working as Lobby men for provincial newspapers, been in partner-ships involving for instance a big Midlands paper and a big Northern paper. Such partnerships may carry over into the national Lobby field; the 'new' correspondent may enter the national Lobby already belonging to a partnership, but in other fields such a pattern is unusual. There are examples of two young correspondents co-operating on a basis of common inexperience. Some novitiate specialists fall into a pattern already set by their number one or their predecessor. Sometimes a specialist entering a field is approached by an individual, or a pair, with a straightforward partnership offer.

Some specialists join a partnership immediately; others join gradually – an agreement to share one difficult news source may later extend to others. Partnerships may also be terminated – either after a dispute or with cordial agreement. The shifting of personnel in any specialist field leads to a reshuffling of partnerships. A specialist who has belonged to a lengthy partnership may lose his partner and not find another:

'No. A matter of personal relations: I worked closely with a specialist who later left the field.'

The theme of co-operative partners as friends recurs frequently.

c. *Partnerships and news organizations*

The 23 per cent of all the specialists who described themselves as co-operating partners were heavily concentrated among correspondents working for *The Times, Daily Mail, Daily Express* and *Daily Mirror*; between a third and a half of the responding specialists from each of these newspapers (and 39 per cent from all four) said they were co-operating partners. This is nearly twice the proportion of specialists working for all other news organizations. All four of these news organizations were regarded by specialists in general as unusually *competitive* (Table 6.1).

Specialists on news organizations in multi-media ownership are more likely to be co-operators than are specialists who work for independent organizations. The four large multi-media organizations, International Publishing Corporation, Associated, Beaverbrook and Thomson, in 1968 owned twelve national newspapers, and specialists working for these organizations were nearly three times as likely to be co-operating partners as were specialists working for other news organizations. A possible explanation is that the multi-owned news organizations on the whole were in the mid-stream of competition (*The Times, Daily Mail, Daily Express* and *Daily Mirror* were all multi-owned) which is associated with more co-operation.

Among those specialists who said they had co-operating partners two-thirds had partners of similar seniority – number ones co-operated with number ones, and numbers two and three with numbers two and three. This finding is consistent with the hypothesis that co-operation is related to directness of competition.

Table 6.5 shows what happens when the reports of competitors are added to the reports of specialists about themselves.* The evidence on Foreign correspondents is in several ways too weak to include in this Table, but the total *number* of co-operators among London-based specialists nearly doubles from 38 to 73. The *proportion* of co-operators among London-based specialists is 25 per cent on the basis of self-reporting; when the other evidence is added this rises to 48 per cent of questionnaire respondents – or to 36·5 per cent of the total sample (including non-respondents to the questionnaire).†

Further problems arise if one looks at *partnerships* rather than individual partners – since in most cases the questionnaire responses do not reveal the precise identity of the co-operating partner. However, most respondents did complete the details about the *type* of organization and from these combined with information in the un-

---

* Also added are a few specialists who in the interview gave details of their partnership, but denied it in the questionnaire – or did not answer, or refused to complete the questionnaire.

† There are other anomalies – arising, for instance, from personnel changes between the interview and questionnaire stages.

structured interviews – mainly from competitors – come the figures
below for 45 of the partnerships between organizations:

TABLE 6.5

CO-OPERATING PARTNERS: SELF-REPORTING
AND REPORTED BY COMPETITORS
(*Excluding Foreign correspondents*)

	Specialists reporting THEMSELVES as co-operators	Self-reported plus reported as co-operators by competitors in same field	Total size of field
Political Lobby	15	20	46
Labour	4	8	33
Education	3	6	14
Aviation	3	8	16
Crime	2	10	20
Football	8	13	30
Motoring	2	6	22
Fashion	1	2	19
Total N	38	73	200

Popular newspaper* with popular newspaper	21
Quality newspaper with quality newspaper	7
Quality newspaper with popular newspaper	9
Popular newspaper with agency/broadcast	4
Quality newspaper with agency/broadcast	3
Agency/broadcast with agency/broadcast	1
Total number of partnerships†	45

* Including London evenings, as well as dailies and Sundays.

Three-fifths of partnerships are of either the popular-popular or
quality-quality sort. When the evidence of the unstructured interviews is added to the self-completed questionnaires there is only one
change in the five organizations involved in the most partnerships.
The total number has doubled for the leading five organizations –

† Each partnership is of two specialists; thus 2 men co-operating together count
as 1. Three men co-operating together (if each co-operates with the other 2) counts
as 3.

but these figures are for *partnerships,* allowing in some cases more than one partnership per partner:

Daily Mail	14 partnerships
Daily Express	10
The Sun	9
The Times	8
The Daily Telegraph	7

These figures once again point to the meeting point of the larger circulation qualities and the more middle market of the popular newspapers. The same point is also made if we look at the partnerships between specific newspapers. These are all the cases where at least two partnerships exist:

The Financial Times	and	*The Guardian*	2 partnerships
The Times	and	*The Guardian*	2
The Times	and	BBC *News*	2
The Times	and	*Daily Mail*	2
The Daily Telegraph	and	*Daily Mail*	2
The Daily Telegraph	and	*The Sun*	2
Daily Mail	and	*Daily Mirror*	3
Daily Mail	and	*Daily Express*	3
Daily Mail	and	*The Sun*	2
Daily Express	and	*Evening Standard*	3
Evening News	and	*Evening Standard*	2
			──
			25 partnerships
			──

These figures are a major underestimate in the case of the fields with which this study deals – for instance it was impossible with certainty to identify the partners of nearly half of the 45 specialists who replied in the questionnaires that they had co-operating partners; and these have thus been omitted.

The figure of 36·5 per cent of London-based specialists being co-operating partners is probably also a major underestimate:

(1) The base total of 200 specialists (London-based only) is unrealistically large in view of non-response.

(2) The general sensitivity of the topic may have meant that in some cases both members of a co-operating partnership either became non-respondents or did not fully answer the relevant questions.

(3) Many specialists were reluctant to discuss the co-operative behaviour of their competitors; their knowledge of all the partnerships in the field also seemed to be incomplete.

(4) Some specialists who co-operate with partners working for separate news organizations under the same ownership may think this does not 'count' and not bother to report it.

(5) In at least one field there was a strong impression that a collective exchange of views had taken place among specialists with a resulting decision to play down the topic of partnerships.

(6) In some cases a partnership is difficult to keep secret – especially if between two of the most prominent and central specialists in the field. But a partnership involving one or more specialists less central to the daily activity of the competitor-colleague group can more easily be shielded from view; for instance, the prevalence of partnerships between Sunday specialists is probably underestimated.

4. COMPETITION AND INFORMATION EXCHANGE

a. Does exchange reflect competition?

For a specialist journalist there are the contradictory requirements of first getting all the 'known news' which the competition will have, and secondly getting the 'exclusive' news which the competition will not have. The first requirement will be most easily met by co-operating with the direct competition; but the second requirement will be sacrificed. Two polar possibilities are:

(1) Co-operating with what the news organization regards as a direct competitor.

(2) No co-operation.

The obvious compromise course is:

(3) To co-operate with the third or fourth most direct competitor.

All of these occur. There are other opportunities provided by the general colleague exchange phenomenon; and possible patterns are multiplied again by the presence of teams in which the number one, two and three may adopt differing forms of competitor-colleague behaviour.

If one accepts the specialists' assessment of the competitiveness of particular news organizations – which inevitably include an estimate of the individual specialists involved – how does this compare with co-operative behaviour? Table 6.6 shows that the higher the level of competitiveness – as seen by competing specialists – the more likely is a specialist team to include at least one co-operating partner. The proportion of co-operating partners increases from among the *four* organizations regarded as most competitive (a total of 32* teams), to the *three* most competitive (25 teams) to the *two* most competitive (18 teams) organizations in each of the seven† London-based fields.

TABLE 6.6

'MOST COMPETITIVE' SPECIALISTS AND
PARTNERSHIP CO-OPERATIVE BEHAVIOUR

'Most competitive' organizations as seen by other specialists in seven London-based fields	Percentage of specialist teams in which at least one member is a co-operating partner	
	Self-reported partners Questionnaires only	Partners as reported by self or competitors – Interviews and Questionnaires
	%	%
Four most competitive organizations	37	69
Three most competitive organizations	40	72
Two most competitive organizations	50	78

The increasing proportions including one co-operating partner among increasingly competitive news organization teams holds whether one uses information provided by the co-operating partners only, or whether this is combined with the reports of competitors as well. Were it necessary to make no qualifications Table 6.6 would show strong evidence that *the hotter the competition provided by a specialist team the more likely is it to contain a co-operator.* But even though the 50 per cent figure on self-reported information appears unrealistically low (in view of no answers and non-response), there are qualifications to be made. The news organizations regarded as most competitive tend to be those with the larger teams of specialists – and obviously a three-man team is more likely to contain at least one partner than is a one-man team.

* 32 and not 28, because there are some cases of 'fourth equal', etc.
† Fashionis not included

If the specialists' own definition of competitive directness is adopted the representative case is of a co-operating partner who works for the *second most direct competitor*. Going on to a more 'objective' indicator of directness of competition, the criterion of percentage of readership overlap gives a somewhat different picture – the most common partnership axis being with the *third* most direct competitor. The implications of such co-operation thus vary according to whether one takes the audience's point of view or the news organization's. But the news organization editorial executives themselves tend to reject the audience overlap criterion; indeed these executives largely set the 'usually regarded as most direct competitor' criterion and in terms of this criterion the representative case of co-operation with the *second* most direct competitor is striking.

b. *'Scoop merchants' and 'syndicates': a false dichotomy*

A dichotomy between collective exchange behaviour (or 'collusion') and the individualistic ('scoop') behaviour of a few virtuous specialists is often made by other journalists (including some news executives) and by outsiders with some 'inside' knowledge of one specialist field. This dichotomy, however, is not supported by the present evidence. Such discussions tend to refer to named individuals. Having given firm undertakings of anonymity, one cannot reveal the information which would demolish such arguments – in the case of most, but not all, such named individuals. But the contrast of corrupt 'syndicates' and heroic individualistic 'scoop merchants' is a false dichotomy:

Firstly, a specialist who gets what are acknowledged by competitor-colleagues and others as 'exclusive' stories may also himself be a co-operating partner.

Secondly, the majority of specialists work in teams of two or more correspondents. One man may concentrate on exclusive news while protected for purposes of more routine coverage by a number two who co-operates with a direct competitor.

In the first case there are certain partnerships which include a specialist who is regarded among competitor-colleagues as a leading gatherer of exclusive news; but the individual who on perhaps three days a year gets what is regarded as an exclusive story may nevertheless on most days of the year hand over all or nearly all of his information to a partner – the partner indeed providing security against the missing of routine stories.

In the second case a certain division of labour between the number one specialist and a number two (and/or three) is common. The number one man concentrates on 'big' stories and tries to produce exclusive predictions about major personalities or organizations in the news source area; the number two man covers more obvious stories – and perhaps more routine gathering situations, such as press conferences, meetings, and documents. This kind of division of labour made it difficult for some specialists to answer whether or not they belonged to a partnership:

> (b) 'No. In fact my number 2 does belong to a partnership, and I am not quite so concerned with current news stories, unless they are fairly significant! Suppose I am part of a partnership by proxy.'

At least in the London-based fields, a substantial *majority* of correspondents regarded within their fields as the leading gatherers of exclusive news either belong to a co-operating partnership themselves, or belong to one 'by proxy', through another member of their news organization team. The popular 'scoop merchants versus syndicate' dichotomy is false.

c. *News sources and exchange*

Collective exchange of information between specialists can have either positive or negative connotations for source organizations. The specialists' propensity to hand on information to each other can simplify getting information quickly into all the national media. A source organization may be disappointed that only two or three correspondents appear to cover a particular event, but gratified to see stories in all the national press next morning. However, collective exchange also works against the sources. When two or three specialists know about some item of bad news, it 'can't be kept quiet'.

Partnership exchange, similarly, can be either welcome or unwelcome to new sources. It may provide a saving in a prominent source individual's time. The appearance of a fairly exclusive piece of information in the output of two or three news organizations may provide a favourable ratio of spread and friendly treatment. But again the news source may be less pleased with a co-operating partnership if what the source believes is an untrue, damaging or unfair story appears not just in one isolated publication but in two or three.

Does the existence of exchange and partnership co-operation make for more or less penetrating and comprehensive coverage of the news source? There are two opposite possibilities: (1) The breadth of coverage is greatly reduced because the effective number of specialist teams is less than the apparent number. (2) Co-operation will strengthen access because routine coverage is handled by partnerships while the energies of the most experienced and capable specialists are released for digging out exclusive stories and maintaining contact with irregular sources. The assumed baseline position of perfect competition with 20 equally equipped specialists each pursuing alone one of 20 equally important stories has never occurred. But it seems probable that both of the above hypotheses would be true of certain situations. In certain situations – especially those which would interest only one category of national news organization – the apparent total number of news organizations might exceed the effective number; if there seemed to be five organizations involved the effective number might be only two or three. But on the other hand, co-operation both of the general exchange sort and partnership co-operation will probably strengthen access and especially the speed at which some stories emerge. If two or three number one specialists – freed for a day by the co-operative partnership of their number twos – combine together on piecing together different parts of a major story, they may be much more successful than could one correspondent by himself.

On the question of adequate breadth of coverage and depth of access in the news source area, exchange and co-operative activities probably add to both the weaknesses and strengths of daily and weekly journalism – adding sometimes to its arbitrary, chaotic, uneven, and chancy coverage, but also sometimes to its accurate, thorough and, above all, early informativeness.

d. The Editor and exchange

National Editors expressed a wide variety of opinions about exchange and co-operation. One Editor said: 'I want my specialists to do what is best for the paper.' This objective is, however, more easily enunciated than is a ruling upon certain specific situations – as the same Editor was well aware. Another Editor at first said he would fire any specialist engaging in partnership behaviour; later he said that if the partner was not very direct competition he would probably disapprove officially but do nothing to stop it. Finally the same Editor revealed that one of his leading specialists co-operated in partnership with a competitor (fourth most direct) – the Editor moreover showed not merely tolerance but a certain pride in this partnership (the co-operating partner worked for a more 'up-market' news organization).

This last Editor's general attitude to co-operation, however, has been classified as basically 'against'. The attitudes of 15 Editors towards partnership co-operation can be classified as follows:

Against	6 Editors
Mixed, intermediate	7 Editors
In favour	2 Editors

The two Editors who were in favour of co-operation both specifically named the most directly competing news organization and said they did not mind their specialists co-operating even with it. Both said that co-operation on balance resulted in more gains than losses.

The seven Editors with mixed or intermediate views about co-operation tended to say that some co-operation was both inevitable and impossible for an Editor to eradicate. Certain practices in this area were officially disapproved of, but there was also some turning of blind eyes. Two of these Editors gave some details of co-operating partnerships in which they had themselves been previously involved.

The six Editors who were against co-operation tended to express these views with considerable vigour. Some of these Editors insisted on regarding co-operation as a personal affront. But there was also some agreement that Editors could do little to prevent specialists from co-operating. The Editors' strongest disapproval was of specialist associations; there is, however, a general editorial realization that specialist associations provide useful help – for instance in circulating addresses to lesser sources. One Editor said that he was opposed to such groupings because they obviously diminished his authority. Other Editors said that specialist associations encouraged correspondents to conceal stories which might cause specialist-source embarrassment at an interpersonal level.

e. Specialists and exchange

It is possible to view information exchange between competitor-colleagues as resulting from excessive competitive pressures brought to bear on correspondents by news organizations. Some specialists spontaneously explain both exchange and partnerships in this way. The present study's data cannot confirm or disprove this. Experimentally one might increase the competitive pressures within a specialist group and predict that exchange and co-operation would also increase; but the opposite hypothesis might be just as promising – that increasing co-operation would bring increasing competition.

Certainly some stories will be 'suppressed' by specialists, but on politically salient subjects this seems unlikely to happen frequently; most pieces of information will be possessed by two or more news source individuals who will usually find alternative publicity outlets. Moreover most specialist groups contain at least one or two extremely individualistic correspondents; and there are fringe specialists, half in and half out of the group. Another factor is the specialist's self-image; like other men, he will generally try to minimize the gap between his idealized self-image and his everyday behaviour. Even though exchange partnerships may be regular and longstanding, there are always exceptions for 'exclusives'. But in any case co-operation seems more likely to produce exclusive news than to bury it, more likely also to strengthen the hand of correspondents not only against their news organizations but also against their news sources.

Effective 'suppression' is more likely to spring from the conventional wisdom of the specialists in the field. The belief may be accepted uncritically by all the competitor-colleagues that so-and-so may be the case but lacks a 'news peg' or wouldn't make a news story; if used a story might not be regarded by the competitors as an 'exclusive', but as an 'old story' not worth following up and thus lacking in prestige within competitor-colleague group and news organization alike. The suspicions which national Editors have of specialists' associations may perhaps be only partly misplaced.

Some norms of the specialist group may follow from the combination of one prevalent ideological approach, and the common occupational socialization in news values which are strengthened by collective exchange of information between competitor-colleagues and sustained by constant oral dipping into the collective group memory. Some norms may reflect the physical circumstances of newsgathering work – for instance that Lobby correspondents are crammed together into offices at Westminster. Other group norms may follow from the specialist group's overall output as seen by competing executives, the consequent prevailing view of the field, and its playing back to the specialists in the form of news organization policy and news values. Such re-inforcement and the group shaping of news values may be further set by recurring patterns of competition and co-operation.

7

Newsgatherers for whom?

The last three chapters have looked at the three major work roles of the specialist journalist – as employee, as newsgatherer, and as competitor-colleague. This chapter will present some evidence about the specialist journalist's relationship with his audience.

This chapter also returns to some of the basic questions which were posed in the opening chapter. The broad findings of the study are reviewed and are related to suggestions for further research on a variety of mass media topics.

a. The specialist and his audience

Seeing the flow from the production end correspondents are inevitably more specifically aware of news sources and other journalists in the same news organization. They also see their own newsgathering role as more active than the rather passive term 'gatekeeper' might suggest. Most correspondents seem aware of at least four types of audience:

(1) Journalists
(2) The news source area
(3) The highly interested audience sector
(4) The total audience.

(1) *Journalists* include executives and news processors within the correspondent's own news organization, his competitor-colleagues, and journalists in general. He knows these are very active audience members with some control over him.

(2) *News source area* includes both organizational and individual news sources, both regular and irregular news sources.

(3) *The highly interested public* is less clearly defined. Many correspondents see themselves as aiming primarily at only a fraction of the total news organization's audience. Some Lobby men say they are aiming at the 10 per cent or so who take a serious interest in politics; on any one story an Aviation correspondent may be aware that substantial fractions of the audience (e.g. engineers) understand more about specific stories than he does. Some Football corres-

pondents are aware of the substantial number of young football players who understand modern tactics at first hand. In each case there is also the less highly interested audience group – those who are bored with political detail, have rarely or never flown on a plane, or are among the majority (say the correspondents) of football fans who do not understand modern tactics.

(4) The *total audience* will vary more from one news organization to another than will, for instance, the news source area. For most sorts of news 100 per cent of the total audience cannot be expected to pay attention. But in many cases, say, 60 per cent seems a possible target. It is this 60 per cent that many correspondents try to swing towards the views and/or information level of the 10 per cent or so of highly interested audience members. This is how many journalists see their informative role:

'No power. Influence on opinion forming by crystallizing thoughts of reader.' (Lobby)

'My job is to educate the public so their children can be educated.' (Education)

'In educating public to need for reform in the administration and playing of the game.' (Football)

The specialist correspondent has daily contact with news executives, news sources and competitor-colleagues; but he cannot have daily contact with a representative cross section of the national audience. The correspondent cannot meet this whole audience even if he wants to. Should his next-door neighbour, or his friend, or his wife comment on a piece he has written the correspondent may be flattered. But his experience as a reporter has taught him that few 'members of the general public' remember reporters' names accurately; journalists are used to being blamed for a piece which really appeared in a competing newspaper. The audience of the whole news organization is so general and the direct involvement of one out of 300 journalists on a national newspaper is so specific that there is little contact. The individual audience member – one out of millions – has low marginal utility to the news organization and little power over the individual journalist.

Those readers of the newspaper, or viewers of the TV news, who will regularly have noticed the individual correspondent's piece, remember what it said, and are able to comment upon it to him are in most cases either news sources or other journalists (especially executives and competitor-colleagues). Because these people not only can expect punishments and rewards but also are the only audience members who provide a regular detailed feedback of comment, the specialist pays more attention to news sources, executives and competitor-colleagues than to the millions of audience members.

His most regular experience of members of the general audience is from their letters. Average (mean) answers to the question, 'How many letters do you get (addressed to yourself) from your general audience?' were as follows:

AVERAGE NUMBER OF GENERAL
AUDIENCE LETTERS PER WEEK

Washington	2 letters per week
New York	2
Bonn/Rome	1
Political Lobby	8
Aviation	10
Education	12
Labour	4
Crime	26
Football	19
Fashion	71
Motoring	24
Average for all fields	14 letters per week

The 174 correspondents who answered claimed to receive 2,529 letters a week (or about 125,000 a year). These letters were very heavily concentrated in the revenue fields.

The word 'crank' occurs frequently in comments about letters; many letters are abusive; others ask for very simple advice or information available in reference books:

'These are mostly requests for information. They increase very noticeably when one has written something about pensions or pay.' (Lobby)

'Mostly disagreement or factual queries and the odd bit of praise.' (Aviation)

'Usually asking for educational advice.' (Education)

'Majority from the enthusiastic and biased young. The average tends to go up after any event involving the Scots.' (Football)

'Depends on what I've written. Many ask technical questions.' (Motoring)

Correspondents often complain of having to send polite replies to abusive letters; most replies are dictated. The *Daily Mirror*, for instance, circulates extracts from letters within the office plus a league table of numbers of letters received; the star columnists usually come top, followed by revenue goal specialists. Several correspondents spoke with pride of a single piece which had produced, say, 300 letters, and some deliberately ask their readers to write.

But specialists are, of course, aware that the media organization regards audience research figures – based on sample surveys – as much more objective than letters. Asked, 'Do you ever see audience research figures?' 34 per cent of specialists said they did. These included the majority of Fashion specialists, half the Education specialists, and nearly half of political Lobby, Labour and New York correspondents. The *majority* of specialists on the *Daily Mail, Daily Mirror, The Sun, Sunday Times* and BBC *News* saw audience research figures of some kind; some specialists quoted 'page traffic findings' (70 per cent of men readers look at the sports page) or audience composition figures (5 per cent of our readers are students).

In some news organizations there is reluctance to show research findings to journalists (possibly for fear of divisive results or leaks to the competition); but one or more specialists from 18 of the 23 separate news organizations claimed to have seen such research. The most general response to such research details is one of in-difference. There is a general belief that the broad nature of the audience is relevant, but that specific details – whether 50 or 70 per cent of men read the sports page, or whether 5 or 10 per cent of readers are students – are irrelevant to the production of news stories. To test the hypothesis that correspondents would have an inaccurate image of their news organization's audience, we asked the simplest specific question we could think of – what proportion were manual working class.* When compared with the National Reader-ship Survey figures on social class composition for the specific correspondents' news organizations the proportion of working class audience members was *underestimated* by nine out of ten specialists. Specialists typically underestimated the proportion of working class audience members by about 20 percentage points.† In the case of every national newspaper the average of specialists' replies was a substantial underestimate of working class readers. This

---

* 'What proportion of your editorial organization's audience (readers or viewers), would you say, are manual workers and their families? . . . % of our audience are manual workers.'
† Half the specialists did not reply to this question or said they did not know; the contrast between the specialists' figures and those of the audience researchers seems sufficiently large to outweigh any problems of definition or non-response.

strong tendency for correspondents to think their audience more middle class than research figures indicate is in line with the general non-revenue tendencies of the correspondents.

b. Audiences and news organization 'face-lifting'

An obvious weakness of the present exploratory study is, of course, that while adopting a broad comparative approach to national journalists, it has neglected other stages in the news flow. What are now required are research designs which fill the middle ground between careful studies of a single stage in the news flow and the other extreme – the case study of a single, unusual, news event.

One illustration of an urgently necessary type of research strategy must suffice: a comparative study of a number of *face-lifting* operations within news organizations. At intervals from a few months to a few years most news organizations decide upon a change of format – a re-styling of the front page, a re-ordering of pages through the publication, a changed emphasis in a major area, a new type or length of news bulletin or programme; the extreme cases are the axing of a programme or publication and/or the launching of a new one. The study of a number of such face-lifting operations would involve several research advantages: there is a neat 'before and after' situation; audience research is usually available; one can expect a debate within the news organization in which different groups put forward their goals – and from which a coalition goal emerges. Given reasonable safeguards, media organization managers could be expected to benefit from the outside study of the face-lifting process. A reasonable compromise between media organization caution and the articulate public's insistence on its 'right to know' might be the retrospective publication of studies of face-lifting operations after an interval of two or three years. Until such studies are conducted, managers of large media and news organizations can expect increasingly strident criticisms of their excessive secrecy and their denial of responsible public scrutiny. Until such studies are conducted the contribution of social scientists to public debates about most 'media crises' will continue to be either non-existent or largely ill-informed and irrelevant.

c. Audiences, goals and the number of media voices

The above suggestion focuses on a type of recurrent process within news organizations where a number of stages in the news flow are 'brought together', in which the coalition goal is redefined, and where specific organizational decisions are taken. Such projects would still not focus upon 'monopoly' and 'competition' which in one formulation or another has always been the central mass media question.

The final section of this chapter will return to the question of media monopoly. Perhaps at this stage it is worth making three broad points which are relevant to the general issue:

(1) There is no single audience or 'typical' audience member. Any one news organization has a very varied audience. The link between any individual specialist journalist and ultimate audience members is extremely tenuous.

(2) No news organization – even the most popular – tries only to 'give the audience what it wants'; however the wants of the audience are defined, news organizations have several goals, of which the audience revenue goal is only one.

(3) The 'number of media voices' is another phrase of very imprecise meaning. Moreover a phenomenon such as competitor-colleague exchange makes it clear that the number of effectively competing 'voices' within a specific field is unlikely to be the same as the number of news organizations or ownerships.

2. CORRESPONDENTS' LIFE STYLE

What right, if any, do journalists have to speak to audiences of millions? In what sense are they representative of their audiences? Are these specialist journalists cut off from ordinary people? Do they live in an unreal frenetic inside-dopester world whose values are alien to those of the rest of the nation's population?

a. The train to the suburbs

Nine out of ten specialist correspondents are married. With 30 as the average age for starting national specialization, most specialists were married while they were still general reporters. The most frequently quoted wives' occupations (before marriage) were nurse, secretary, schoolteacher and journalist. The married specialists averaged just under two children each. Most of the London-based specialists lived in the London suburbs – with more in the outer than the inner suburbs. Six-tenths lived *outside* the Greater London postal area; less than one-tenth lived in Central London.

The majority of Foreign correspondents entered that specialist field *before* marriage. Indeed, being already married at this stage appears to reduce the chances of a 26-year-old reporter being sent on foreign assignments (as a 'fireman', war correspondent, or rover).

Foreign correspondents also tend to have followed an élite and precocious career pattern; their higher level of education and more privileged social background, plus the low average age for first permanent foreign posting combine to make Foreign correspondents more likely than other specialists to marry only *after* national specialization. A number of Foreign correspondents had met their wives while in a foreign posting. These wives' occupations before marriage were of noticeably superior status to the occupations of some London-based specialists' wives. For instance, among the wives of Football and Crime correspondents the highest status previous occupations were nurse and secretary; but these were the lowest status occupations among the Foreign correspondents' wives – more of whom at their marriages had been full-time students, teachers, journalists or professionals. The wives of Foreign correspondents may thus be more predisposed to be interested in their husband's work; taking the children to school, shopping, or talking to friends may enable a wife to provide her husband with useful information – especially in a political capital like Bonn or Washington. In North-west Washington, where most of the British correspondents live, the housewife next door may be the wife of a useful news source. But it is in entertaining informants in the home that Foreign correspondents differ most from London-based ones:

(Q. 'HAVE YOU INVITED WITH ANY
REGULARITY, IN THE LAST YEAR,
INFORMANTS TO YOUR HOME...?')

Foreign correspondents	56% said 'Yes'
London-based correspondents	38%
(N = 192) All selected specialists	42%

This is another way, then, in which the wife is drawn into the Foreign correspondent's work. In both Washington and New York Foreign correspondents are anxious about the children's schooling. Fears of their children's schooling being affected are a major factor in the anxiety of Foreign correspondents on the question of being posted elsewhere. Some Foreign correspondents send their children to the French Lycée which offers the prospect of continuity from one capital to the next; but not all British correspondents, even with French wives, want 'French children'. The other obvious possibility of a boarding school in England has equally obvious possibilities for tension. Among Foreign correspondents stresses in the first years of marriage may be less than for other journalists, but this may be balanced by greater stresses in subsequent years.

The wife of a London-based correspondent tends to be less involved in her husband's work. Impressionistic evidence suggests that the extreme cases are Crime and Football correspondents; these specialists spend many evenings away from home – and some correspondents say that their wives' interest in Crime or Football is rather limited.

Correspondents live on a suburban level of income, but lead a metropolitan kind of life at work. While there is an element in the correspondent's life of going to 'work' to have 'leisure', there is also an element of going home to work. The train journey is only part of the time spent away from 'work' in which the correspondent catches up on work. Between arriving home in mid-evening and leaving in mid-morning he watches TV news, and starts to plough through the newspapers at the breakfast table. In addition he gathers and sends stories over his home telephone.

Books – both reading of and writing of – are another aspect of 'work' which spill over into the domestic sphere. Specialists overall claimed to read almost exactly one book a week. Foreign correspondents read more, and Crime correspondents (great book *writers*) read less. Political, Labour, Education and Aviation correspondents all averaged between four and five books per month. Many complained that they would like to read more. 'All for review or connected with work. No time for novels', was a common regret. So the non-work part of life is used not only to recuperate from the strains of work, but also to prepare for work and to make 'extra earnings' related to the specialist field. Few specialists mention hobbies. Asked about neighbours, only one correspondent in ten claimed to see neighbours more than occasionally.

Any occupation that requires its members to work unusual hours must timetable their leisure into unusual shapes. Daily newspaper correspondents get Saturday off, but at least one of the Lobby team has to be on duty on Sunday. An unpredictable and one-man-team field like Aviation seems to produce much interruption of 'days off'. The Football men claim to have the fewest days off; this is largely because daily newspaper correspondents must cover Saturday games for retrospective pieces in Monday's papers. But the most usual case is of the daily man who has Saturday completely free and one other day, Sunday or a day in midweek, when he may get 'consulted' on the phone by the office. In the case of big stories in their field on a normal off-day, most correspondents automatically assume that they will cover the story.

Many of the complaints from correspondents about the impingement of work on leisure are from morning newspaper men who complain that their evenings are disrupted. A common complaint is that mid-evening deadlines make it impossible to get to theatres, concerts and films. Dinner dates, it is said, are often disrupted. A further complaint is that Fleet Street hours prevent a father from seeing his young children – except at breakfast. Although some correspondents – especially the single and those living in inner London – minimize the incursions of work on leisure, the replies of many correspondents indicate considerable strength of feeling, sometimes bitterness, about the extent to which they see work as dominating and impoverishing their lives outside work.

b. *The friends of correspondents*

Just over two-fifths of these specialists' friends were themselves journalists. This question was asked in two different ways with very similar proportions resulting. Asked 'What are the occupations of your three best friends?' 71 per cent said at least one of these friends was a journalist. 42 per cent of the three best friends of all the specialists (N=184) were journalists; audience goal specialists had the most – 53 per cent – journalist friends, and advertising goal the least – 32 per cent.

There is little comparable data for other occupations. But the data seem to fall somewhere between two extreme hypotheses sometimes put forward about the social life of journalists. These are:

(1) Journalists only talk to other journalists.

(2) Journalists are ordinary people who know a cross-section of society.

The first point is not supported since just over half of specialists' friends are not journalists – and this may be substantially higher than in some occupations. But the second, cross-section of society, point is hardly supported either. Although some journalists clearly are friendly with members of various occupations well represented in the London suburbs, they quote few friends who could be described as 'working class', and few who are involved in manufacturing industry. The humblest types of occupations quoted with any frequency are lower white-collar such as 'clerk' or self-employed such as 'shopkeeper'. There is a fair sprinkling of doctors, lawyers, engineers, company directors, accountants, school and university teachers, salesmen, and social workers. About one-tenth of friends' occupations are in the news source area (e.g. education correspondent's schoolteacher friend) and about another one-tenth of quoted friends are in parts of the communications industry other than journalism (book publishers, PRO, TV producer). Added to the

42 per cent of friends who are journalists, this makes almost two-thirds of all 'three best friends' who are connected with the specialist journalists' work, broadly defined.

c. Work and its rewards

In the unstructured interviews correspondents were asked about likes and dislikes. Most commonly quoted *likes* about the work were involvement with nationally known personalities and important events; the satisfaction of seeing the field from the inside and perhaps exerting some influence on it; the experience of being in an active relationship to events and seeing deals and manoeuvres often involving large sums of money; the excitement of conflict between powerful opponents – or, as one Labour correspondent said, 'the taste of blood'. The most commonly quoted *dislikes* were of sometimes being manipulated; of 'doorstepping' – standing in the street waiting; the unpleasantness of having to dig for stories in the face of active source hostility; the pace, discomfort and sometimes danger (one Aviation man claimed that all his competitor-colleagues had forebodings about plane travel). It is noticeable that both the likes and dislikes emphasize excitement, physical stress, and emotional wear – both arise from the work's non-routine character.

These correspondents give a strong impression that their lives are dominated by work. This can be seen as having both a positive and a negative aspect. Their work involves obvious strains – deriving from deadlines, competition and the conflicting interests of news organization, news sources and competitor-colleagues; work also overlaps into the sphere of leisure. All of this encourages correspondents to use what leisure they have for purposes of recuperation. But there is also the *negative* aspect – the kind of work these journalists do may lead them to regard available social and leisure activities as relatively dull and unattractive.

d. Mass communicators: work domination, social segregation?

These specialists live in the London region and could be accused of being too concerned with London, but Northern editions are produced in Manchester and Glasgow; Foreign correspondents are stationed abroad. In terms of educational qualifications these specialists are rather varied; they are less well educated than members of the older professions but better educated than members of some other white collar occupations. Living in London may lead them to over-emphasize certain suburban concerns such as news about mortgages, education, train crashes, airport planning, transport in general, and gardening. But millions of other people do share such suburban concerns.

The correspondents emerge as overwhelmingly middle class – stretching from the upper to the lower middle class. They have experienced some career uncertainty, they are aware of numerous strains at work – but have developed ways of containing these; they tend to be worried about their future careers and at not seeing enough of their children. The argument that they do not see enough of 'ordinary people' might be rebutted by the contention that they are themselves ordinary people. But this is only true if 'ordinary people' is equated with 'middle class'. Whether or not a broad range of middle class backgrounds, and a broad domestic spread through London suburbia is a suitable non-work background for specialist newsgatherers can only be decided in relation to some criteria as to the proper or appropriate social backgrounds for senior communicators in a western democracy.

There is the accusation that mass communicators lead work-dominated lives which socially segregate them from ordinary people and reality. But if their friends were not primarily other mass communicators, who else would they be? Can one expect members of these occupations – unlike those of other occupations – to choose their friends on some kind of random sampling basis? Moreover, even if the communicators did meet socially more 'ordinary' or working class people, what difference would this make? Compared with this, readers' letters might appear an almost sophisticated form of keeping in touch with their general audience.

Accusations of work domination and social segregation involve two contradictory implications – firstly the implication that communicators are sufficiently important or powerful or influential, that their social backgrounds and life styles are of legitimate concern to the general public; the second implication is that people in such important positions should either come from, or be in intimate social contact with, 'ordinary people'. Yet if these jobs are so important it is naïve (in view of the evidence about social stratification in both western and eastern industrial societies) to expect that the people who do such jobs will come from some cross-section of the population. Such expectations are not widely held about politicians or doctors or other occupations often believed to be of some social or political importance.

Nevertheless concern about the social backgrounds and life styles of communicators does exist and may well increase. Studies which compared the social backgrounds of various kinds of communicators with members of other occupations would be welcome. One can put forward the following hypothesis for such a study: specialist newsgathering journalists come from more varied social backgrounds, have less education and more varied current social contacts than either seniorish TV producers (outside news), or editors in book publishing, or executives in advertising agencies. However, another promising hypothesis would be that there is probably a very wide range of social backgrounds and life styles *within* each communicator occupation – according to the mixture of organizational goals prevalent in the relevant type of output.

Were this shown to be the case any subsequent public debate might more remuneratively focus upon such questions as: Should we have more broadcast producers like those in TV light entertainment or like those in educational radio? Should we have more journalists like present Foreign correspondents or like Football correspondents?

3. News values: dominance and discretion

Are the 'news values' in relation to which correspondents shape their stories merely a projection of the suburban values and neuroses of the journalists themselves? Are news values completely arbitary and unpatterned (as some journalists sometimes contend)? Or are news stories socially patterned (as sociologists would claim)? Or are news values simply a mass media version of social values held by millions of audience members?

a. News values and social systems

Just as it is simplisticly assumed that there is 'an audience', a similar mistake is often made in assuming that 'news values' are somehow standardized and uniform. If one compares newspapers from two different countries it is quickly obvious that, say, French news values differ from British news values. But do they have a similar relationship to the nation or social system within which they operate?

Studies of news in the USSR suggest that official news values – as reflected in the content of Russian newspapers and news bulletins – may not fit very well with the kind of news which Soviet citizens want. Soviet audiences, it seems, want more 'negative' news, whereas the Soviet news media concentrate on positive news and only contain certain restricted sorts of negative news. Consequently foreign radio broadcasts supply some of the bad news which Soviet citizens want, and the official media to some extent adjust to this competition.[1] Clearly there are major differences between the news values which developed under different political systems. Nevertheless it would be misleading simply to contrast Soviet uniformity and western variety;

there is some variety in Soviet news values – and there is also much uniformity in western news values.

Before dismissing the standardization produced by 'excessive competition' in the case of British national journalism, it is well to remember the uniformity to be found in the much larger number of daily newspapers across the United States. 'Hundreds of newspapers, though published in cities scattered from coast to coast, were as alike as so many peas in a pod', wrote the editor of *Editor and Publisher* in 1933. Warren Breed twenty years later explained the phenomenon in terms of an arterial process by which Editors of small dailies followed the lead of Editors of big city dailies, who in turn followed news choices made by news agencies and other national media.[2]

The 'flow of news' whether across the world, across a continent or across London – from Scotland Yard or Westminster to Fleet Street and beyond – is a flow of standardization. This standardization is in part a reaction of journalists at various stages in the flow to the uncertainties and ambiguities of news definitions. News is more highly regarded the earlier and more exclusively it is available – but earliness and exclusiveness involve the risk of unreliability; news is regarded more highly the more conflict it contains – but conflict means differing points of view, and hence ambiguity. Just as the small-town American 'wire-editor' gets a feeling of security from using stories which the Associated Press has announced in advance as the big stories of the day, so the London specialist correspondent gets a feeling of security if he follows the stories that his competitor-colleagues will be covering.

Not all news values result from imitative competition. Competition and imitation are both defined in terms of the other. Some news media neither compete with nor imitate each other. An aspect of news in the United Kingdom especially noticeable to American visitors is the similar news values of several popular daily newspapers which together have many millions of readers. It is well to remember that both the common American phenomenon of the monopoly *local* daily which concentrates on the middle of the market, and the high circulation British *national* daily, both follow from a combination of geographical and technological factors. These factors cannot be easily discounted in any intended comparison, because central social values in any society are also influenced by geography, technology and history.

The relationship between a whole society and its mass media can only be adequately studied on some kind of comparative basis. Especially if it is to include comparative study of the *content* of different sorts of media output, this is a formidable task. But until such studies are conducted most statements by social scientists about news values will remain either speculative or related to very limited areas of output.

b. Discretion: news organizations and journalists

News organization executives and specialist correspondents all operate within what they regard as some set of news values – news values which are in general fairly vague, but which in the individual journalist's specific work situation are more clear-cut. These news values constitute only general guidelines; there is always some discretion. Just how much discretion (or autonomy) exists in any particular case is unclear because what constitutes the guidelines (or controls) is also unclear. Uncertainty is inherent in both the news values and the degree of discretion in relation to news values.

This study has attempted to locate the major areas of autonomy and discretion; in comparing groups of specialist journalists it has focused on patterns of behaviour over a whole year. The study has not dealt with tactics employed in particular situations, nor the strategies which individual correspondents adopt over long periods of time. It would be extremely interesting to have such studies available. However, the number of variables, the time pressures, and the problems presented by confidentiality, the telephone, and by other basic characteristics of newsgathering would constitute formidable difficulties for such studies; certainly established 'participant observation' techniques would be quite inadequate.

In the meanwhile one can list some of a number of different levels at which news values impose some constraints, but at which discretion also exists:

(1) The individual newsgathering correspondent has some discretion in relation to the news values of his competitor-colleagues.

(2) The group of competitor-colleagues in relation to news values which might be expected to operate in their field also have some collective discretion.

(3) News processors within a news organization also have substantial discretion.

(4) At the news organization level there is discretion as to what area shall be covered, which news areas will have specialist correspondents, and what emphasis will be given to the non-revenue goal.

(5) At the level of the mass media industry there is discretion as to certain sorts of competition or newsgathering activity which may be collectively outlawed.

c. Are news values social values?

Seriously intended general discussions of the mass media usually adopt the news values of journalism. This is the case, for instance, with most discussion of the media in the London weekly papers – as well as in such American publications as *Columbia Journalism Review* and *Nieman Reports*; the approach is anecdotal, personalized, and 'what's new?' Nevertheless such discussion is usually based on some close acquaintance with the subject matter. The recurrent weakness of so much 'academic' discussion of the news media is a preference for over-sophisticated explanations in general and conspiracy theories in particular; conspiracy theories are all the more damaging, a weakness in much academic writing, for usually being implicit rather than explicitly stated.

While not forgetting the warnings of the last few pages, it might be worth adopting the following hypothesis:

That much news output can be explained in terms of responses to audience demand for, and available supplies of, 'negative' news. One type of news output to which this hypothesis is relevant is the news coverage of strikes and trade unions in Britain. Did Britain in the 1960's have a fairly ordinary strike record but an extraordinarily large amount of its news devoted to strikes? If this contrast did occur it might be preferable to reject hypotheses which attribute political motives to journalists, executives or media owners. Britain is a country with only very small supplies of violent death, disasters, or overt 'conflict' of any kind. The daily question which confronts News editors and Editors (and Foreign correspondents based in London) is 'Where's the bad news?' – or 'Where's the violence?'[3] On most days there is very little violent conflict in Britain, which could be expected to appeal to a national audience. On many days in the year, then, the News editor has to search for the next best thing – and quite often it seems to him that this is a strike story. Strikes in industry get coverage then (according to this hypothesis) not because strikes are especially common in Britain, but because violence and overt conflict are uncommon.

How should such a hypothesis be tested? Studies of single unusual events in which the news media are found to have 'exaggerated' public enthusiasm, or the potential for violence, are of great interest;[4] such studies, however, can be interpreted in several ways. The author of the present study visited the site of the Aberfan coal-tip disaster and watched journalists watching miners digging out and removing the dismembered bodies of dead schoolchildren. Direct observation of a number of such disasters might well lead to the conclusion that major disasters involving many deaths are usually handled with great restraint.

However, the research design favoured by mass media researchers does not follow the procedures of disaster researchers. Mass media researchers tend to select their 'event' in advance. This procedure rules out major disasters (which are usually relatively unexpected); moreover it places the researchers at the mercy of those very journalism news values which their research reports subsequently decry. If the 'case study' is selected on the basis of advance news stories which predict unusual violence or enthusiasm, then there is a strong initial bias in the direction of an ultimate 'non-event' finding.

Future studies relevant to news values should select for analysis a number of news events or issues – in a manner which is sufficiently explicit to make replication and comparison possible.

4. SPECIALIST AUTONOMY
AND THE COMPETITOR-COLLEAGUE ROLE

How much autonomy do specialists have? How does it vary according to the news organizational goal? Do journalists write only for their colleagues?

a. *Role strain and specialist autonomy*

Specialist journalists are involved in boundary positions – positions for which some of the role senders are located in another unit of the same organization, or a different organization (e.g. news sources, competitor-colleagues). Diedrick Snoek has found in such boundary roles as salesmen and purchasing officer, a connection between tension on the job and the required interaction with a diversified set of role senders. Likely problems include: (1) Direct conflict between incompatible role expectations. (2) Overload problems resulting from role senders being unaware of each other's expectations or evaluating tasks differently. (3) Ambiguity when implicit assumptions are not shared, unspoken rules are broken or communications failures occur. (4) The necessity to exert influence without legitimate authority.[5] All four of these types of role strain may be experienced by specialist newsgatherers. 'Incompatible role expectations' may exist, as between the role of newsgatherer and the role of employee; 'overload' problems clearly exist in the face of deadlines; 'implicit assumptions' are often not shared, and norms are usually vaguely held, while exceptions are both prevalent and impossible to codify; the necessity to exert influence without authority is another problem.

But the very multiplicity of possible types of role strain in itself is used by the individual specialist as a buffering device. Some of the role strain can be short-circuited by explicit or implicit understandings with competing colleagues. Moreover on any one day, in relation to any particular news story the relevant role senders are extremely poorly informed of each other's intentions. Simply because he is placed in the several roles and is engaged in the full-time activity of communicating with several sorts of role-senders – new sources, news executives, and competitor-colleagues – the specialist may use his more comprehensive and later information to resist certain demands; by manipulating the timing of his interaction and the amount of information he provides or withholds, and by his knowledge of his competitor-colleagues' activities, he can expand autonomy and reduce control.

News sources may realise that other sources are trying to get favourable coverage, news organizations and executives are trying to exert positive directing as well as processing control, and the correspondent is also subject to both competitive and co-operative pressures within the competitor-colleague role. Consequently in relation to any particular role-sender the specialist has some credible excuse, in the form of 'I wrote a balanced story but the sub-editors hacked it to pieces' or the other way round – 'The source is keeping quiet and none of the specialists can get the story'.

This ability to play off some of the pressures against other pressures varies according to the specific news organizations, news sources, specialist group and individual corespondent. But the potential amount of strain will usually not occur, because one type of role strain may act as a cushion against another. Further research might show that role-defence operates in such a way that the specialist gives especially positive emphasis to one role and uses this role as a defence against pressures exerted in the others. There are at least three possibilities here: (1) The correspondent allies himself with certain prominent sources and resists the pressures of both competitor-colleagues and news organization, using as a weapon the information his sources provide. (2) The correspondent allies himself with the news organization and uses his strength in the employee role to resist other pressures. (3) The correspondent emphasizes the competitor-colleague role and buffers himself against sources and news organization. But these possibilities are made considerably more complex by the prevalence of different goals in different fields of news.

b. The more revenue goal, the more source control?

At the beginning of Chapter 5 the following hypothesis was put forward: 'The greater the element of non-revenue goal, the more autonomy will the newsgatherer have in relation to his news sources; and the greater the element of revenue goal, the more will the news-gatherer be under the control of his news sources'.

In view of the inevitably uncertain definition of 'autonomy' and 'control' one must not expect any clear-cut proof or disproof of the hypothesis. But some general statements about the broad shape of the data in this study can be made.

(1) *Advertising* goal fields. In the case of Motoring and Fashion, strong control is exercised by major news sources; there is an important conjunction between news sources and advertisers. Some news source organizations are potentially able to deny not only news but also advertising. Advertising goal specialists who submit to this control feel relatively autonomous in relation to their news organizations – because there is no major conflict between the news organization's advertising goal and the advertiser/news sources.

(2) *Audience* goal fields. Here the news sources again are able to exert a substantial element of control. Football and Crime specialists are to a considerable extent controlled by news sources which have information in urgent demand by news organizations for audience goal reasons. But firm control is also exercised by news organizations in relation to these specialists – and this control is in explicit conflict with the interests of news sources. Thus Crime and Football correspondents find themselves being subjected to vigorous pressures from both news sources and news organizations. The result is considerable role strain and general discomfort.

(3) *Non-revenue* goal fields. Foreign correspondents would, according to the hypothesis, be less under the control of news sources than any other kind of specialist journalist. News sources have particularly few sanctions against Foreign correspondents from friendly nations. The data on Foreign correspondents suggested, however, that they were firmly under the control of their news organizations; to some extent this follows from the news organization's definition of the prevalent goal. But another way of viewing this control is to see the control as coming from the main international news flow (in which the international news agencies are prominent); this control, however, reaches the individual correspondent via his news executive's surveillance of the international news flow.

(4) *Mixed goal fields.* Aviation, Education, Labour and Political Lobby correspondents are much less under the control of news sources than are either the audience or the advertising goal correspondents. The mixture of goals provides especially favourable conditions for playing off the pressures in one role against pressures in another role. As domestic fields these are not under the control of international definitions of news. News values are to a great extent shaped by the competitor-colleague group. Especially in the case of the high status Lobby and Labour fields, correspondents go unusually far in maintaining their independence from both news organizations and news sources.

c. Newsgathering for newsgatherers

The previous chapter reported evidence that specialist newsgatherers often gather news in alliance with competitors. Competition itself is defined in terms of relations between individual specialists within a competitor-colleague group. This occurs partly because when they seek to exert control over specialists in a particular competitive direction news executives do so through the news output of the competitor-colleague group in the particular field.

But specialists are dependent upon competitor-colleagues from their first day in the field. Specialists to a considerable extent are initiated into the specialist role by their new competitor-colleagues. A new specialist follows the learning-by-doing pattern which is standard practice in this non-routine occupation. Specialists were asked how long they took to become confident on most stories. Just over a third took six months or less; another third took up to twelve months; and another third took up to or over two years.

Some specialists were taken round and introduced to all the predecessor's most helpful news sources, as well as receiving all of his files and – some say most useful of all – his personal book of source telephone numbers. But in many cases the specialist did not have any help from a predecessor; this could be because there was no specialist in the field previously, because the predecessor became ill or died suddenly, or just did not choose to assist his successor. When asked who helped them 'when you were still settling into the field', specialists (N=191) said they received 'considerable help' as follows:

'From predecessor in the post'	19% (received considerable help)
'Colleagues in the field working for other editorial organizations'	43%
'Certain news sources'	37%
'Your own No. 1 or No. 2 if you were a No. 2 or No. 3'	30%

These categories are not necessarily exclusive. But 43 per cent did receive 'considerable' help from competitor-colleagues:

'Colleagues in other organizations above all. The "brotherhood" both British and American.'

'Sports fraternity seems always anxious that a "new boy" should not fall down on the job.'

'I found people on rival papers most considerate and helpful in the early days, but basically it was a question of finding my own feet.'

'It's not quite the rat race it's made out to be.'

The competitor-colleague helping relationship is thus of importance to a specialist from his early days. These colleagues – for whom, and against whom a specialist gathers news – differ considerably from field to field. Crime correspondents, for instance, belong to a declining field; they are lowly educated; markedly older than most specialists; strongly Conservative in politics; concentrated on the popular newspapers. Education correspondents by contrast belong to a growing field; are highly educated; markedly younger than most specialists; strongly Labour in politics; concentrated on the quality newspapers. There are other important differences – in previous career, pay, promotion prospects and so on. So marked are these differences that Education correspondents have a group ideology which is sharply different from the ideology of the group of Crime correspondents.

Some of the factors which influence these different social characteristics and ideologies have been indicated. Different fields have different predominant goals; so the same news organization expects different things from specialists in different fields – its expectations of its Fashion correspondent differ from its expectations of its Lobby correspondent. Specialists gather news from different news source areas; one might expect people who gather news from policemen to differ from people who gather news from the education world. News organization executives select promising journalists to become specialists; there is an element of self-selection on the part of would-be specialists. Both groups anticipate the likely response of news sources.

But another important influence on the characteristics and ideology of the specialists who enter a field are the existing specialists. These specialists set the tone of a field within journalism; it is in response to these current specialists that news sources adopt their stances. There are also more direct influences by current specialists – who initiate new men into the ways of the field, including the practice of exchanging news with competitors. Any individual's experience within a specialist field must be influenced by the interpersonal behaviour of his competitor-colleagues in that field; after a short time in the field a correspondent may ask to be moved – and this must sometimes be because he dislikes the group's ideology. The men in the field not only influence and maintain the character and ideology of the group in various subtle ways; existing specialists also play a part in the selection of new specialists.

The ideology of a particular competitor-colleague group appears to be carried forward in a largely oral tradition. It is probably all the more potent for not being written down. The group's ideology cannot easily be challenged by outsiders. It also cannot easily be challenged by members of the competitor-colleague group. Indeed the group ideology – strongly influenced as it is by news organization goals, news sources, and by the previous careers of competitor-colleagues – is in its very nature likely to be well adapted to occupational realities and to the forms of pressure which are regularly exerted on group members. The group ideology is expressed in conventional wisdoms, some of which appear so obvious, or are so strongly held by a majority of members, that they are never challenged.

What can be done to change or challenge the prevalence of such group values, memories, and competitor-colleague patterns? How can the values and ideology of any social group be changed? Presumably by changing recruitment, and occupational socialization, by altering the balance of the roles in which the occupation places workers, or perhaps by removing workers from the work situation for phases of re-socialization elsewhere. Both Editors and specialists are aware of such possibilities, but also stress likely costs in terms of money, career disruption, and additional strain and insecurity. Moreover it would be mistaken to believe that competitor-colleague behaviour can be broken down (even if this were desirable) by such simple measures as bringing in more highly educated specialists. Group processes are not different in fields (such as Education and Labour) where there are the most university graduates, and the latter in these or other fields are no more or less likely than other correspondents to belong to co-operating partnerships. Competitor-colleague behaviour within groups would not be easy to change because it is consistent with fundamentals of the occupation, such as definitions of news.

d. Communicating for communicators?

Do all communicators really direct their main efforts towards impressing their colleagues? Do Lobby correspondents write for Lobby correspondents, do book editors seek only to impress other book editors, and do TV drama producers think only of other TV drama producers?

Specialist correspondents – according to the evidence of this study – do indeed gather news partly for (and with) other specialists in the same field. But they also work with the news organization and its executive in mind – as well as the news sources. Journalists do not work directly for particular audience members; audience research can only reveal audience responses to broad areas of coverage.

It seems probable that other communicators also work with the judgements of competitor-colleagues in mind. Competitor-colleagues define the competitive situation; they are members of the same segment of the occupation; they cover the same subject matter and deal with the same outside people – including performers; some competitor-colleagues can reward group members in very direct ways, such as promotion opportunities. Exchange behaviour with colleagues employed by competing organizations enables competitor-colleagues to strengthen their collective autonomy and to resist organizational controls.

Despite the existence of some studies of communicators which do not report competitor-colleague exchange behaviour, the hypothesis would still predict that exchange behaviour takes place between competitor TV producers, book editors, magazine writers and so on. The important comparative question is how its incidence varies between different areas of the mass media.

A high prevalence of exchange behaviour with competitors, a high level of autonomy and high prestige within the occupation are likely to be strongly correlated; furthermore all of these factors can be expected to correlate with the strength of mixed goal. Following this the hypothesis would be that competitor-colleague behaviour in TV, for instance, would be highest among mixed goal (quality-pop) programmes regarded as carrying prestige in the broadcasting world. Competitor-colleague exchange behaviour would be least common among the makers of outright 'commercial' programmes (and wherever the audience rating is the sole criterion of success). As between different segments of the mass media, the hypothesis is that competitor-colleague exchange would be very prevalent in 'general' hardback book publishing companies (with their strong non-revenue goal element) – and such behaviour would be uncommon in advertising agencies which have an unambiguous profit goal and are 'client' dominated.

5. JOURNALISTS AND POWER IN THE MASS MEDIA

Are journalists powerful people in contemporary western democracies? The general theme of this section is that journalists are probably more powerful and more politically important than is often supposed. This argument has two main steps:

(1.) It is 'journalists' broadly defined, rather than journalists narrowly defined, who are powerful.

(2.) Journalists broadly defined are powerful especially within the mass media industry itself.

a. *Correspondents' perceptions of own power*

Specialist journalists themselves made quite modest claims when asked: 'In what sort of circumstances, if any, do you think specialists in your field wield significant power or influence?' Many answers took the form of 'Very little, except when. . . .'

Short term power or influence was believed to operate in relation to certain situations – such as a political crisis or a particular delicate set of negotiations:

'Very seldom, perhaps marginally in specific tight situations.' (USA)

'No power, but some influence on their own government, if their stuff is inherently plausible, on questions where they may have franker sources of information than diplomats do – e.g. what kind of reception a British minister can expect.' (USA)

'In revealing in advance and interpreting major party and government policy changes. During a party leadership crisis or contest.' (Lobby)

'Only in producing revelations which politicians wish to keep quiet.' (Lobby)

'Only in bringing things into the open – and so sometimes prompting a decision.' (Labour)

'Rarely, because educationists are usually convinced they know best (classroom tradition). Occasionally during major squabble: comprehensives, students, school leaving age.' (Education)

'When planning decisions (e.g. East of Suez strategy, Third London airport) are subject of parliamentary or public debate.' (Aviation)

'No great power or influence but we do sometimes help to catch villains.' (Crime)

'Presumably could have some influence on initial acceptance of a new car model; or in such factors as use of seat belts.' (Motoring)

A number of specialists also quoted cases of injustices to individuals.

In terms of *long-term power* or influence many correspondents saw themselves as collectively helping to decide what became the major issues and who became the leading individuals, within the field of specialization. It was also believed that ideas initiated by correspondents were later taken up by leading individuals in the field, and *vice versa*.

'What they write must have some influence on what English people think about the United States.' (USA)

'No power except selectivity: i.e. concentrating public attention on a particular story or angle and ignoring or playing down others.' (Lobby)

'In politics they create a climate, friendly to or critical of ideas and persons.' (Lobby)

'Presumably trade unionists learn more about their own union's activities and their leaders through newspapers and TV than from attending branch meetings. . . .' (Labour)

'Power – no. Influence – may arise through informing teachers of new techniques or exposing facts about educational opportunities. I think education correspondents played a part in the movement against the 11+ exam.' (Education)

'Getting over the vital part the British aircraft industry plays in the nation's technological advance.' (Aviation)

'We mould public opinion on major issues. This has led to greater freedom for managers, and helped players obtain a fairer contract system.' (Football)

But some correspondents also believe that they have a direct influence upon decision-makers within the news source area – by asking questions, by handing on information, by giving advice, or because senior people in situations of uncertainty seek the national correspondents' support and are prepared to make some concessions and changes in presentation in order to achieve such support. One Foreign correspondent claimed that through personal contact with a key British Minister, supported by news stories on the issue, he had influenced the British Cabinet into taking its first serious interest in a major international defence issue. Others said:

> 'Our views do influence politicians' tactics and to a lesser extent their decisions. But not big decisions – only their presentation.' (Lobby)

> 'A certain amount through questions asked at press conferences and in putting forward possible solutions of labour problems in articles – which are often quoted at meetings.' (Labour)

> 'Even hard-bitten sports officials are – like politicians – conscious of their need for an efficient public image. Consequently they are very touchy about criticisms and through this fear the sports press wields considerable power in the background.' (Football)

> 'On new car models in pre-production stage; and during drafting of some legislation.' (Motoring)

Such direct influence on policy makers is quoted by only a minority of specialists. Moreover a somewhat smaller minority say that correspondents have no significant power or influence, or only negatively – through inaccurate stories, or through predictions (such as of a resignation) which cause the predicted decision to be reversed.

b. *Two forms of leadership: business men and communicators*

The classification of news organization goals put forward in this book involves the concept of a 'coalition goal' – which is composed of advertising revenue, audience revenue and non-revenue elements. Journalists are major supporters of the non-revenue goal, and the obvious proponents of revenue goals are relevant categories of business executives.

In the nineteenth century many newspapers were dominated by a founding individual who himself set not only the revenue goal but also the non-revenue goal (often of a political partisan kind). But dominant individuals of this kind, even in newspapers, became less and less common after the second world war. The commercial broadcasting organizations (although not entirely devoid of tycoon founding father figures) operated under new constraints – such as governmental powers over licence renewal. The BBC also has a some-what similar constraint – its finances depend upon government approval.

Thus even in the broad area of finance, broadcasting organizations were ultimately dependent upon skills other than financial ones. These 'political' (broadly defined) skills were largely looked for in the persons of 'journalists' (broadly defined). Moreover broadcasting organizations which were forced for long-term political reasons to produce a 'balanced' output came to give special prestige emphasis to various kinds of 'factual' output. 'Factual television' (news, news background, documentaries, outside broadcasts of events) assumed increasing importance; in this broad area journalists, broadly defined, were in control. The BBC perhaps provides the extreme example of a major media organization which during the 1960's came to be controlled mainly by men with broadly journalistic backgrounds. But this process was not confined to the BBC; it also happened, to a lesser extent, in ITV.

In the case of commercial broadcasting and newspapers in most advanced western countries there now appear to be two main forms of leadership; firstly business men broadly defined; secondly communicators. Among the 'business men' the relative strength of accountants, salesmen, advertising men, 'production' men, and owning families varies from organization to organization. But among the communicators there is only one dominant category – the journalists.

The relative strength of business men and journalist communicators clearly differs not only between organizations but also in different parts of the same organization. Certain sorts of output have 'pure' revenue goals – and here business men dominate. Other sorts of output of a broadly news, factual, cultural, educational or informative character have a strong element of non-revenue goal (and an overall mixed goal). It is in such areas that journalists predominate; these areas are, of course, the very areas which concern politicians. In those areas of media output which are generally thought to be most politically important journalists have predominant control.

c. Journalists: new men of power?

The purpose of this section is to list some promising hypotheses in the areas just discussed.

(1) *There are two dominant mass media – newspapers and TV;* in both journalists are the dominant communicator occupation. Despite the death of newspapers, there is little evidence that newspapers have been killed by TV (rather than by other newspapers).[6]

These dominant media of newspapers and TV have, however, squeezed the lesser media – such as magazines, films and radio.

(2) *The media have increasingly become 'factualized';* this has led to increased prominence for journalists. The increasing 'factualization' has been seen throughout the media – especially in TV and radio, but also in magazines and books.

(3) *Much 'factual' broadcasting is heavily dependent upon press journalism.* With the one major exception of the televised 'event', most factual television depends on press journalism for its basic information, its editorial angle, the definition of what 'balance' is, and often for its performers. Where it does not depend upon press journalism, factual broadcasting often depends on newsagencies – whose output is heavily slanted towards the requirements of newspaper customers.

(4) *Journalism as an occupation is weak, but certain categories of journalists have influence.* Discussions about journalists – especially about their possible power or influence – tend to turn on the definition of 'journalist'. Chapter Two of this book argues that journalism is an indeterminate occupation; journalists engage in a very wide range of tasks; most journalists work for specialized or localized publications. But several categories of journalists do appear to have very considerable influence. *Firstly* there are the leading individual figures in national journalism; in the United States most of these men are columnists and commentators, while in Britain they are the Editors of the major publications. *Secondly* there is a somewhat larger category of other senior executives – in Britain these would include men like Night Editors of national newspapers, the men in charge of major factual television programmes, and the Editors of a few influential magazines. *Thirdly,* newsgatherers – some of whom are the subject of this book; there are grounds for believing that the Lobby correspondents play an important part in the evolution of rivalry within the British Cabinet and in the definition of political crises.[7] *Fourthly,* there are the more loosely defined journalist/politician/public figures.

These four categories taken together add up to only a few hundred men. Some future study may investigate these differing categories of influential journalists. Such a study might find that the whole question of the power of journalists turns on the issue of whether the more loosely defined prominent 'journalists' are included or not.

(5) *What has increased most significantly is the number of individual journalists who wield political influence.* Behind this hypothesis lies

the assumption that at least some British journalists wielded influence well over a hundred years ago. The 1970's differ from the 1870's or the 1820's, however, in the greatly increased scale of the media; clearly this is related to major historical changes in the complexity of modern societies. Some journalists have long wielded some influence both within the media and without. It is the great expansion of the media in the last century which has led to increased total influence for journalists; in a hundred years the number of influential British journalists may have risen from a few dozen to a few hundred. Of those few hundred, specialist news-gatherers (from mixed goal and non-revenue fields) probably make up the largest category.

6. SOCIOLOGISTS AND JOURNALISTS

There are differences between the places where journalists work, such as newspapers, and the places where sociologists work, such as universities. There are differences also in their conceptual frameworks and methods of gathering data; there is a major difference in time perspective. Journalists are occupationally obsessed by personalities and specifics, whereas sociologists look for general theories and only reluctantly concede that individual human personalities can play a major part in the development of societies.

Nevertheless there is more in common between sociologists and journalists than either side might care to admit. Both sociologists and journalists often mislead outsiders with their rhetoric into believing that they are revolutionaries, socialists and reformers. These latter labels may indeed fit a minority of sociologists and journalists, but in both occupational ideologies there are long established and potent traditions of conservatism. Both occupations are interested in the seamy side of life; both occupational ideologies stress that reality is shielded by façades, things are not what they seem, and that many social appearances have been deliberately contrived. Both sociologists and journalists often anticipate deceit, self-seeking and corruption in public life. With their expressions of anarchistic sentiments, sociologists and journalists frequently mislead not only their audiences but also themselves.

There is considerable mutual suspicion between sociologists and journalists; but much of this mutual suspicion is based on ignorance. Neither occupation seems fully to recognise the extent to which it is dependent upon the other. Journalists are dependent upon sociologists and other social scientists in an increasingly high proportion of stories. Surveys, studies, reports, and investigations by various sorts of social scientists play a larger and larger part in political and semi-political journalism; yet the journalists who produce the stories sometimes show a startling ignorance of the simplest conventions of such work, and a failure to search for the most easily available published sources. Many journalists – despite their professed hostility to government organizations – when faced with government publications and statistics often accept them with complete credulity.

But if journalists know little of social science and social science approaches to evidence, the ignorance of journalism which most university sociologists display is even more complete. Yet much of a social scientist's broad map of the society in which he lives comes to him through journalism. Although most sociologists are quite willing to absorb a regular daily and weekly ration of journalism, they are remarkably lacking in curiosity as to how news gets into newspapers or on to TV screens. When sociologists do venture opinions about journalism these opinions often reveal ignorance of the most elementary details.

Within social science during the last decade or two research on the mass media has tended to carry low status. In the case of journalism little recent sociological research of a reasonable standard exists. In consequence several broad areas of sociological theory and research have not taken the mass media into account. The existing sociological literature in such areas as organizations, the professions, and small group exchange is the weaker for this neglect.

The mass media badly need the help and assistance of social science. Journalists, for instance, would be less dependent on public relations men and major source organizations if they had more broad knowledge of social science evidence and how to find it. The managers of media organizations could also benefit from social science in many ways – in understanding not only their own organizations but also the society in which they operate. This is probably especially true of Britain's large media organizations whose senior managers in the last two decades have consistently ignored easily available bodies of relevant evidence – sometimes with disastrous commercial results. One especially obvious example of this is the extraordinarily short-sighted policies of the newspaper industry in relation to the recruitment and training of journalists.

7. Definitions of monopoly

In the first chapter the question of 'How many media voices?' was introduced with a quotation from de Tocqueville – who saw the power of the American press in the 1830's as being neutralised by the number of newspapers. Now it is time for some concluding remarks on the relevance of this study to the media voices issue.

a. The case of the Lobby correspondents

In *The Westminster Lobby Correspondents* the present author argued that the Lobby phenomenon should not be seen as a conspiracy against the public:

> 'The inadequacies of the Lobby correspondents are disturbing not because they diverge from, but because they are so similar to, the inadequacies of the wider intelligence system into which they fit.'[8]

The Lobby system fits into the extremely centralized patterns of both British national politics and Britain's national mass media system. Just over 100 journalists – representing all the daily newspapers, plus the Sundays, major agencies, BBC and ITN – are allowed special access to 10 Downing Street and other Ministerial briefings; Lobby men also receive documents before MPs. Other journalists (notably from non-daily papers, magazines and foreign news organizations) are excluded.

This Lobby system could be seen as reflecting certain central tendencies and values in British society. There is the 'truly British compromise' element – in this case between an open and a closed system. There is the famous British insularity (no foreigners). There is the proverbial British smugness (it's illogical, but it works). There is the British stress on a traditional and oral culture – some of the leading political journalists in the land ply their trade without benefit of secretarial assistance or filing system.

Another aspect of Lobby journalism was the high level of exchange partnerships; two-fifths of the national Lobby correspondents said they had exchange partners. In some cases these partnerships appeared to increase the level of competitiveness; but in other cases the opposite probably occurred. This was made the more likely by an unusual feature of Lobby partnerships – namely that partnerships involving journalists from three (not only two) separate news organizations were common. In the case of partnerships involving three popular newspapers, the partnership was, then, likely to have a vast total ultimate audience. One particular popular newspaper partnership in the Lobby had as its collective audience over half the British adult population.*

This extreme example illustrates the general point that, despite

---

* According to the National Readership Survey (JICNARS) evidence for 1968. This piece of information was deliberately not reported in *The Westminster Lobby Correspondents*; some of the journalist personnel involved have now changed jobs.

23 national news organizations, in some cases a few specialist journalists can shape the flow of a certain kind of information to tens of millions of people. The number of voices may be much smaller than it appears.

b. Non-revenue goals and national media policy in Britain

Centralization of the media in Britain is obviously related firstly to the small geographical size of the country and secondly to the economies of scale in the mass media industry. But centralization has gone much farther than these two factors alone would favour. Much of the centralization of the British media has occurred historically because of the strength of non-revenue goals. Prestige seeking has been so strong in relation to profit seeking that more and more newspapers and other communications organizations have become absorbed by a few profit-seeking multi-media organizations.

Another aspect of the national media scene in Britain has been the extraordinarily potent influence of government, Royal Commission, and government committee decisions. The history of broadcasting in Britain is, of course, the major example. But a prime factor in the last half century of British press history was government paper rationing from 1939 onwards. To the mechanism of Royal Commissions on the press have also been added various other kinds of official reports on monopolies, prices, and so on. Most, but not all, of these reports are examples of the weaknesses of *ad hoc* 'common sense' investigations. Commercial television in Britain for instance – as a result of a series of major government miscalculations – has for most of its years of existence shown either embarrassingly large profits or actual losses. The quality and quantity of information available to successive governments for making national media policy has been unsatisfactory.

c. Media oligopoly and specialist competitor-colleagueship

Competitor-colleague groups of specialist newsgathering journalists must be seen in the context of five major features of the national media industry:

(1) National dominance of 'provincial' media. Provincial newspapers are mainly London owned; both BBC and ITN are London dominated. The group of *national* competitor-colleague journalists has no provincial rivals of any significance.

(2) National newspapers and TV are the two dominant media in Britain. The specialist correspondents of both media are to be found in the groups of national specialists; with only a few exceptions the broadcast specialists are relatively unimportant in terms of competition and exclusive news.

(3) Multi-media organizations owning national newspapers, provincial newspapers, magazines, commercial TV and book interests are increasingly important. The competitive level within the whole British media industry has been reduced by one particular organization – the International Publishing Corporation. Partly because this organization owned the main pro-Labour national newspapers it has paradoxically been allowed to grow to a size which appears inappropriate for any single media organization in a country the size of Britain. In a number of important fields IPC owns the leading specialized magazine or magazines. This, put beside the competitor-colleague phenomenon in the national general media, means that the level of competition may be very low indeed over a broad industrial or technical field.

(4) *Daily* media dominate the British media industry to an extent not known elsewhere. This is all the more serious from the point of view of the 'number of voices' – since co-operation between competitor-colleagues is most often between specialists of similar daily frequency. Probably no change would more effectively guard against the possible dangers of competitor-colleagueship than the strengthening of *weekly* publications.

(5) Although in 1968 the grounds for disquiet were not extensive, one must consider the likely changes over the next decade. This includes a further decline in the number of national newspapers and a further strengthening of a few multi-media organizations; especially important are the new video-electronic media which multi-media organizations seem likely to dominate.

The competitor-colleague phenomenon may not by itself constitute a cause for disquiet, but, seen against the overall media industry picture of oligopoly, any additional restriction of competition is serious. In this book it has been argued that competitor-colleague exchange will sometimes in effect increase the positive aspects of competition; but the same phenomenon will also *sometimes* decrease the 'real' amount of competition. Especially since the data reported in this study probably underestimate the level of co-operative activity, it is – at the very least – possible that the effective level of competition in some specialist fields of news is considerably less than the 'number of voices' represented in the particular fields would appear to indicate.

J.A.W.—K*

d. New definitions of monopoly: a task for social science

Some broad hypotheses which are relevant to specialist journalism and concerned with the level of competition are as follows:

(1) A law forbidding companies owning national newspapers from also owning provincial dailies might lead to a revival of an independent British provincial press; many highly profitable provincial dailies have in recent years been milked to subsidize other activities.

(2) Since co-operative behaviour and imitative competition are both responses to uncertainty, new measures which increased the job security of journalists might increase the effective number of voices.

(3) Greater co-operation between specialists working for a single news organization and covering neighbouring specialist fields might have several consequences – less co-operation with competitors, less dependence on particular news sources, and better-informed stories.

These three hypotheses are merely intended as illustrations of an important task facing social scientists involved in mass media research. Future research must undertake a broad redefinition of the criteria used to judge the level of competition or degree of monopoly within particular areas of the mass media. Until such research is conducted both sociologists and journalists will, in relation to the 'number of media voices', probably be justified in one of their common ideological assumptions: everything is not as it seems.

References

1. Introduction

1. 'The World Outside and the Pictures in Our Heads', Walter Lippmann (1922) pp. 3–20.
2. Jeremy Tunstall, *The Westminster Lobby Correspondents* (1970) pp. 101–2.
3. For a general discussion of mass media research in the United States and Britain see the editorial introduction to Jeremy Tunstall (ed.) *Media Sociology* (London: Constable) 1970 pp. 1–38.
4. Some now exist: See Tom Burns, Jay Blumler, Philip Elliott.
5. See Oliver Boyd-Barrett.
6. E.g. Richard D. Altick, J. Edward Gerald (1956), Alfred M. Gollin.
7. Charles Perrow (1967).

2. Journalism: Occupation and organization

1. Joseph R. Gusfield.
2. Ibid., p. 580.
3. Winston Fletcher (1970).
4. Political and Economic Planning (1938) p. 18.
5. *Royal Commission on the Press, 1947–9* Evidence p. 1.
6. National Board for Prices and Incomes (1969) p. 19.
7. An excellent summary is Einar Östgaard (1965).
8. Tamotsu Shibutani, p. 17.
9. Arnold M. Rose.
10. D. Butler and D. Stokes, pp. 229–30.
11. Elihu Katz and Paul Lazarsfeld.
12. Bradley S. Greenberg and Edwin B. Parker.
13. Raymond A. Bauer and David B. Gleicher.
14. Melvin De Fleur.
15. Johan Galtung and Mari Holmboe Ruge.
16. Kurt Lewin (1951).
17. David Manning White (1950).
18. Lewis Donohew, p. 66.
19. Aleksander Matejko.
20. Malcolm Warner (1968).
21. Charles Perrow (1967) p. 196.
22. *Royal Commision on the Press, 1961–2*. Report pp. 219–22.
23. S. M. Lipset, J. Coleman and M. Trow (1957).
24. Economist Intelligence Unit (1966).
25. Charles Perrow (1967) p. 197.

26. Leslie Sellers, *Doing it in Style* (Pergamon 1968) pp. 279–82.
27. Warren Breed (1955) p. 183.
28. Rodney W. Stark.
29. *UK Press Gazette* 4th September 1967.
30. Colin Seymour-Ure (1969) provides a useful discussion.
31. The Monopolies Commission (1966) p. 25.
32. Ibid., p. 18.
33. Colin Seymour-Ure (1968) p. 63.
34. Maurice Edelman (1966).
35. Talcott Parsons (1960) pp. 44–58.
36. Amitai Etzioni (1961) p. 52.
37. Peter Blau and Richard Scott (1963) p. 42.
38. Ephraim Yuchtman and Stanley E. Seashore (1967) p. 898.
39. Robert E. Park (1922) p. 360.
40. E. Yuchtman and S. Seashore (1967) p. 898.
41. Ibid., p. 900.
42. Ibid., pp. 901–2.
43. Issued by the National Council for the Training of Journalists.
44. Rafael E. Gill.
45. Tom Burns and G. M. Stalker (1966) pp. xviii–xx.
46. National Board for Prices and Incomes (1969) p. 22.
47. Leo Rosten (1937) p. 328.
48. For a survey of 100 journalism students, see Oliver Boyd-Barrett (1970).
49. A. M. Carr-Saunders and P. A. Wilson (1933) p. 270.
50. *Editor and Publisher* 27th April 1968.
51. Oliver Boyd-Barrett (1970).
52. L. Broom and J. H. Smith (1963) pp. 321–4.
53. International Press Institute (1962) pp. 161–70, 233.
54. *Report of the Tribunal appointed to inquire into the Vassall Case and Related Matters* (London: HMSO Cmnd. 2009 1963).
55. Ceredig Hughes in *New Society* 28th December 1967.
56. International Press Institute (1966), pp. 35–7, 57–66.
57. *Royal Commission on the Press, 1947–9* pp. 164–74.
58. H. Phillip Levy (1967).
59. *Royal Commission on the Press 1947–9*. Evidence Q 7, 478.
60. Ernest Greenwood (1957) pp. 45–55.
61. F. J. Mansfield (1943) pp. 33, 37.
62. Seymour Martin Lipset, *et al.* (1962) p. 162.
63. F. J. Mansfield (1943) pp. 42, 60.
64. Morris Janowitz (1960) pp. 223–4.
65. Ibid., pp. 41, 27.

3. *Specialist correspondents: goals, careers, roles*

1. Jeremy Tunstall (1970).
2. J. Galtung and M. H. Ruge (1965).
3. J. Tunstall (1970) pp. 3–6, 109–18.

4. Political and Economic Planning (1938) p. 293.
5. Lord Burnham (1955) p. 24.
6. Frederick J. Higginbottom (1934) pp. 148–9.
7. Lord Burnham, pp. 72–4.
8. Ibid., pp. 77, 85–6.
9. Ibid., pp. 87–8.
10. Bernard Falk (1951) pp. 43–4.
11. This was written by the (retiring) Motoring correspondent of *The Guardian*. Adam Raphael, 'Confessions of a Car Tester', *Punch* 16 Oct. 1968.

4. Specialist correspondent as employee

1. Fred E. Katz, pp. 19–20.
2. Ibid., p. 21 (italics in original).
3. Dan Nimmo, p. 77.
4. Jeremy Tunstall (1970) pp. 27–8, 112–13.
5. Harold Wilensky (1967) p. 57.
6. Jeremy Tunstall (1970) p. 126.
7. Rose Laub Coser (1961) p. 35.
8. Fred E. Katz (1968) p. 24.

5. Specialist correspondent as newsgatherer

1. Frederick J. Higginbottom, p. 201.
2. Colin Seymour-Ure (1968) p. 168.
3. Marjorie Ogilvy-Webb (1965) pp. 47–66.
4. Jeremy Tunstall (1964) pp. 155–92.
5. Henri Stephan De Blowitz (1903), pp. 128–55; *The History of the Times*, Vol. 2, pp. 524–6.
6. Henry Brandon, *Sunday Times* 13th April 1969.
7. Michael MacDonagh (1913) p. 64.
8. David Halberstam, *The Making of a Quagmire* (London: Bodley Head 1965) p. 20.
9. Leo Rosten (1937) p. 106.

6. Specialist correspondent as competitor-colleague

1. Henri Stephan De Blowitz (1903) p. 149.
2. Ibid., pp. 154–5.
3. Economist Intelligence Unit (1966) Part I, p. 62.
4. Leo Rosten (1937) p. 251.
5. Warren Breed (1952) p. 224.
6. John Pendleton (1890) pp. 155–6.
7. Frederick J. Higginbottom (1934) p. 150.
8. Leo Rosten (1937) pp. 88–9.
9. Kurt H. Wolff (ed.) (1950); Marcel Mauss (1954); B. Malinowski (1932).
10. George C. Homans (1961) pp. 74–5.

11. As in Peter M. Blau (1955).
12. Edmund Dählstrom (1965–6) p. 278.
13. Warren O. Hagstrom (1965) p. 52.
14. Nihon Shimbun Kyokai, *The Japanese Press '67*, p. 87.

7. Newsgatherers for whom?

1. Gayle Durham Hollander.
2. Warren Breed (*Journalism Quarterly*, 1955).
3. See Chapter 2 above.
4. K. Lang and G. Lang; J. Halloran *et al.*
5. J. Diedrick Snoek.
6. James Curran (1970).
7. Jeremy Tunstall (1970) pp. 98–108.
8. Ibid., p. 122.

Bibliography

Richard D. Altick, *The English Common Reader*: a social history of the mass reading public 1800–1900 (University of Chicago Press) 1957.

Raymond A. Bauer and David B. Gleicher, 'Word-of-Mouth Communication in the Soviet Union', *Public Opinion Quarterly*, 17, 1953 pp. 297–310.

Bernard Berelson and Morris Janowitz (eds.), *Reader in Public Opinion and Communication* (New York: Free Press; London: Collier-Macmillan) 1966.

Peter M. Blau, *The Dynamics of Bureaucracy* (University of Chicago Press) 1955.

Peter M. Blau, *Exchange and Power in Social Life* (New York: John Wiley) 1964.

Peter M. Blau and W. Richard Scott, *Formal Organizations* (London: Routledge and Kegan Paul) 1963.

Jay G. Blumler, 'Producers' Attitudes Towards Television Coverage of an Election Compaign: a case study', *Sociological Review Monograph, 13.* (1969) pp. 85–115. Reprinted in Jeremy Tunstall (ed.) *Media Sociology* (London: Constable) 1970, pp. 411–38.

Oliver Boyd-Barrett, 'Journalism Recruitment and Training: Problems in Professionalization' in Jeremy Tunstall (ed.) *Media Sociology* (London: Constable) 1970, pp. 181–201.

Warren Breed, 'The Newspaperman, News and Society', unpublished doctoral dissertation, Columbia University, 1952.

Warren Breed, 'Social Control in the Newsroom: a functional analysis', *Social Forces,* 33, 1955, pp. 326–35.

Warren Breed, 'Newspaper "Opinion Leaders" and Processes of Standardization', *Journalism Quarterly*, 32, 1955, pp. 277–84.

L. Broom and J. H. Smith, 'Bridging Occupations', *British Journal of Sociology*, 14, 1963, pp. 321–34.

Lord Burnham, *Peterborough Court: The Story of the Daily Telegraph* (London: Cassell) 1955.

Tom Burns, 'Public Service and Private World' in *Sociological Review Monograph, 13* (1969) pp. 53–73. Reprinted in Jeremy Tunstall (ed.) *Media Sociology* (London: Constable) 1970.

Tom Burns and G. M. Stalker, *The Management of Innovation* (London: Tavistock) 1966.

David Butler and Donald Stokes, *Political Change in Britain* (London: Macmillan) 1969.

A. M. Carr-Saunders and P. A. Wilson, 'Journalists' in *The Professions* (London: Oxford University Press) 1933, pp. 265–70.

William O. Chittick, *State Department, Press and Pressure Groups* (New York: Wiley-Interscience) 1970.

Bernard Cohen, *The Press and Foreign Policy* (Princeton University Press) 1963.

Rose Laub Coser, 'Insulation from Observability and Types of Social Conformity', *American Sociological Review*, 26, 1961, pp. 28–39.

James Curran, 'The Impact of Television on the Audience for National Newspapers, 1945–68' in Jeremy Tunstall (ed.) *Media Sociology* (London: Constable) 1970.

Edmund Dählstrom, 'Exchange, Influence and Power', *Acta Sociologica*, 9, 1965–6, pp. 237–74.

Henri Stephan De Blowitz, *My Memoirs* (London: Edward Arnold) 1903.

Melvin L. De Fleur, 'Occupational Roles as portrayed on Television', *Public Opinion Quarterly*, 28, 1964, pp. 57–74.

Melvin L. De Fleur, *Theories of Mass Communication* (New York: David McKay) 1966.

Lewis Donohew, 'Newspaper Gatekeepers and Forces in the News Channel', *Public Opinion Quarterly*, 31, 1967, pp. 61–8.

Economist Intelligence Unit, *The National Newspaper Industry* (London: E.I.U.) 1966.

Maurice Edelman, *The Mirror: A Political History* (London: Hamish Hamilton) 1966.

Philip Elliott, 'Selection and Communication in a Television Production—A Case Study', in Jeremy Tunstall (ed.) *Media Sociology* (London: Constable) 1970.

Amitai Etzioni, *Complex Organizations* (New York: Free Press) 1961.

Bernard Falk, *Bouquets for Fleet Street* (London: Hutchinson) 1951.

Winston Fletcher, 'Britain's National Media Pattern', in Jeremy Tunstall (ed.) *Media Sociology* (London: Constable) 1970.

Johan Galtung and Mari Holmboe Ruge, 'The Structure of Foreign News: The Presentation of the Congo, Cuba and Cyprus Crises in Four Foreign Newspapers', *Journal of International Peace Research*, 1, 1965, pp. 64–90. Reprinted in Jeremy Tunstall (ed.) *Media Sociology* (London: Constable) 1970.

J. Edward Gerald, *The British Press under Government Economic Controls* (University of Minnesota Press) 1956.

Walter Gieber, 'News is What Newspapermen Make It' in Lewis Anthony Dexter and David Manning White (eds.) *People, Society and Mass Communications* (New York: Free Press) 1964, pp. 173–82.

Rafael E. Gill, 'Press Corps of Israel, Statistical Trends, 1955–59' *Gazette*, 7, 1961, pp. 283–90.

Alfred M. Gollin, *The Observer and J. L. Garvin 1908–1914* (London: Oxford University Press) 1960.

B. S. Greenberg and E. B. Parker (eds.), *The Kennedy Assassination and the American Public: Social Communication in Crisis* (Stanford University Press) 1965.

Ernest Greenwood, 'Attributes of a Profession' *Social Work*, 2, July 1957, pp. 44–55.

Joseph R. Gusfield, 'Occupational Roles and Forms of Enterprise' *American Journal of Sociology*, 66, 1961, pp. 571–80.

Warren O. Hagstrom, *The Scientific Community* (New York: Basic Books) 1965.

J. D. Halloran, P. Elliott, and G. Murdock, *Demonstrations and Communication* (Harmondsworth: Penguin) 1970.

Frederick J. Higginbottom, *The Vivid Life* (London: Simpkin Marshall) 1934.

Gayle Durham Hollander, 'Recent Developments in Soviet Radio and Television News Reporting', *Public Opinion Quarterly*, 31, 1967, pp. 359–65. Reprinted in Jeremy Tunstall (ed.) *Media Sociology* (London: Constable) 1970, pp. 252–8.

George C. Homans, *Social Behaviour: Its Elementary Forms* (London: Routledge and Kegan Paul) 1961.

Everett C. Hughes, *Men and Their Work* (Glencoe: Free Press) 1958.

International Press Institute, *Press Councils and Press Codes* (Zurich: IPI) 1961.

International Press Institute, *Professional Secrecy and the Journalist* (Zurich: IPI) 1962.

Morris Janowitz, *The Professional Soldier* (Glencoe: Free Press) 1960.

Fred E. Katz, *Autonomy and Organization: The Limits of Social Control* (New York: Random House) 1968.

Elihu Katz and Paul F. Lazarsfeld *Personal Influence* (Glencoe: Free Press) 1955.

Kurt Lang and Gladys E. Lang, 'The Unique Perspective of Television and its Effects: a pilot study', *American Sociological Review*, 18, 1953, pp. 3–12.

Daniel J. Leab, *A Union of Individuals: The Formation of the American Newspaper Guild, 1933–1936* (New York: Columbia University Press) 1970.

H. Phillip Levy, The Press Council: *History Procedure and Cases* (London: Macmillan) 1967.

Kurt Lewin, *Field Theory in Social Science* edited by Darwin Cartwright (New York: Harper) 1951.

Walter Lippmann, *Public Opinion* (New York: Harcourt, Brace) 1922.

Seymour Martin Lipset, Martin Trow, and James Coleman, *Union Democracy* (New York: Anchor) 1962.

Eugene Litwak, 'Models of Organization which permit Conflict', *American Journal of Sociology*, 67, 1961, pp. 177–84.

Michael MacDonagh, *The Reporters' Gallery* (London: Hodder and Stoughton) 1913.

Denis McQuail, *Towards a Sociology of Mass Communications* (London: Collier-Macmillan) 1969.

Bronislaw Malinowski, *Argonauts of the Western Pacific* (London: Routledge) 1932.

F. J. Mansfield, *'Gentlemen, The Press!' Official History of the National Union of Journalists* (London: W. H. Allen) 1943.

James G. March (ed.) *Handbook of Organizations* (Chicago: Rand McNally) 1965.

Aleksander Matejko, 'Newspaper Staff as a Social System', *The Polish Sociological Bulletin*, 1967, pp. 58–68. Reprinted in Jeremy Tunstall (ed.) *Media Sociology* (London: Constable) 1970, pp. 168–80.

Marcel Mauss, *The Gift* (Glencoe: Free Press) 1954.

Dan C. Nimmo, *Newsgathering in Washington* (New York: Atherton) 1964.

Marjorie Ogilvy-Webb, *The Government Explains* (London: Allen and Unwin) 1965.

Einar Östgaard, 'Factors Influencing the Flow of News' *Journal of International Peace Research*, 1, 1965, pp. 39–63.

Robert E. Park, *The Immigrant Press and Its Control* (New York: Harper) 1922.

Robert E. Park, *On Social Control and Collective Behaviour* edited by Ralph H. Turner (University of Chicago Press) 1967.

Talcott Parsons, *Structure and Process in Modern Societies* (Glencoe: Free Press) 1960.

Charles Perrow, 'A Framework for the Comparative Analysis of Organizations', *American Sociological Review*, 32, 1967, pp. 194–208.

John Pendleton, *Newspaper Reporting in Olden Times and To-day* (London: Elliot Stock) 1890.

Political and Economic Planning, *The British Press* (London: PEP) 1938.

Arnold M. Rose, 'Rumor in the Stock Market', *Public Opinion Quarterly*, 15, 1951, pp. 461–86.

Leo C. Rosten, *The Washington Correspondents* (New York: Harcourt, Brace) 1937.

Colin Seymour-Ure, *The Press, Politics and the Public* (London: Methuen) 1968.

Colin Seymour-Ure, 'Policy-Making in the Press', *Government and Opposition*, 4, 1969, pp. 427–525.

Tamotsu Shibutani, *Improvised News: a sociological study of Rumor* (Indianapolis: Bobbs-Merrill) 1966.

Georg Simmel, *The Sociology of Georg Simmel*, edited by Kurt H. Wolff (Glencoe: Free Press) 1950.

J. Diedrick Snoek, 'Role Strain in Diversified Role Sets', *American Journal of Sociology*, 4, 1966, pp. 363–72.

Rodney W. Stark, 'Policy and the Pros: An Organizational Analysis of a Metropolitan Newspaper', *Berkeley Journal of Sociology*, 1962, pp. 11–31.

The Times, *The Tradition Established 1841–1884* (The History of the Times, volume 2) 1951.

Jeremy Tunstall, *The Advertising Man in London Advertising Agencies* (London: Chapman and Hall) 1964.

Jeremy Tunstall, *The Westminster Lobby Correspondents* (London: Routledge and Kegan Paul) 1970.

Jeremy Tunstall (ed.) *Media Sociology* (London: Constable) 1970.

Max Weber, *From Max Weber*, edited by H. H. Gerth and C. Wright Mills (London: Routledge and Kegan Paul) 1948.

David Manning White, 'The Gatekeeper: A Case Study in the Selection of News', *Journalism Quarterly*, 27, 1950, pp. 383–90.

Harold L. Wilensky, *Organizational Intelligence* (New York: Basic Books) 1967.

Malcolm Warner, 'TV Coverage of International Affairs', *Television Quarterly*, 7, 1968, pp. 60–75.

Joan Woodward, *Industrial Organization* (London: Oxford University Press) 1965.

Ephraim Yuchtman and Stanley E. Seashore, 'A System Resource Approach to Organizational Effectiveness', *American Sociological Review*, 32, 1967, pp. 891–903.

OFFICIAL PUBLICATIONS

Royal Commission on the Press, 1947–9. Report (London: HMSO) 1949. Cmnd. 7700.

Report of the Committee on Broadcasting, 1960 (London: HMSO) 1962. Cmnd. 1753.

Royal Commission on the Press, 1961–2. Report (London: HMSO) 1962. Cmnd. 1811.

Monopolies Commission, Report on The Times Newspaper and the Sunday Times Newspaper (London: HMSO) 1966. H.C. 273.

National Board for Prices and Incomes, *Costs and Revenues of National Daily Newspapers* (London: HMSO) 1967. Cmnd. 3435.

National Board for Prices and Incomes, *Journalists' Pay* (London: HMSO) 1969.

Appendix on methods

This study was made possible by a generous grant from the Leverhulme Trust. The author's application described in general terms an occupational study of journalists, but added: 'Because of the great variety of different kinds of journalism, particular attention will be confined to a limited number of journalistic specialisms'. The application had been supported by Peter Townsend, chairman of the department of sociology at the University of Essex – and work began on the project in that department in October 1965.

a. Preliminary interviews with journalists

Preliminary unstructured interviews were conducted with 186 journalists in 1965 and early 1966. About half of these journalists were working for national news organizations – and the other half for provincial newspapers and national magazines or specialist publications. They were involved in a wide variety of journalism – and included sub-editors, feature writers and photographers and Editors.

b. Direct observation

Direct observation sessions – varying from a day to ten days in length – were carried on inside seven national and four provincial news organizations.

The author attended the daily press conferences given by the three major political parties during the General Election campaign of March 1966. He also attended the press conferences during the last two weeks of the Pollok (Glasgow) Parliamentary by-election in March 1967.

c. Specialists: unstructured interviews

In summer 1967 Oliver Boyd-Barrett joined the project as a research assistant for a period of 18 months. During this time he played a substantially more active and responsible part in the research than is usual for research assistants; in particular he conducted half of the next round of interviews.

From autumn 1967 a new round of 140 interviews commenced – this time devoted only to national specialist newsgatherers from the selected fields. The preliminary interviews had included another 22 London-based specialists in these selected fields, plus 16 Foreign correspondents who were interviewed by the author in New York and Washington. In 1968

20 other Foreign correspondents were interviewed in Bonn and Rome by the research assistant. 12 further unstructured interviews were conducted late in 1968 with Fashion correspondents.

These unstructured interviews (like the preliminary interviews) mostly took place at or near the specialist's office. The median duration was 100 minutes; many interviews took place partly in a bar or restaurant. An interview guide was used which covered these 23 points: Entry into journalism; starting specialism; daily routine; major annual events; travel; main news sources; source relations; minor sources; own office situation; news organization's attitude; main competition; how competitive; co-operation; competitor-colleague group; audience; image/ status of specialist field; image/status of journalism; worries and insecurity; effects on social life; 5 years' time – expectations; dislikes about job; likes. After each interview a commentary was tape-recorded and typed up on a separate sheet for each of the 23 headings.

d. Design of final stage

At this stage the author wrote a 50,000 word rough draft report on the research so far. This report served to finalize the conceptual framework and main hypotheses. It had originally been intended to return to the same specialists for a second face-to-face interview; but at this stage it was decided to switch to a mailed questionnaire.

This was designed in early 1968 and piloted on at least one specialist from each of the selected fields. The final version of the mailed questionnaire was 22 foolscap pages long.*

e. Mailed questionnaire completed by specialists

This was the main round of data collection. Questionnaires were sent out in May 1968. (Football, Fashion, Bonn and Rome were sent out later in 1968). The numbers and response are shown overleaf.

Thus 207 usable questionnaires were returned – an overall response rate of 70·2 per cent; the response rate for London-based specialists (excluding Foreign correspondents) was 76 per cent. The substantially lower response rate of Foreign correspondents was to be expected – especially since fewer of them had been interviewed face-to-face. Among the home-based fields it is noticeable that the response rate falls from Lobby, other mixed, and audience to the advertising goal fields.

f. Additional interviews with executives

Additional interviews were conducted with the following categories of senior executives:

* Since many of the questions have already been included in the text and tables, it is not repeated here. The author will supply a copy of the questionnaire on request.

15 Editors of national news organizations
12 City (financial) editors
15 Advertising and Circulation directors and managers
In addition 20 news source individuals were interviewed.

	Possible number	Number of usable questionnaires returned	Successful response rate
Non-revenue (Foreign)			%
Washington	27	18	⎫
New York	34	19	⎬ 61
Bonn	17	8	⎭
Rome	17	10	53
TOTAL, FOREIGN	95	55	58
Political Lobby Total	46	39	85
Other Mixed Goal			
Labour	33	23	70
Education	14	14	100
Aviation	16	11	69
TOTAL, MIXED	63	48	76
Audience Goal			
Football	30	24	80
Crime	20	14	70
TOTAL, AUDIENCE	50	38	76
Advertising Goal			
Motoring	22	16	73
Fashion	19	11	58
TOTAL, ADVERTISING	41	27	66
All Correspondents	295	207	70·2

g. Recruitment survey

The research assistant took charge of a survey of journalism recruits. 99 trainee journalists attending courses in Harlow and Sheffield completed questionnaires. A report on this survey and on journalism recruitment has been published.*

* Oliver Boyd-Barrett (1970).

h. The access problem

Obviously a study such as this could not have taken place without the active support of many journalists. The author is extremely grateful to them.

i. An exploratory study

Perhaps it is worth repeating that this has been intended as an exploratory study. The major data collection stage produced questionnaires completed by 207 specialist journalists. But a total of 430 journalists (and some non-journalists) were interviewed face-to-face. These interviews, plus direct observation sessions, produced approximately one million words of typed notes.

Index

DATE DUE